Praise

"How to guide young people during times that confound us all? This era of bullying, sexting, active shooter drills, mental illness struggles, death threats, and persistent crisis? Jim Zervanos's *Your Story Starts Here: A Year on the Brink with Generation Z* answers this question with a frank depiction of Zervanos's days as a father to two young boys and as a creative writing teacher in a high school outside of Philadelphia. If his classroom lessons were distilled into commands, they would be: observe, go deeper, be empathetic. His parenting lessons: love, pay attention, be patient, and forgive. Even as an A+ student of his own teachings, he daily negotiates situations that require a careful balancing of his values. Watching Zervanos stay steady in unsteady waters, with good humor and strength, is the central pleasure of this moving, engaging book. I loved every page."

DEBRA SPARK, AUTHOR OF *DISCIPLINE*

"*Your Story Starts Here* offers an alternative to the polemics on public education: an insider's view of the complex reality of a public high school in the United States in the 21st century. This book is as rich in humor and compassion as it is in dismay at the reality of school shootings and children ushered, sometimes forcefully and prematurely, into adulthood. These glimpses into the daily life of a husband, father, and English teacher give us reasons to be grateful that people like Jim Zervanos embrace the challenge."

PETER TURCHI, AUTHOR OF

MAPS OF THE IMAGINATION: THE WRITER AS CARTOGRAPHER

"Masterfully paced and wonderfully rendered, *Your Story Starts Here: A Year on the Brink with Generation Z* is a slender gem, a book that should be required reading for parents, for teachers, for artists ... for anyone who's wondered what it means to be human in a world that daily challenges our humanity. It is a testament to Zervanos's skill that we can't help but be drawn into the lives we encounter: the students he mentors, the sons he parents, the wife he supports as she dives into her doctoral program. There's never a false note rising from the deft, often lyrical prose that ferries us along in short, journal-entry-like chapters. The raw (often humorous) honesty on the pages is palpable. Zervanos ultimately pulls off the memoirist's greatest sleight-of-hand; that is, he opens a ground-level window to the most intimate, vulnerable moments of his life, and as we peer through, we magically see pieces of our own lives reflected in the glass. This book is irresistible."

Scott Gould, author of *Idiot Men*

"High school students, full of anger and pain, come alive through their words and their teacher's insights in this eminently readable memoir in essays as a teacher navigates his classroom, his family life and career at the same time. Packed with empathy as well as literary lessons, we have a front-row seat to watch the world fall apart as these kids come of age. This book is insightful, heartfelt, and authentic. The world needs more teachers, and more writers, like Jim Zervanos."

Kelly Simmons, author of *Not My Boy*

About the Author

Jim Zervanos is the author of the memoir *That Time I Got Cancer: A Love Story* and the novel *LOVE Park*. His award-winning essays and short stories have been published in numerous literary journals, magazines, and anthologies. He is a graduate of the MFA Program for Writers at Warren Wilson College and Bucknell University, where he won the William Bucknell Prize for English and was an Academic All-American baseball player. He teaches at a high school in the suburbs of Philadelphia, where he lives with his wife and two sons and has risen in the baseball pantheon as coach of two Little League teams.

www.jimzervanos.com

YOUR STORY STARTS HERE

A YEAR ON THE BRINK WITH GENERATION Z

JIM ZERVANOS

www.vineleavespress.com

Your Story Starts Here: A Year on the Brink with Generation Z

Print Edition
ISBN: 978-3-98832-047-6
Published by Vine Leaves Press 2024

Cover design by Jessica Bell
Interior design by Amie McCracken

To my students,

and to Mary Ellen Goldfarb, Andy Wineman, and Dan Loose,

who showed me the way to be a teacher

To Winnie,

Lover of books! Thank you for all your support and enthusiastic interest in my work... and in the process, from writing to publication ... and beyond. Your help and insight has been invaluable to me!

Jim

Dec. '23

Docendo discimus.

By teaching, we learn.

Don't just do something, sit there.

—Thich Nhat Hanh

Give me a child until he is seven and I will show you the man.

—Aristotle

Author's Note

This book is a true account of a year in my life as a teacher and a father. I have changed names and altered identities to protect people's privacy.

Ryan's Lament

Ryan Henry comes to see me at the end of the day. He practically tiptoes into the classroom to be sure he's not bothering me, checking to see if the coast is clear before making eye contact.

"How do you make a point you're trying to make?" His gaze shifts about, as if he's casing the place and we're about to make some kind of secret deal. A junior already, he's grown tall since his mysterious month-long hospitalization last spring. Now he's skinny, sinewy—developments that make it more difficult for him to disguise the discomfort I know he feels with personal interactions like this.

"Well..." We lock eyes. He crosses his arms, hovers just beyond my desk. I'm stumped. *How do you make a point...?*

He goes on, "I'm working on tone." He's entirely earnest. "I've been reading Joyce. You know, there's, like, an Irish early twentieth-century tone." I assume he's into *A Portrait of the Artist as a Young Man.* "I'd like to write in that tone," he says.

Me too, I think.

He says, "It's so funny. So great."

"I agree. Don't worry about tone. Let your tone grow out of the story you have to tell. You've got your own voice, your own tone. Remember that story you wrote in ninth grade?"—the last time he was my student, technically. Since then, he's paid me the occasional visit, like this one, shot me the occasional email, attaching some cryptic draft for me to read. I say, "It was funny, warm, but also biting, with a real edge, but not cynical. A real tenderness, I remember, between the teenage son and the parents. He's abroad, right? They visit? He's going through something, but he's really happy to see them."

Ryan nods, absorbed in thought, seemingly mesmerized by my description, perhaps impressed by my memory of his story. But there's something else he's trying to wrap his mind around.

"I don't want to be too cynical," he says. "I feel like I'm too cynical. My stuff lately, I mean. You said it was warm and tender. I wish I could still write like that. Like I did then."

I take in this heartbreaking insight and feel a pang of regret—for the fact of the insight and for having led him to it.

"You *can* still write like that," I tell him, and I want to believe this is true.

I can read his pained expression. *I wish I could be that way again.* I offer an understanding smile. I want him to be happy—with who he is becoming. I remember my own son, seven-year-old Christopher, not long ago, crying on his bed after I scolded him—too harshly, I thought, until he said, "I used to be *good,* but now *I'm bad."* Time stopped, or I wanted it to stop, as he heaved miserably and I implored him to believe me, *"You're good. You're good."*

I ask Ryan what he's reading now.

"Saul Bellow. He's a lot like Philip Roth. You told me about Roth. I just finished *The Plot Against America."*

I nod. What the hell was I thinking? He's just a kid!

"Now I'm into *The Adventures of Augie March,"* he says. "I like it."

"It's great," I agree, and we leave it at that.

There's no turning back, I think, as he exits.

A moment later he reappears in the doorway. "I just sent you a new story."

"I can't wait to read it," I say. Immediately, I check my email and see an attachment entitled "Somebody Please Help Edwin." When I look up again, he's gone.

THE ZEITGEIST

Today it begins. The motor starts. On the first day with students, in the first class. I've presented the syllabus, given an overview of Modern Literature, talked about the big themes—moral ambiguity, anxiety, confusion—that mark the modern age we still live in. While the students are filling out a personal-information sheet that includes a list of books they've read over the summer, two boys are talking about *Jude the Obscure,* required reading for this course, AP Literature and Composition, aka Modern Lit. One kid says he found the ideas clear enough, the language dated and difficult, but he liked it overall.

I'm hovering nearby. I dare to chime in, "Thomas Hardy's a great place to start our conversation about modern lit, even though it's 'dated,' as you say." Hearing myself, I hope that he doesn't think I'm a complete dork—or at least that my dorkiness is matched by his.

The kid grins. "Because it's *obscure."*

"That's *it."* There's the spark. The engine revs, and I'm fired up, to see what these kids have in store, to see what *this kid* has.

In the minutes before the bell, we read the opening of F. Scott Fitzgerald's essay "The Crack-Up," in which he asserts, "The sign of a first-rate intelligence is the ability to hold two opposed ideas in the mind at the same time, and still retain the ability to function." For homework they'll reread this introduction and write about what they think it all means, what Fitzgerald was going through, what was on his mind, when he "cracked up" at age thirty-nine.

This question will segue into a class discussion of the "zeitgeist," whose meaning I'll ask them to figure out by the root words. This line of reasoning has become predictable. One kid who knows some German will announce that *zeit* means time. As for *geist,* I'll egg them on toward the one word they're all thinking of, *poltergeist.* Skeptically, a few will guess, *Ghost?* "Not ghost exactly," I'll say, "but spirit. Spirit of the times. That's it. Zeitgeist means the spirit of the times. That's what we're talking about here."

Then it's back to the Fitzgerald quote. I'll ask them what "opposed ideas" are battling it out in *their* minds these days. I'm always both thrilled and unnerved by what they have to say. "We apply to colleges that we know we probably won't get into." "We vote even though we know it won't really make much of a difference in the way things are." "We come to school every day, even though we know there's a chance we could get shot." Most of these kids are experts in "retaining the ability to function," despite these mind-twisting contradictions. They are also experts in disguising their anxiety, as I imagine Fitzgerald was before he "cracked up" a decade short of forty-nine, the age he was sure he'd be all right.

At lunch I tell my teacher-friend Dean Garrett how I feel already charged up by my AP students, many of whom Dean shares in AP Government. As usual, I don't know anyone's names, since I teach only seniors, whom I've just met, whereas Dean teaches most of them as juniors in AP U.S. History. I tell Dean how impressed I was by the boy who observed that *Jude* was *obscure.* When I describe his hip, thick-rimmed glasses, orange madras shirt, and khaki cargo shorts, Dean smiles and informs me that "Miles is the real deal," surprised I don't already know him somehow. Apparently, Miles's reputation precedes him. "He's applying to Harvard early decision," Dean says, "and he'll probably get in."

The gauntlet has been thrown down.

Alone at my desk after school, I think of Fitzgerald before he cracked up, at thirty-nine still believing he had a good ten years left to fulfill his dreams, which he later realized had already eluded him. What defeated him exactly? What two opposed ideas was he no longer able to hold in the mind at the same time? He writes of hope colliding with pessimism, of the world facing conditions once considered impossible, of his own dreams revealing themselves to be embarrassingly unimportant. As I approach forty-nine, I see that for a decade or more I, too, have been balancing in my mind, with increasing effort, two opposed ideas: my gratitude for my general satisfaction in life and an anxious recognition that my own dreams have eluded me, or at least my youth has. These days, that old driving desire to *achieve*, perhaps once fueled by vanity and blind confidence, has been met with an unfamiliar desire that I recognize as peculiarly unselfish and not entirely unwelcome. It is a desire that competes with the artistic impulses, or that at least demands shared space with them. It is a mysterious, growing desire not to *be inspired,* as a writer and artist (an identity I'm loath to relinquish), but to *inspire,* as a teacher and father, to be an optimistic encourager of dreams, a shameless promoter of romantic ambitions, a sage guide for my students and sons, as we confront the impossible.

While I've been sitting here, my mind has opened a crack to make room for something I deliberately neglected all summer—my own writing. I had trusted an unprecedented compulsion to free myself from the Byzantine trials of stringing words together, in hopes that I might clean the slate for something unexpected. I believe this plan has paid off because it has helped me to realize that it's my life as a teacher I want to write about, now, after twenty-one years, through the eyes of a father of two young boys, during this unfathomable time in America, where a Dream deferred seems at risk of becoming a Dream destroyed before it can ever become a Dream fulfilled; where women are still rising up and facing down the bullish, boorish tyranny of men; and where the pen is no longer necessarily mightier than the sword (if it ever was), let alone the gun—the semiautomatic rifle, to be precise. And yet it's hope that compels me. Hope in the ideals of America as I see them embodied in these great, smart, creative, compassionate kids.

I've decided to keep a diary, of the sort I might ask of my Creative Writing students, of each day's memorable details, recorded faithfully, somehow, if not typed on my laptop or in my Notes app after the last bell, then dictated into my iPhone while driving to pick up Michael from pre-school, or in the parking lot after getting the groceries, or at the curb outside the elementary school before going inside to get Christopher, or at home after I've put the boys to bed, lying next to Vana, who's exhausted after a full day's work even before she's started her full *night's* work required for her intensive two-year doctoral program, sitting up in bed reading another chapter or cranking out a paper due by midnight.

After watering the plants and tidying up my classroom, I slip out of school at 2:30, twenty minutes before the contract day is over, understanding that the tidal wave of student work I'll have to read will begin to build tomorrow, after which it will crash and ebb and swell in relentless cycles until June.

Oncologist Visit

No school today. It's snowing again. Tomorrow I'm flying to Tampa, Florida, for a writers' conference. Or at least that's the plan, depending on the weather conditions. But first I have to break out the snow blower. And I still have to pack. And I have an appointment with my oncologist at Penn at 3:00. Before I go to Florida, I want to confirm that last month my lymph nodes were swollen because of a sinus infection, not because of a recurrence of lymphoma. I might not be able to make it into the city if the snow keeps falling like this. I email the nurse practitioner, who tells me to come in right now since all the other patients have canceled their appointments. Her offer would be funny if she were joking. Instead, I'm wondering why she doesn't tell me to stay home like everyone else. I take a deep breath and brace myself for a treacherous ride.

Christopher is home from school, too. I inform him he's coming with me to the hospital. "Can we go to McDonald's?" he asks, in a tone that suggests this is a negotiation.

"Deal."

After a brief examination, my doctor says, "You don't have cancer," and reminds me that now, after five years in remission, I've got the same chances of getting it that he has.

In the elevator on the way out, we see a bald little boy in a wheelchair. I smile hello to his parents.

"Last treatment today," they say.

"Congratulations," I say.

In the parking garage Christopher says, "Do you think I'll get cancer?"

I say, "I hope to hell not."

"How do I get cancer?" he asks.

I say, "If you figure *that* out, you'll be famous."

He says, "Why don't you just look it up on Google?"

In the car I call Vana and announce, "All clear."

Instantly she's crying, and it takes me a moment to remember that I'm not alone in this ongoing plight. It's a cry she's obviously been storing up since last month's ambiguous results. She'd given no sign of her fears. Which would explain this surprising expression of relief. "Everything's okay," I say, happy to soothe, as we drive out of the city.

As we enter the McDonald's drive-thru, I'm expecting Christopher to ask me why Mommy was crying.

But the news on the radio has our attention, and now I'm expecting questions about the porn star suing the president.

Instead, as I hand Christopher his Happy Meal, he says, "I wonder what the toy is," and I'm relieved of my burdens.

GRADUATION DAY

Today is Benfield's Graduation Day, an official school day devoted to the ceremony held at Scanlon University, where all school district faculty, from K-12, are expected to report by 8:30 a.m. for breakfast, and then to participate in the pomp and circumstance, the high-school teachers in black robes alongside the seniors in royal blue robes.

Today is also the day Vana will be presenting her dissertation proposal at the University of Pennsylvania, at 2:00.

But this morning, with the early summer sun warming the living room, Christopher says he's not feeling well enough to go to school, despite the outdated prescription pink stuff we dug out from the refrigerator and put to use last night when he complained of a sore throat, all while Michael was honking his horn into a hefty pile of Kleenex and repeatedly calling me into his bedroom. "Daddy, can you blow my nose?" Now Michael is sitting here with us in the living room, eyes glued to the TV, sounding like a clogged drain, in a fog with his brother.

I'm not buying the act.

"They're both fine," I tell Vana, gazing skeptically at the zombie-faced boys, "fine enough to go to school."

Christopher moans, "Nooo," unpersuasively, lying on the big chair, forcing himself to break eye contact with the TV, which I mute. Michael honks his horn again. I shake my head, calling bullshit on all of this.

"Well, what are we going to do?" Vana asks.

"Babysitter?"

Vana shrugs.

I text Karolina, who comes on Saturdays to help with laundry. She's not available. I call my mom, then my sister, in Lancaster. Neither can make it.

"Your mom?" I ask.

Vana replies, "Is it really that big of a deal for you to miss graduation?"

I sigh, exaggerating my devotion. "I teach all seniors," I remind her. "Semester courses. So that's two-thirds of the graduating class, about two hundred out of three hundred students." I want to believe I'd be as heartbroken as I'm pretending to be to miss their big day. I want to believe *they'd* be heartbroken to discover that I was missing their big day. "So, yeah, it's kind of significant. Not to mention Candi MacPhearson, the *Pegasus* editor, is keynote speaker and Hailey Villamaria, another one of my AP kids, is giving the class-president speech I helped her with."

Vana sweetly mirrors my sigh. I'm pleased she's sympathetic to my plight. I've nearly convinced myself that missing graduation is simply not an option. So the question remains: What do we do with these two rascals, who continue to make a stronger case than I'm able to make?

I can see how this stalled ordeal is beginning to consume Vana. At some point, and soon, this bomb needs to be defused.

I ask Christopher, "Do you want me to stay home with you?"

He nods vigorously.

I ask Michael, "Do *you* want me to stay home with you?"

He nods lethargically.

I ask Vana, "Do you want me to stay home?"

She smiles. "Yes, but I don't want you to miss graduation. I know it's important to you."

I say, "I'm staying home."

"Yay!" from all.

Vana goes upstairs to get dressed.

I go on to the school district website to report my absence, but the next official workday has already begun. It's too late to enter my request. But I don't need a substitute teacher and there's no practical reason for my attendance, which for all intents and purposes will make no difference to anyone.

I text Assistant Principal Serenity Davis to let her know of this unfortunate development.

Almost instantly she texts back, "Hope the little guys feel better!"

I feel relieved—free for the day, just like that—then disappointed, to have my hunch confirmed, my absence so quickly determined to be of no real consequence.

I decide to go for a run before Vana has to leave. It's a beautiful day. When I return, she's sipping coffee on the porch, wearing a light gray dress and high-heeled orange sandals, hair up, looking subtly spectacular, altogether relaxed, despite what's at stake for her today. *A prelude to summer,* I think, notwithstanding the two "sick" kids glued to the TV inside. We sit together until noon, when she says she should probably get going.

She says her goodbyes to the boys, and then out by the car, with her giant bag strapped over her shoulder, she hugs me and says, "Thank you for everything. You're a good daddy. I love you"—as if there were ever any doubt that this is the way the day would play out.

"I love you, too," I say. "Good luck. You're going to be great."

After she's gone, Christopher is soon in shorts, dribbling the basketball out on the porch, and it's bombs away. He's hitting threes, grabbing rebounds, and slamming the Little Tykes hoop into submission.

"*Someone* feels better," I say. "I missed graduation for *this?*" He can hear that I'm not disappointed.

He grins, feigning confusion. "*What?*"

"Yeah."

"I *was* sick, this morning. Now I'm like seventy or eighty percent."

"Uh-huh."

After lunch I lie down for a nap with Michael in his bed. The two of us wake up together three hours later at 5:00. Much-needed sleep for both of us, apparently.

Downstairs I find Christopher pleasantly sprawled on the hardwood floor amidst colored pencils and markers and dozens of scattered sheets of computer paper, impressive drawings of fantastically serpentine, meticulously toothed creatures, apparently marking the start of his Reptile Period. He looks up and tells me they're all for sale, but he hasn't priced them yet.

In the meantime, Vana has texted photos from her successful proposal. "Passed!"

As if to celebrate, we boys go to the nearby frozen yogurt joint and eat our late-afternoon snack outside on plastic Adirondacks under an umbrella. Then we decide it's time for dinner and head across the street to the new Domino's, where they have tables for customers not calling for home delivery. While the pizza bakes, we slip out to the Starbucks for fresh bags of Daddy's favorite whole-bean coffee, and we pick up Mommy's dress from the dry cleaner next door.

Back in our booth at Domino's, Christopher, not an experienced soda drinker, suddenly gives his orange Fanta a frenetic shake. I let slip, "*Don't,* you dumb shit!" so spontaneously that he looks up and laughs at the fresh and silly sound of this curse, and of course Michael is laughing, and so now I'm laughing too, until Michael repeats, "you dumb shit." I take the bottle and gently unscrew the cap to avert disaster. The pizza arrives, and it appears so over-spiced that I ask the man if he's sure this is the one we ordered. He says, "Large plain?"

I nod.

I tell the boys, apologetically, that this is not the same Domino's pizza I used to scarf down years ago. I'm guessing the company tried to get fancy to compete with Papa John's. Michael, who eats anything, nibbles the tip of a slice, winces, and sets it down.

"You feel okay?" I ask him.

"I'm *fine,*" he insists. "Don't like this pizza." He touches a finger to the garlic-covered crust. "I want French fries."

Christopher and I each eat a slice and we box the rest. We all agree that this is the last time we'll eat here.

At home I put a bag of frozen fries into the oven and find the Phillies game just starting on the TV. All in all, it's been a great day. There's not the slightest sense that the world missed us for a single moment—or that we missed it.

Summer Reading

"How do you know when your students have learned?" That's what Freddy Whetts, our principal, has been asking us recently. I'm not sure what the answer is exactly. It's easier to know when a student has *not* learned. Like when she leaves a quiz blank or stares at you dead-eyed when you ask her a question in class. But even then, you never know what might have sunk in, even if she can't demonstrate the learning gain you only dimly suspect.

Eighth period, Jasmine, a senior Creative Writing student who was absent Friday, takes her summer reading test in the hallway. She returns minutes later, teary-eyed, nose ring glistening, and asks if we can talk after class. The other students are working quietly on their "rant" assignment, so I sit at the empty desk next to her and say, "No time to read this summer?"

Tears are falling now. "My summer was terrible. I meant to do it. I like to read. I just couldn't." She's choking on her words.

I have no doubt she's been through something rough. "Okay, let's come up with a new plan, a new deadline." Her eyes widen. I say, "You think about it, and I'll think about it, and we'll talk again tomorrow."

She nods, warily, as if she half-thinks I'm going to throw her a curveball now with a lecture on living in the real world and digging herself out of the hole she's already in. Instead, I recap for her the instructions for today's assignment since she was out in the hallway when I explained them earlier, and she gets right to work on her laptop.

Twenty-one years of teaching and seven years of being a dad have gotten me to this point. It used to be that I was the cool young teacher, or at least that's what I was led to believe. But it's really *now* that I'm cool, or cooler than I was then, whether the kids think so or not. In the early years, I wasn't the kind of cool that took this kind of action, sitting down like this to hear a student out, to really listen, and then to propose a modified plan specific to her needs—as if I were actually running the show here, as if I actually had the freedom to take command of how this or that student might best be served by the educators charged with teaching her. Now I understand that, in this classroom, this moment is mine to seize or to squander.

"Thank you so much," Jasmine says when I get up from the desk next to her.

When I return to my lectern at the front of the room, I pretend to be grading papers though I've got my eye on Jasmine, who's wasted no time starting her "rant"—that terrible summer, no doubt, igniting the imagination and firing those furious fingers. When one hand rises to wipe a damp cheek, the other drums ceaselessly at the keyboard.

School Shooting

Another school shooting. Texas. Ten dead. Kid wore a trench coat. Used his dad's legally purchased shotgun and pistol. The kid killed his ex-girlfriend in art class. He announced, "Surprise!" when he entered the room.

His T-shirt said "Born to Kill."

A girl who survived was asked if, while witnessing the shootings, she was thinking "This cannot be happening here," and she replied, "No, I never thought that. It's happening everywhere. I had a feeling it would happen here eventually."

This girl's comment is the *New York Times* headline, an attempt to capture where the horror lies, if any remains. It lies in the earnest expectation of a teenage girl. More kids have been shot in school this year than American soldiers have been killed in Iraq and Afghanistan. Maybe kids will quit school and join the military to be safe. Twenty-two school shootings so far this year. You can count on one per week. Going to school is like playing Russian Roulette. Who will be next? Will it be us?

After school I spend three hours at my classroom desk, searching websites for literary contests and independent presses that accept unsolicited submissions. The hallways are quiet. Outside my window the courtyard soaks in the afternoon sun. I'm surprised by the long list of potential publishers I've accumulated. I send my recently finished cancer memoir to a few of them to beat their deadlines, and I feel something like hope.

MADELINE AT THE WHITE HOUSE

Tonight, in bed with Michael, I read *Madeline at the White House.* On page three, the president's daughter, Candle, is frustrated because she can't see her father, who is literally invisible but for a yellow puff of hair, behind a wall of advisors in the Oval Office.

Michael points and says, "Donald Trump."

This afternoon on the drive home from soccer practice, Christopher blurted, "Donald douche bag!" when he heard Trump's name mentioned on the radio. "Don't say that," I said, secretly thinking that if "douche bag" is the worst he repeats of what he's heard from my mouth, I can live with that. Over the holidays, my friend Roger's kids called the president "Donald fuck face" in the home of their Trump-supporting cousins, who live in Florida. Roger grinned when he told me the story. The episode caused quite a row at dinner and possibly a permanent rift in the family, thus Roger's seeming pleasure at the prospect of not having to travel south again for the holidays.

Michael and I also read *Good Night Washington, D.C.* Michael points and says, "The White House" and "I want to go to Washington, D.C." He understands from TV that there is a real White House and that these drawings represent that real place. He understands that Donald Trump is in some close association with that real white house, where the American flag flies on top. He points and says, "Megan flag." He also spots the Megan flag on telephone poles and on front porches. A year ago, he pointed to an American flag and said, "Donald Trump!"

That was the moment I knew Trump was going to win the election, or at least that the man had branded himself so successfully that my two-year-old son identified him as synonymous with the American flag, with America itself, having spotted him on TV how many dozens of times before a wall of American flags while giving whatever speech. I remember thinking, *Oh shit*, picturing Hillary waving confidently in her white pantsuit.

Bo Chang's College Essay

After school I meet with Bo Chang, a student in my AP Modern Literature class, who wants help with his college-application essay. Bo speaks with an accent that suggests he's not only the son of immigrants, but an immigrant himself. I haven't heard much, or read much, from him in class so far. My expectation that his essay will be unimpressive is based solely on my unwise correlation between his seeming second language and his inexpert-sounding use of it. I should know better. Two years ago, the student who scored the highest grade on my English final exam was a Chinese girl who, throughout the year, had appeared to know only the fewest English words necessary to deflect the questions I asked her in class.

Bo sits with me at my desk while I read his essay aloud and take scant mental notes. His writing is superb. The essay is about his newfound passion for baking bread. He describes how on his first attempt the bread came out hard on the outside and undercooked on the inside. He proceeded to experiment and to become such a master baker of bread that his mother began to ask him to write down the recipes so that she could replicate his baking style.

I begin to formulate a theory about Bo, even feeling a sense of pride for him because he has discovered this passion for baking that might lead to winning a scholarship to culinary school and perhaps one day owning his own bakery, or even a chain of bakeries, or a restaurant. I ask if he cooked other things prior to the bread, and he says no. I ask if his mother had baked bread before or even influenced his desire to try to bake bread himself. He says she'd never baked bread before. He explains that she'd once cooked homemade corned beef, which he criticized—an episode he recounted in the essay's first paragraph.

"Your mother cooked corned beef just that once? That's it?"

I suggest that there's a gap in causation between his criticizing of the corned beef and his subsequent undertaking of bread-baking. I suggest he clarify his motivation; perhaps, for example, in response to his criticism of her corned beef, his mother says, "Okay, big shot, why don't *you* give cooking a try?" and then, not to be outdone, you decide to try making something that is notoriously difficult to make, bread, something you knew she had never tried, and maybe never would. I tell him to disregard the *specifics* of my suggestion, of course, and instead to appreciate the larger point I am trying to make about his vague motivation.

Smiling, he says, "That is actually very close to what happened, almost exactly what she said. I will make the changes." We nod, both satisfied. I ask him where he hopes to go to school. He says, "I am applying early admission to the University of Pennsylvania. For engineering."

I raise my eyebrows. "Engineering? You've got talent to burn, man. You're a baker, a writer, a future engineer."

He nods considerately. "Thank you." Packing up, he repeats, "Thank you."

I shouldn't be surprised to learn later from his guidance counselor that Bo Chang is ranked number one in his class.

I chuckle to myself, *at* myself, happy to be reminded that, despite my high (and usually met) expectations, I can still underestimate a kid by a mile.

Clearing Out the Closet

I'm clearing out the right side of my closet to make room to hide in the event of an armed intruder. This is where I'll go if I'm alone during a lockdown. It seems insane that I'm emptying a nook large enough for me to situate myself comfortably. I've imagined the case in which I get in there to hide, and the old map and scrolled-up posters fall down, and an old coffeemaker and piles of corkboard block the space where my legs should go. I imagine slipping into the closet, hoping I won't be in the middle of teaching a class if this maneuver ever becomes necessary. I can't exactly crawl into the closet to be safe all alone while my students brace themselves against the classroom wall. Or maybe we'll have time to draw straws for this perfect hiding spot.

At lunch, Dean reports the news of the eleventh school shooting of the year. It's Jan 23. A fifteen-year-old is in custody in Kentucky. A girl and a boy are dead. Many injured. It's interesting, we all agree, that the kid didn't blow his own brains out.

"We know the suspect is white, too," Dean says.

"How's that?" I ask.

"Because it says he's in custody." Dean looks up from his phone. "Not shot dead."

TOOTH

At four in the morning, I awake to my three-year-old son Michael's call-out for a fresh bottle of milk. "I want moke!"

It turns out that sitting on his night table is a full bottle of milk. I say, "There's a bottle right here." Weeks ago, I began leaving a bottle for him at bedtime, to spare me these wake-up calls. I take a swig. "It tastes fine."

He frowns. "I want cold."

Downstairs I open the bottle. One whiff and I nearly retch. No wonder Michael decided yuck. The kid has a bloodhound's sense of smell. He's always asking, "What's that smell?" with either a smile or a frown, before I discover coffee brewing or an apple rotting.

When I return to bed, Vana whispers, "Put money under Christopher's pillow."

"My God," I say. "Great call. I forgot."

How could I have forgotten again? And how did Vana remember? The same thing happened the last few times Christopher went to bed with a tooth under his pillow: Vana remembered less than an hour before he woke up. One time we both forgot, and Christopher cried out at the crack of dawn, "My tooth is still here, but no money!" Vana and I swapped glances. "Uh-oh." I got a dollar from the dresser drawer and went to investigate. I palmed the bill and searched under the bed. "Maybe it fell," I guessed, then presented him with the dollar. "Look, Mommy!" He beamed at Vana in the doorway. Order restored.

This morning I fetch a five from my wallet downstairs and tiptoe into Christopher's room. Fortunately, he's a deep sleeper, but he is hugging his pillow for dear life, so this isn't going to be easy. Sunshine is beginning to creep through the blinds. I fold the bill and manage to sneak it barely under the edge of the pillowcase. The rest of the ritual is a bust: The Tooth Fairy must have forgotten to take the tooth with her, I'll have to tell him.

I backpedal in relief.

At six o'clock, Christopher blasts into the bathroom and says, "Daddy, look!" holding up the five-dollar bill.

I'm in the shower. I wipe the glass wall to see. "Who's that on there?"

"I don't know," he says, gone in a flash.

"Abe Lincoln!" I call out.

He returns. "This is my fifth tooth. Maybe that's why I got five dollars. Get it? Fifth tooth? Five?"

I say, "We'll see if next time you get *six* dollars."

I better remember!

Last night we were horsing around on the bed. I was trying to grab the football from his hands. He snatched his hands away and the next thing I knew he was screaming in horror, "You broke my tooth! You knocked my tooth out!"

Oh shit. His mouth was bloody. I honestly hadn't felt my hand so much as graze his face, but this was no time for pleas of innocence. Vana came in and promptly found the tooth on the white bedspread. I thought for sure that Christopher and I were both going to get in trouble for playing football in the house. Instead, Vana whisked Christopher into the bathroom and instructed him to spit in the sink. He cupped cold water to his lips, and before long he was smiling, pleased with the new gap and the prospects of the Tooth Fairy's visit.

He's seven years old, whip-smart, and yet he believes in the Tooth Fairy—and, I suppose, why shouldn't he? Meanwhile, he's grown skeptical of Santa Claus, but mainly because he's a geography whiz and understands the unlikelihood of a whole toy-delivery operation situated on the North Pole, which he also understands is shrinking because of global warming. And flying reindeer? Lugging all those toys? But a Tooth Fairy carrying bills a thousand times its size and weight he accepts without questioning. "She's small but strong," he explains to me.

"How do you know it's female?" I ask.

"Fairy," he says. "*Fairy?*" and gives me a look. Duh.

All Throats Are Red

At lunch in the faculty dining room, the school nurse says she read a *New York Times* article about kids' increasing anxiety. This trend is familiar to us teachers. The nurse describes how kids text their parents, claiming their throats are red. "Of course, they're red," she says. "All throats are red." She tells us that the parents take their children's calls at work, then come promptly to pick them up. "The question is, what test did they forget about next period?"

American Flag

During AP Modern Lit, I notice, beyond the window, the flag at half-mast. *For Veterans Day tomorrow?* I'm wearing my American-flag sweater today in early celebration. We happen to be discussing *The Great Gatsby*. Half the class, musicians in the marching band, are at a Veterans Day parade downtown. There's an apparent link between the brightest students and musicianship. Meanwhile, Sue-Lin, who has played piano at Carnegie Hall, is in class today. I wonder what other instruments not suited for the marching band the rest of the students in attendance might play. The flag droops, then whips up, perfectly horizontal, flattened for a long moment in a burst of wind, and sinks again.

Then I remember—the reason for the flag at half-mast—the shooting at the Texas church, 26 dead, children, et cetera. Yesterday's news.

We're sitting in a big circle. Bo Chang is going on about the dying of the American Dream, the death of Gatsby's optimism, the green light, because of corruption, immorality ... "the dark fields of the republic" ... no chance at that "orgastic future"... but "tomorrow ..."

I glance at Madison, sitting beside me. Yesterday she let out an earnest "ugh" when I told the story of my father handing out tiny American flags, instead of cigars, on the day I was born, November 11th, Veterans Day, 1969. "Why *'ugh'?*" I asked her. I could tell she meant no offense. She was half-grinning, as if to convey her sympathy at the irony I wasn't grasping.

"The flag," she said, "it's so depressing..."

"No!" I let out, in this year of Colin Kaepernick, now unemployed quarterback who "took a knee" during the National Anthem and was recently labeled a "son of a bitch" by the President. I say, "Don't let anyone take the flag from you. It's *yours!"* I thought of Catholics renouncing their faith because of predatory priests. *Don't let them steal your souls! Your love of country!* "Look at that flag up there." I pointed to my giant cloth flag tacked to the cinderblock wall above the bulletin boards on the side wall. "That big, beautiful flag is all of ours."

Beside the flag on the left hangs my aerial-shot poster of Manhattan taken from atop One World Trade Center and on the right the framed Abraham Lincoln portrait I claimed from my grandfather's house after he died. Next to Abe is Martin Luther King, a hand-drawn portrait composed of the text of his "I Have a Dream" speech. Below these images, on a wide strip of corkboard, hang Mark Twain and Jack Kerouac, Bogart and Bergman in *Casablanca,* the black silhouettes of Rocky and Adrian, and the Brooklyn Bridge from Woody Allen's *Manhattan*—all complicated American myths, not without their dark sides. From the opposite corner, in the black-and-white photograph above my desk, James Baldwin looks down his nose, wide-eyed and unsurprised, cigarette smoke curling at the ceiling.

Today Madison is eyeing my American-flag sweater and smiling. I smile back.

Cameron and Hunter Are High

When I enter the faculty dining room, chuckles are dying down, shaking heads coming to a stop. Evidently, a good story has just been told. I go to the microwave and heat my spaghetti.

"If you weren't in education, you wouldn't believe it," says Carolyn Winters, guidance counselor. Others at the table nod. A few faint sounds of agreement. "A day in the life of Winters," she adds. "Could be a one-woman show. Or a sitcom."

I sit down and ask, "What'd I miss?"

My beloved lunch crew is made up of eight or so colleagues: Half of them are guidance counselors, school psychologists, and emotional-support staff, who happen to take their lunch sixth period as well; the other half are teachers like me who, because we teach seniors, are scheduled to eat during the same period our students eat—all of us seasoned Benfielders, who have come to cherish these thirty or so minutes when, day after day, year after year, we can, in the middle of the work day, enter a room populated by people who are not teenagers. This is our sacred space—this overlarge, usually frigid cinderblock refuge, with a conference table, a microwave, and a refrigerator—where we vent our complaints, share our triumphs, confide sworn secrets, spew our criticisms, offer punchlines, rehearse the tirades we'll never deliver to their intended targets. We like each other. We like our jobs, especially this part.

Today my colleagues appear consumed by their phones, if not by their lunches, but I know they just heard my request for a recap. I also understand that this is the time during which we break all the rules we seek to enforce in our classrooms. We curse, talk smack, tell fart jokes, reveal secrets, and—the horror—obsess with our phones. This is our lunchtime routine, our way, if only briefly, of reconnecting with the outside world, catching the latest headlines, texting our loved ones, all while chowing leftovers from steaming Pyrex containers or scarfing cafeteria lunches from Styrofoam trays. A long silence follows my request to be let in on the Big Story, and I know from experience that it is coming, in due time, in snippets contributed by each of them, between bites and diversions, and almost inevitably the retold story will take on new life.

I'm not surprised to learn that they have been talking about Cameron Scordato, who they say reeked so intensely of pot during first period that he was sent to Assistant Principal Everest Toole, in charge of Discipline. And then, if you can believe it (we all do), Cameron returned to class by second period, apparently unpunished. We all lament the nearly impossible task of busting a kid for smoking grass when the only evidence is that he smells like a bong.

I inform everyone that by fourth period Cameron and his sidekick, Hunter Simmons, smelled like a *pair* of bongs. I confess that I don't bother anymore even to *attempt* to discipline a kid for whatever odor he's giving off. They've always got some excuse that's impossible to disprove. Years ago, a kid made the case, with firsthand testimony from his father, that his clothes smelled like pot, like everything else in the house, because his dad was constantly smoking it. But in my class this morning I was pretty sure Hunter hadn't just absorbed Cameron's scent; in fact, he seemed more stoned than Cameron, not bothering to contain his laughter as he described, from *The Things They Carried,* Tim O'Brien and his platoon buddies picking Curt Lemon's splattered remains out of a tree—maybe the least funny thing in the book.

Carolyn looks up from her iPhone. "200,000 gallons of oil spilled in South Dakota. Keystone pipeline."

Neil Gillespie looks up from his iPhone. "Elephant hunting is legal again. Thank you, Trump."

I cheer, "Our spring break plans are back on."

Dean laughs. "No need to smuggle our trophies in anymore."

Carolyn says, "How about that picture of Don Junior with that pathetic elephant tail in his hand. Nice trophy, you dick."

Neil says, "That should be the GOP's new symbol—a dismembered elephant."

SWASTIKA

On my way out, I spot a swastika scribbled in ballpoint-pen ink on the floor outside Penny Verlander's door. Standing there, I examine it for a moment. It's "only" about two square inches. I wonder how big a drawn swastika must be to be a punishable offense. I've seen a group of kids sitting around here in the mornings before homeroom. There's no one around now. It's five minutes after four o'clock. I look up at the ceiling to find that the nearest camera is poised just overhead, hidden inside a small black glass bubble. I walk through the main office to alert someone. There is no administrator to be found. I text Assistant Principal Serenity Davis. I tell her she might want to check the video to see who drew a swastika on the floor outside Penny's classroom. She thanks me for the tip. I wish her a lovely evening. I'm already imagining Principal Freddy Whetts coming to the conclusion that the swastika is too small to make an issue of it.

TOOTH №6

While I'm getting ready this morning, Christopher enters the bathroom with a little cloth baggie tied shut.

"Daddy, look what the tooth fairy brought me. Can you untie this?"

"Wow." I untie it. He peeks in. I say, "Count it."

He dumps the coins on the bathmat, makes two piles of quarters and four piles of dimes.

"Each pile is a dollar," he says. "Six dollars, see? For my sixth lost tooth!"

In bed last night, Vana told me six bucks was nuts. *She* only got a dollar at that age. Christopher's friend Parker gets only a dollar *now.*

"Last time he got five," I reminded her.

"That's all I *had,*" she said.

"It's all *I* had." I told her I could prove it with contemporaneous documentation from these pages. Just as I could show he was expecting six bucks this time. "I think it'll be okay this once."

She gave me the small jewelry bag. I deposited the dollar seventy-five in quarters she scraped from a bowl on the dresser. I rounded out to six bucks with a quarter and forty dimes from the old jewelry box in the upstairs office. I figured we're not paying a kid six bucks so much as transporting six dollars in change from one room to another.

Now he's thrilled, of course, more so with the thoughtfulness of the tooth fairy than with the value of the loot. "She remembered," he says. "You think next time I'll get seven?" And then, "She is *strong,*" holding the bag before his face, imagining a fairy the size of a clipped fingernail but with the strength of his index finger. "Why does this say *Chanel* on it?"

"I don't know," I say. I was afraid he wouldn't miss that detail, but I'm prepared to dismiss it—as I do.

He doesn't pursue the matter.

While I'm getting dressed, he finds Mommy sleeping in the guest room, where she relocated after Michael got "scary" last night, dreaming of monsters. Maybe the Wild Things came to life in his bedroom, as they did for Max in the book we've read the last two nights.

"Look, Mommy," I hear Christopher say. "The tooth fairy gave me six bucks cuz it was my sixth tooth."

"That's good, honey."

Michael enters the guest room, and I follow.

"Looth tooth," Michael says, repeating what he said last night after he collided with his brother during another game of ready-set-hike in the living room. Christopher came running into the kitchen looking like a little Dracula, with a bloody, symmetrical smile.

"Not anymore," Christopher beams now, healed—and paid.

Miles's Poem

In the waning minutes of AP Modern Lit, I rush through introducing the first two pages of *Gatsby* in the vain hope that I'll have time to return their graded poems. Nevertheless, Miles lingers after the bell and asks if he can see his poem, whose surprisingly low grade, an A-, he already saw recorded online. I read aloud to him my handwritten note: "I love the third stanza, your best, where you shift gears and make the explicit connection: 'I'm like the hummingbird.' But then in the fourth stanza the metaphor gets lost or confused, as you say you would pollinate *other* plants. So now you're *different* from the hummingbird, which is fine, but now what? There's no sense that you're contemplating this newfound distinction. Why not weave in language that captures the value of this? Preferably not just how this makes you better, like you're outdoing the hummingbird, which you've already portrayed as impressively busy and ambitious, pollinating at least 100 flowers a day, wings constantly fluttering. Maybe get at something bittersweet here, where you recognize that you're even more ambitious than the hummingbird after all, that you can't stop at just the flowers; you're different from all the other hummingbirds, and this distinction comes with a price; you're not part of the species after all; your ambition has no limits."

I look up from the paper in my hands. Miles appears speechless.

This is not the first time I'm talking with a student about his work when I realize I'm accidentally conducting a therapy session: by excavating the subtext, I'm unveiling the truth not only of the poem but of the kid...and, in this case, not just Miles *in general,* but Miles *specifically,* right here, doing what he's doing right now: not grade-grubbing exactly, but trying to understand the rationale behind the 46 out of 50. I ask him if my comments make sense, if the grade seems fair. He nods and admits it struck him as low when he spotted it on Gradebook earlier. I posted the grades just minutes before last period. I wonder how frequently he's checking his grades. And how often he sticks around after class to ask his teachers about the grades that fail to meet his standards—or Harvard's. I know he must be thinking about his early-admission application. I don't blame him. At the moment, I'm glad to have put the time and thought into the feedback, relieved to have been prepared for this encounter.

What I'm offering Miles is not a defense of a low grade, a grade that for some students would be cause for celebration. My "criticism," I explain to him, reflects my enthusiasm for the work, for how good I believe it can be—how good *he* can be. He's quiet. He glances at me. *Who is this guy?* I can't pinpoint the exact source of his uneasiness. Here's the moment where I give the student an offer he can't refuse, or, rather, an offer he's quite *free* to refuse—in either case, one bound to resolve the matter. I say, "I'd love to see a revision if you're interested. That's why I offer such detailed feedback." I extend the paper toward him. He takes it and shrugs.

If a student says the comments are clear and fair but doesn't revise, then case closed. No hard feelings. I hope the feedback made him think about what's working well and what might work better. If he shrugs, as Miles does, and takes the paper with him, then, well, we'll see. Miles is obviously not happy about having more work to do, either to improve the poem or to improve the grade. But he knows I'm not messing around. The worst a student can say about me at this point is that I'm more excited about his work's potential than he is. Indeed, after rereading those comments out loud, I'm wishing the poem were mine so that I could revise it myself. I want that passion to come through in these conversations, so that the student's reaction might be, *hey, hands off, this is MY poem*...and maybe I'll see a revision tomorrow.

Losing Stars

Today Christopher had some trouble with his teacher. At the dinner table he tells Vana and me about the sticker system, designed to discourage misbehavior. You start with ten stars, he explains. Each time you call out without raising your hand, you lose a star.

I ask. "Who's 'you'? Just *you?* How about the other kids?"

"Only Justin and Chase. Nobody else."

"How many stars did you end up with today?"

"Four."

"*Ended up* with four?!" I say.

"That's it," Vana says. "No screens."

"*What?!*" Christopher looks to me for backup.

"Sorry," I say.

Later Christopher comes to me and, with a hint of grave concern, says, "Daddy, I don't know what to do." He means, literally, he does not know what to *do*—with his time—when TV isn't an option.

I'm at the desk in the kitchen, trying to get some writing done. "See?" I say. "No-screens forces you to come up with ideas for other activities."

"Like play a game?" he asks.

"On my *phone?* Are you kidding? Mommy just said—"

"No! *Together.* Like, a real game."

"Oh. Okay."

He says, "I have a new favorite game, actually. It's called Spoons."

"Oh yeah? Cool."

"It's a card game. With spoons."

I nod. "Sure." It's only fair, I figure, that I drop whatever I'm doing to do whatever he wants to do, since this is the kind of meaningful activity I mean to encourage.

He says, "Can we get it?"

"*Get* it? We have cards. We have spoons."

"Nooo," he says. "It's, like, a real game, that comes in a box. Let me show you..." He gestures to my pocket, where I keep my phone.

I sigh, lamenting the familiarity of this ritual. He's playing me like a violin right now. I open the Amazon app. I type in "Spoons," and there it is.

"Yay, Daddy, look!"

This is all wrong, I know. The kid's teacher designed a sticker system just for him. He thinks he was rewarded today with his four remaining stars. Whatever happened to demerits? Starting with zero and getting strikes called against you when you screw up. Three strikes and you're out. Nowadays the kid starts with a trove of assets, and the burden is on the grown-up to take one away from him.

"Are you going to start raising your hand in class?" I ask firmly.

He nods.

Even more firmly, "You can't just blurt out whatever you want whenever you feel like it."

He nods.

I'm pathetic, about to buy this game for him, trying to convince myself that I'm using this unearned reward as leverage. I swipe: Order Now. Fifteen bucks. In the interest of *meaningful activities,* I tell myself.

"So now what do we do?" I ask.

"I'll teach you," he says, and finds a regular deck of cards in the junk drawer. In the dining room he stoops for the half-soccer ball that slides on the hardwood floor like a hockey puck. He sets it on the table between two chairs. It looks like the buzzer you smack when you have the answer. *Family Feud?* He points to it and says, "It's the spoon."

I bite my tongue for the moment. He explains the rules. The game is not complicated. I realize I just spent fifteen bucks on a deck of cards and six plastic spoons.

I can't resist any longer: "We can use spoons from the drawer? Maybe we can cancel the order—"

"No! We'll use magic markers." He gathers them from the nearby art table. "They need to be different colors."

On Friday he's disappointed when there's no package from Amazon on the porch when he gets home from school.

"How many stars did you end up with today?"

"Eight," he says proudly.

"So, you *still* didn't raise your hand *twice.* It's *that* difficult for you to raise your hand?"

He nods. "I get frustrated because I know the answer and my teacher doesn't call on me."

"Because you're blurting it out before she has a chance to call on *anyone!*"

All day Saturday he's asking if Spoons has arrived yet. Again and again, he checks the porch. Finally, he returns with a box and tears it open. It's exactly one deck of regular cards and six large plastic spoons in assorted colors. And a directions sheet. He wants to play pronto, of course. The directions contradict most of what Christopher taught me the other day, the half-soccer ball and magic markers notwithstanding, so I google "spoons" and the game comes up as the top hit, i.e., *before the utensil.*

How have I not heard of this game? It's as rudimentary as can be. The spoon could just as well be a fork or a penny or a peanut. You take a spoon when you get four of a kind. The player with the most spoons wins.

Some genius decided to market this in a box for cavemen like me who don't know about a game that's more popular on the internet than its namesake tool.

But Christopher couldn't be more excited, fanning the spoons between us, shushing me, "No, no, Daddy, listen," as I try to comprehend the rules.

Cynical Girl

In Level-Two Creative Writing, or, "Honors Level," the high school's latest euphemism for Not-Quite-"Advanced" (like the middle child, lost between Level One, aka "Advanced," and Level Three, aka "College Prep"), Angie announces, as if to her friends, "I still have no idea for my story!" The plot outline and first two pages are due today.

"Come on over," I say, "and sit on the hot seat—the *idea* seat."

She joins me at my desk while the others get busy on their laptops.

"Anything?" I ask her.

"Nothing."

"Not even *bad* ideas you ditched?"

She ponders this possibility. "Well, only…about how I feel like I was born in the wrong time…"

Instantly I'm intrigued. "What time would you prefer?"

"Any!" She reconsiders. "Okay, like, the seventies to the nineties."

Makes sense. Basically before 9/11.

"How I hate Millennials," she adds, "even though I *am* one."

"Millennials are older than you. You're Generation Z."

"See! It's like I was born in the wrong time. I can't relate to *either*. I'm constantly cutting through all the bullshit on everything and everyone, including myself. It's exhausting."

I'm smiling. "Um, I think you've got a story here."

"Really?"

"Or at least a character with a voice."

"It's just me ranting."

"If everything you just said were your first paragraph, I'd be hooked."

"So how do I make it fiction?"

"You can start by changing characters' names. What would be the perfect name for your narrator? Ashley? Shelly. *Sheila."*

"As if that's going to fool anyone." She laughs, but she's thinking now.

I'm trying to nudge her toward the demands—and freedoms—of fiction, referring to her, or to her *character,* in third-person. "She's a likable character, smart, interesting, self-effacing, with a clear, impossible, even romantic goal."

Angie smiles, maybe even blushes a little.

"So now what?" I ask her.

"*Now* what?"

"You need a plot."

"I suck at plot. That's my problem. I wouldn't know where to begin."

"Begin anywhere. Don't worry about chronology. It's all about how the parts work together to create a whole."

I remember recommending a story from my students' Greatest Hits collection bound on the back counter.

"Did you read Rachel Elliot's 'Cynical Girl'?"

She nods, yes, but sheepishly, perhaps hoping I'm not about to quiz her on it.

"Think about it. The girl is pregnant and doesn't want to be. The *plot* is just a trick to contextualize all this great stuff you have to say. You just need a hook, a question, to drive the story. What are the circumstances of your character's life that would trigger all these interesting and funny observations? She can be a seventeen-year-old girl, just like you. There's no need to disguise that. The plot is where you can make stuff up, make things happen, to fire up that voice of hers—*yours."*

Angie smirks. Something good is going on behind those widening eyes.

I go on about "Cynical Girl": "Remember the opening scene, the girl scoffing at all the lowlifes at the Planned Parenthood? But she's there *with* them. She knows she's a hypocrite! *There's* the hook. The story can't be over until she confronts her hypocrisy." I hesitate. "Her *bullshit.* It turns out, in the climax, she's *not* pregnant, false alarm, but that question of her pregnancy served its purpose and forced her to recognize that she's been cruel, to her boyfriend and to *everyone,* and why? Because she's *afraid,* right? Not just of being pregnant, but, deep down, of what?"

"Love," Angie says.

Hallelujah.

"*That's* the story, right? In the end she *wants* to change. She goes to her boyfriend, who earlier told her 'I love you' and she laughed in his face. Not this time, though. She loves him, and she wants him to know it."

Angie's looking at me, but her mind is elsewhere.

"What will your character's conflict be?" I ask her.

"I got it," she says, not exactly answering my question. She stands up. "Final copy has to be *at least six pages?*"

"Yes, but don't worry about length. Trust the story."

SAVANNAH'S STORY

After three weeks of working on their short stories, today the students in my three Creative Writing classes have the full period just to read and enjoy each other's finished work. I join them. The first story I read, by Level-One student Savannah Greene, is incredibly great, one of the best student stories I've ever read, I think, or maybe I'm just excited, and grateful, to kick off this long reading period with something so promisingly competent.

The story, entitled *Meg,* is a shoo-in for *Pegasus,* our literary magazine (of which I'm supervisor), unless it's determined, by the student editors or perhaps by Savannah herself, that it's too provocative or risqué for their fellow-student readers, despite the boundaries the magazine has broken in past years. *Meg* is curiously different, startling for its unapologetic portrayal of the first-person narrator, a middle-aged woman who is, against her will, outed as a lesbian by her own daughter, who discovers her mother pleasuring a girlfriend in the family car and who subsequently, acting out in confused rage, stabs a fellow student nearly to death and lands herself in the same psychiatric institute where her mother now tells the story. When I tell Savannah how impressed I am and how I can't wait to see it published, she's both pleased and horrified, grinning and blushing at the thought of others reading her story.

"You really think...? The car scene?" she asks.

"I *like* to challenge our readers. There's never been anything like this story in the magazine before." I smile. "We may need to soften some of the language."

Her eyes widen with skeptical delight. "At *least!*"

Today I'm more impressed than ever by Savannah, who for the past three weeks has worked quietly and perhaps secretively, nodding modestly when I asked how her story was coming along. I'm thrilled that she's entirely at ease with the thought of her story *not* being published, despite my enthusiasm—that her personal satisfaction, with or without my approval, is sufficient reward.

MEN AND WOMEN

This morning I'm reading Joseph Campbell, who talks of how, with our rockets and skyscrapers, we have convinced ourselves that the male preoccupation is "the proper aim for everyone," when actually man is just the agent of female power. This observation reminds me of another book I've been reading, *A People's History of the United States,* in which Howard Zinn describes how certain native societies revolved around the woman, who held the power, how there was no marriage, and how the woman could go from one man to another and the men accepted this flexible arrangement. Campbell explains that the woman used to know how to run the world, that she is, after all, Mother Earth, "the great divinity and the source of all power," and that when she exchanges this position for passage into "the field of male achievement," she loses her real power and this loss breeds resentment.

Man's role is to *act;* woman's, to *be.*

I'm cringing, but only somewhat, at this chauvinistic mythology I can't help identifying with. My brother recently asked how everything's going "as Mr. Mom," during this year of my wife living the life of a full-time doctoral student while maintaining her full-time job. I answered, "Fine," while bemoaning the epithet meant to point up my submission to assuming the woman's traditional role. *Mr. Mom.* Why not "Super Dad"? Or just "Awesome Man"?

And so of course I'm pondering all this when upstairs Christopher is suddenly screaming "No! I'm not wearing a collared shirt!" and by the time I arrive he's coming at Vana from behind like a rabid animal. She's kneeling before an open dresser drawer, folding his clothes. He stops just short of her, with raised hand, as if he would dare, just as she turns her shoulders away from him, instinctively but calmly; and, incredibly, she doesn't let up: "Yes, you *are* wearing it, *Christopher*."

He doesn't let up, either. "I'm not!" His refusals intensify in parallel with the certainty of her demands.

"You're wearing it!" She won't even give him the satisfaction of looking to see his furious expressions.

"No!" He makes fists.

I'm afraid he might actually take a swing at her, but of course he won't. I want her to spin around and wring his neck.

Michael gets what's going on here. Every ten seconds or so he appears out of nowhere to slug Christopher in the upper body, a real thumping blow that keeps Christopher's fire burning. He's seething, retaliation coming out of every pore. Vana folds another T-shirt with stoic lack of interest. I resist the urge to intervene. Michael wants Christopher to bring the fight *his* way, understanding, evidently, that it must be *someone's* duty to act. Someone must *do* something, especially if Daddy's just going to stand there, watching from the doorway.

I've decided to follow Vana's lead. This exchange is an exercise in patience. In detachment. In respect—of the woman's power. In the suppression of my own (primal?) urge to assert control by putting an end to this whole violent male disaster and instead just bearing witness to it—in deference to the mother and in awe of her unique ability just "to be," even, or especially, in the face of the man's (and boy's) need to *physically act.* I understand this is a Catch-22, as I will be (rightly) accused of having done nothing to correct the behavior of our male offspring.

Still, I shove my impulses down, ready to intervene only if absolutely necessary. Christopher doesn't understand why Mommy won't turn around to defend herself. He must be just as mystified by my inaction. In Vana's way, she's showing him how to be a human being. In my way, I'm trying to demonstrate that the woman does not need the man to protect her. And yet, at this point I want to take him down, paralyze him with one arm. Till he calms down. Till he sees that he can't behave like this. Not with me nearby. If she's not going to defend herself, then I must defend her.

I resent this responsibility, even as I hunger to fulfill it. And yet, I tear Michael away from his brother for the third time, hoping that however this ends "naturally" will serve some instructive purpose, just as Christopher whips his collared shirt at Vana, who hollers, "What the hell is the matter with you?" and exits the room, leaving the three of us heaving pointlessly.

FAIR-MINDED

Several of the rants and diary entries that my Creative Writing students wrote are impassioned defenses of Trump. Or, more likely, impassioned complaints, or pleas, aimed at Trump attackers, who refuse to just let the man do his job. He's president now, so get over it. The Right deserves the same respect that the Left expects, or even *received,* argues one student, who makes the point that for eight years of Obama you didn't see the conservatives marching in the streets, claiming "Not my president."

I compliment these rants, the effective stream-of-consciousness style, the passionate voices. I steer clear of political debate and call them provocative or stimulating.

Destiny, who confesses she was "leaning Hillary," admits she doesn't know a whole lot about politics, but now that Trump won, she believes we should all come together as a country and accept him as our leader and respect the office of the Presidency. As she reads her rant aloud in class, the kids are calm, respectful, no signs of stirring or suppressing the outcries I anticipated. My own internal outcries seem to dissipate as I witness their acquiescence to this call for moderation.

After Destiny finishes, I ask the class, as usual, "What's good here? What's working well?"

Noah says, "I admired her fair-mindedness. How she didn't argue for one side or the other."

I want to believe that this kindhearted ambivalence is a good thing. I just hope that one day, when challenged, they'll have the guts to stand up for what they believe in and that they'll be curious enough to try to figure out what that might be.

Aaron's Missing Chapter

Last period, in Level Three, aka "College Prep," Aaron Jackson lumbers by the lectern and asks, "Can you grade that book assignment, cuz it's been a zero for, like, a week?"

I'm speechless. This is the first time Aaron has uttered an unsolicited word to me all semester.

In fact, I already graded his assignment yesterday after school, and I was hoping that the matter might go away on its own, that I might leave the zero and assume correctly that Aaron would never question it, that he'd interpret my silence as a signal, an invitation, to let sleeping dogs lie. I'd asked him yesterday, before class, as I had asked him every day for the past week, if at last he had his paper for me. Instead of the usual head shake, I got "I shared it with you *last Wednesday,*" by which he meant that all this time I'd had *access* to his work, and why the hell hadn't I taken the initiative to read it? I didn't bother reminding him that I'd wanted a submitted hard copy, his physical *paper,* not just his permission to scavenge my Google Drive in search of Aaron Jackson's still-missing assignment. Instead, I let the lie slide and, after class, read the now-shared electronic version.

Originally, he'd elected to write a "Missing Chapter" from the book he'd been reading on his own; now, Aaron's story, or whatever this was, didn't seem at all like an attempted imitation of a chapter from Tim O'Brien's *The Things They Carried.* It seemed more like a page transcribed from a random history textbook.

"The Anglo-Saxon settlement of Britain describes the process which changed the language and culture of most of what became England from Romano-British to Germanic."

Um. Was he serious? What was I supposed to make of this irrelevancy, not to mention the diction and syntax that were obviously not his own? And then I remembered the day Aaron had set aside O'Brien's book in favor of a giant *Norton Anthology of British Literature* that just happened to be sitting on the shelf behind him. Since I was reading Aaron's "paper" in his Google Doc, it was easy for me to copy and paste the whole thing right into a Google search to see if, or, rather, *from what source,* he'd plagiarized it.

"The Germanic-speakers in Britain, themselves of diverse origins, eventually developed a common cultural identity as Anglo Saxons. This process occurred from the mid-fifth to early seventh centuries, following the end of Roman power in Britain around the year 410. The settlement...."

As I do all of this, I keep searching Aaron's document for one shred of a sentence, a phrase, that might conceivably have been formulated in his mind.

"The few literary sources tell of hostility between incomers and natives. ...there is little clear evidence for the influence of British Celtic or British Latin or Old English. These factors have suggested a very large-scale invasion by various Germanic peoples."

And then, there it is, right there in my Google search. Plucked from Wikipedia verbatim. The unaltered opening paragraphs appearing under "Anglo-Saxon settlement of Britain." The ol' copy-paste.

One can't help picturing the student first going to this most obvious of websites, one week after his assignment's due date, making the conscious decision to copy the first paragraphs, paste them into a Google Doc, and then submit this to his teacher. One can't help trying to track the thought process behind these asinine decisions. Aaron must have thought I would read these words and believe he'd written them. He must have believed himself to be capable of writing these words in this order. And he must have believed that it all seemed like a "missing chapter" from *The Norton Anthology of British Literature.*

And yet— Aaron must have known that just the other day his classmate and friend, Zach, got busted for having submitted, as his own "Missing Chapter" (from O'Brien's book), a transcription of an actual letter written by an actual American soldier from Vietnam— an especially dishonorable act of plagiarism, for reasons I didn't need to explain. After school, Zach and I had sat in silence for a moment at my desk, his retyped soldier's letter in my hands, as he awaited the inevitable. He accepted his zero with apparent contrition, and so it was not difficult to give him the speech about integrity and about how in college this offense would be grounds for expulsion, nor was it too unsettling to call his mother, predicting correctly that she would express the proper regret.

With Aaron, I recognize no such signs of contrition. Near the end of the period, I say to him, with great solemnity, "Stick around after class for a minute so we can talk."

He says, "I can't cuz I have to go all the way to the other side of the building."

"To catch your bus?"

He nods. The bell rings.

I say, "We'll talk about it tomorrow," and he's off.

I'll have to harbor my disbelief for another twenty-four hours.

SCHOOL CLOTHES

After his bath, Christopher prepares his outfit for school tomorrow, laying pants and a shirt on the foam chair with the orange fox cover. Vana tells Christopher to pick another shirt.

She says, "No sports attire tomorrow. You need to start dressing like a student. You're going to school, not to the athletic field."

Christopher's IQ test results came back today. He didn't make the cut for the Gifted program, a surprise that came as a blow to Vana, who'd assumed that, at least in this respect, Christopher would follow in her footsteps.

"How is this *sports?!*" Christopher asks about the shirt in his hands. "It says St. Joe's University!"

"It says *Hawks,*" Vana says.

This is how the two frequently go back and forth, an intimate sparring between competitors who relish the provocation.

"The school mascot doesn't just mean sports," Christopher reasonably says, then, "Fine," and lays a T-shirt on top of the long-sleeved Hawks shirt, complying with his mother's demands, or believing he is doing so.

"No T-shirts over long sleeves," Vana says. "It looks sloppy."

"It's like you want me to look handsome every day!" Christopher cries. "Why can't I wear this?" He points to another shirt. "It says *'Penn'! You* got me this from your *school!* I want to wear short-sleeved shirts and not have to wait until spring to wear them."

I think he makes a pretty good case. He's bawling now.

Vana wants him to be preppy. "Like Parker," she says.

"Parker?!" Christopher screams. "Parker takes off his shirt on the bus and he has a basketball jersey on underneath! To trick his mother!"

There's a good long pause here, before he lets out one last cry, which dwindles to a whimper, sadness tinged with regret: Exposing Parker's trick was an unplanned last resort. Christopher meant only to shine light on the great injustice at hand, not to tarnish his friend's image. Let alone to confess to a crime he, too, has committed. But it was worth it, he must be thinking. His mother must learn The Truth!

I AM A HONDURAN

This morning Rodrigo Florez finally shared his "Chapter in My Life" with me. For days I've been warning him that, if he does not finish this assignment, he's going to fail the course, the lowest-level senior English class available. When I implored him to share his Google Doc with me at the beginning of first period today, he conceded, seeing that I wasn't going to start class until he'd made at least this first step toward completing the larger task.

As the document opened on his laptop, he looked up at me. He'd written exactly one sentence. *Growing up as a minority was pretty tough.* I returned his blank stare. I told him to keep writing.

"Tell me about how tough it's been, growing up as a minority."

As he continued to stare at me, I realized that my simplistic summation of his life condition, even though I had basically just quoted his opening sentence, was probably a gross understatement of the challenges he'd undergone. But in the pouty, faintly mustachioed grin that suddenly appeared on his face, I saw that he had forgiven me for my ignorance. I also believed that the grin meant he had a story he wanted to tell.

Now, at the start of second period, I see in the Google Doc that Rodrigo has somehow made exponential progress since only an hour ago. He has written exactly two more sentences. *I was originally from Honduras, but then I moved to America. There are so many problems, and now it has become worse because I can't run a business because I'm more illegal than cocaine.*

Not bad, I think. There's *a voice* here, or at least an attempt to find one—and, I'm guessing, there's a whole lot more to come. There'd better be. I want to find out what happens next.

In September, Rodrigo had attended school the first three days before he vanished for a month. When I learned in a formal email from the guidance department that Rodrigo Florez had gone away for "treatment," I assumed for no good reason it was for alcohol. But later his guidance counselor explained that Rodrigo had tried to kill himself and continued to suffer from depression. It was with pride, then shame, that I recognized that the depth of my sympathy for this Honduran immigrant boy, whose suffering I imagined had been overwhelmingly horrible, was greater than my sympathy for all the other students who'd tried to kill themselves, or even succeeded in doing so. I believed that I could identify with their white suburban pain and that suicide was an overreaction to it; whereas *Rodrigo's* pain I couldn't fathom, and so it took on an exotic authenticity. Rodrigo was new to the school. This past summer his family had moved from the neighboring county to the north, from a remote farm, where Rodrigo had liked living and working, to this gentrified town on Philadelphia's suburban Main Line. His mother works multiple jobs, and so, as the oldest of several siblings, Rodrigo is often left to care for them, when he's not working at the Wendy's, where he puts in forty hours a week.

On a hunch, before heading to the faculty dining room, I check Rodrigo's Google Doc, not that I should expect to see progress; after all, he would have been occupied for the past few hours, along with the rest of his senior classmates, at the annual pre-prom-night Mock Crash assembly. But evidently he's been eager to get back to work. The moment the document opens, I see a fluttering of letters on the screen and then stillness. Rodrigo must see my name at the top of the page, notifying him that the only person with whom he's shared this document has selected *this* moment, of all unlikely moments—

the moment he's decided for the first time in his life to do schoolwork instead of going to lunch—to check on his progress. I imagine Rodrigo staring at the flashing cursor, as I am. It's as if we're looking each other in the eye, unable to see the other staring back. He must be waiting for me to do the right thing and get lost already. I can see I'm interrupting, can't I? Still, I can't resist a glance, and then I keep reading, until I reach that pulsing cursor, hovering at the word "Honduran."

This is an issue because if ICE found out, they would find me and kick me out of America even though I've been living here for about five years. But since I haven't gone through the process of becoming a full-fledged American citizen, they don't care.

Moving from where you lived all your life to somewhere new is tough. Trying to find a job was hard, usually because I would go out in the street with my eletero-cart *and sell* elotes con crema, *which is basically corn with mayonnaise chili powder and* queso molido, *which is like ground-up cheese. It might sound nasty, but it's actually very good.*

We relocated to Tennessee, where the people in the South are very racist towards people like me. Well, whenever I met someone, they said racist comments because I am a Honduran.

Rodrigo is still here, perhaps waiting for me to write something. He could be expecting his teacher's encouraging words to begin flooding the page. No, he just wants me to *vamoose.* To leave him to his work. As I'm about to click out and go to lunch, he beats me to it. His name vanishes. I'm left staring at a half-page of text, already dreading having to face him in the morning, fearing I've interrupted him for good, he'll claim this is it, that's all there is, there's nothing more to tell.

Vape Pens

At the faculty meeting, Carolyn Winters gives us the quick lowdown on PSAT administration next week; the nurse instructs us on using the EpiPen, demonstrating on Serenity Davis's raised thigh how to administer the adrenaline shot in case of an emergency peanut-allergy reaction; and Neil Gillespie, the school psychologist, headlines the program with a thorough presentation on the exponentially growing number of students using vape pens.

"The FDA can't keep up with the chemical combinations and their corresponding names," Neil explains. Almost instantly he captivates an enthralled audience of teachers, of high-school teachers at almost 3 p.m., no less—no small feat. "These drugs are available in stores. When they're discovered, they're banned, and so the 'reputable' vape places—there's one nearby, in Bryn Mawr—have only the FDA-approved ones." I've got one eye on Neil, the other on the PowerPoint presentation. "But these other ones are known killers: K2. Spice. Black Mamba. Mojo." Neil is an engaging presenter. We're like a roomful of law-enforcement officers getting briefed by the chief, who is informing us of ruthless suspects with sexy names. Many of us, myself included, lean forward, elbows on knees, as Neil proceeds briskly from one slide to the next on the projector screen.

"There have been cases of mass overdose—in a whole section of a city where such a drug has been sold in a store, or at a party, where kids are all sharing the same drugs. Or making cocktails of their collected supplies, for a multi-sided high. The behavior can be erratic. Psychotic. Suicidal. There are anecdotes of dozens of people in a single location looking and acting like zombies."

Neil's face slowly darkens. I have come to understand that his days are consumed by such real-life horror stories, while I get to teach fiction.

"Watch out for Cloud 9," he says. "And Darth Vapor. These are the liquid products. The vape pens can cost $350. Parents have come into school to retrieve their kid's confiscated pen. You cannot make this stuff up." He imitates a mom or a dad: "'Hey, I gave my kid 350 bucks for that thing, and I want it back.' I'm serious," Neil says, hitting his stride. He doesn't need to fake his passion; he channels it. And he knows his shit. These are the hallmarks of a great teacher—and of a great administrator. I do not miss the unfortunate irony that he's the school psychologist, not one of us, or, really, one of them, either. He goes on, "The parents have no clue, less of a clue than their kids, who know to lie to their parents about the potential risks, claiming they're"—he makes furious quotation marks with his fingers—"'*just vaping*,' which the parents often *believe* isn't actually 'doing drugs,' which is why they think they're doing their kids some kind of favor. Just look at the packaging."

Our eyes are drawn back to the big screen. "They look like candy and toys and comic books. They smell like watermelon or strawberry." The lure is obvious. I recall those first rushes of independence when I was growing up, dropping five bucks on Snickers bars and Dubble-Bubble, obscene doses of sugar, or, later, pressing my luck, using busboy tips to score Southern Comfort and brand-name wine coolers.

"Meanwhile," Neil says, "they can be laced with phenolphthalein. Fentanyl. Soaked in this stuff. Now you're addicted to opioids."

Tonight, when Michael asks me for a lollipop, I'll savor the sight of him sucking on that cherry Tootsie Pop, flashing me that bright red grin.

SWASTIKA II

I mention the washed-away swastika to Stan the janitor, who shakes his head, says he didn't know about it. His eyes brighten suddenly. But he did find one *inside* Penny's classroom last week.

"You did?" I ask.

He says he scrubbed it off and didn't mention it to anyone, figuring it would be impossible to find the student responsible.

"Probably right," I say. "No cameras in the classrooms."

"Plus," Stan says, "it was so small." He shows me with his fingers, his thumb and pointer an inch apart.

PLASTICITY

In lieu of a spoken prayer before dinner, I do my cross—quick fingers to the forehead, belly, shoulders, chest—as does Vana, and the boys ape the ritual with surprising solemnity. Their dutiful imitation, almost sadly curious in their attentiveness, reminds me that I really must commit once and for all to modeling a lifestyle of spiritual consciousness. I want our sons to grow up feeling whole. The way I felt when I was growing up. I want them to feel connected. But more than that. Safe. Taken care of. Not just by their parents. But by something larger than us.

Of course, we missed church again yesterday.

Saturday nights we almost always plan to go to church. Morning comes and no one rushes anyone else to get dressed. Instead, we make French toast. Vana reads *The New York Times*, taking a break from her doctoral work. I read books I believe do more for me than church does.

Right now, I'm reading Buddhist monk Matthieu Ricard's *Happiness.* On plasticity of the brain. On expanding and training the mind.

Michael asks for a piece of "tushy paper" (*tissue* paper, aka Kleenex), so now Christopher is singing "tushy paper," delighted by his brother's accidental poetry.

Now Michael is repeating "Mine!" about what I don't know.

The boys are playing Legos on the kitchen floor. I ask Michael to please stop saying "mine." I ask Christopher to please stop doing whatever he's doing that keeps making Michael say "mine."

"I'm not doing anything," Christopher says.

I'm reading about how rats' brains grow in more stimulating environments.

Christopher changes his tune. He sings, "Searching for a cup of soup. Searching..."

I ask, "Where's that from?"

He says a word that makes no sense to me.

"What?" I ask, as if hearing the answer again might help.

He says, "It's a show on Nickelodeon"—a riddle inside a riddle now.

I sigh.

He continues, "Searching for a cup— "

Michael yells, "Stop!" and smashes a fist wrist-deep into the bin of Legos.

"Jesus Christ," I let out. "Would you guys—?"

I remind myself to be *present* for all of this, without judgment, in a state of pure awareness. *"When thoughts intrude the meditator does not attempt to interfere with them but allows the thoughts to vanish naturally."* Ricard writes about EEG and MRI tests of meditators, about evidence of precise localization of cerebral activity, of literal changing of the brain through meditation.

I don't want to miss a millisecond.

Mock Crash

Scheduled the week before prom night, the Mock Crash is elaborately designed to scare seniors from driving drunk and may very well scare them from driving sober. This annual event is so effective in achieving its purpose that, after the second time I watched it, a few years ago, I decided there wouldn't be a third time if I could help it. Seeing it once is enough to scare you to death—for the rest of your life.

So, nowadays, while the entire senior class attends the event during all of second, third, and fourth periods, I hide out in my classroom. Bleachers are set up in the grass to make a theater of the parking lot. As the students begin to take their seats, their attention is drawn to the smashed car already sitting crumpled on the macadam. A police officer, an actual fully uniformed Pennsylvania State Trooper, a veteran of the force, sets the scene, offering a kind of prologue before exiting stage right. The whole drama will take about an hour; afterward, everyone will adjourn into the auditorium for a follow-up discussion.

The car would seem at first too completely destroyed to have room for passengers, but behind the crunched and mangled hood are four students, one in the front and three in the back, seniors, actual classmates of the audience, volunteer actors who haven't rehearsed for this, frozen in position, as if awaiting a director's call to action, but they won't be moving once the drama begins because they're all dead, bloodied like the sole survivor, who, once the audience is seated, takes center stage, staggering at first, before growing frantic, seeing, as we all do now, the horror that confronts her.

The survivor of the crash—who was the driver—makes a phone call. She examines, close up, her unmoving friends. She grows frantic. The first police car arrives in the distance, at first unseen, siren blaring beyond the trees that border the campus. The trooper tears into the lot, lights flashing. A new, younger cop emerges, makes a call on his radio. Everyone in the audience is thinking, *my God, how realistic!* The production has only just started. Another car arrives, and from it emerges a woman. The girl's mother? "My darling!" But she goes straight to the wreckage, bypassing the surviving girl. Emergency vehicles arrive. More police cars. A firetruck barrels in. It is organized chaos. EMTs know what to do. Firefighters approach the car with the Jaws of Life. Bodies are carefully removed. The carnage, the lifelessness. The audience is mute, horrified, awestruck.

The mother starts in on the surviving girl. "My son! You killed my son!" It's too much to bear. In past years, the cops managed at this point to escort the grieving mother away and to redirect attention to the cleanup operation. This year, however, the young cop who first arrived on the scene decides, presumably, to improvise. My AP Lit students describe this whole scene to me during fifth period. The young cop approaches the girl and roars, "You killed your friends!" sending the girl into shuddering, convincing hysterics. The proverbial fourth wall has been shattered when the acting transcends artifice and becomes real trauma.

After the Mock Crash drama in the parking lot is complete, the story picks up in the auditorium, where, as is customary, the police officers take questions from the students. This year the students are buzzing—not about the power of their classmates' performances, but about their own shock at the young trooper's aggressive behavior.

A member of the audience asks, "Is that the way you always act at the scene of an accident?"

The policeman, failing to sense the direction of this interrogation, does not take offense at the question. "Yes," he says, "firm," and goes on to give an example of a recently crashed Lamborghini and a drunk driver who, when he gets out of prison in ten years, will have more hell to pay if this trooper gets his way. "I'm going to deport his ass to Mexico!" he promises.

While taking in this whole drama, I imagine Rodrigo Florez sitting in that auditorium, this slight boy with bangs over his eyes, wishing he could disappear, his secrets with him, surrounded by privileged white kids, sixteen of whom are all hopped up in my classroom right now, ignited by the outrageous injustice they just witnessed.

As one student tells the story, there are gasps from his classmates reliving that moment in the auditorium when they heard the cop make his pronouncement. I can see in their hungry, yet also satisfied, eyes that the story ends well for the home team. I raise my eyebrows to signal that I get it, I'm with them, I want them to tell me how it ends, how they got the guy's goat. The last word. "Everybody lost it," they say. It takes the trooper a minute to realize that the hooting is not supportive. These kids are operating on a different frequency, and this guy doesn't have a clue.

I picture Rodrigo shrinking back in his seat.

The girl who asked the question asks a follow-up: "What's your name?"

"Bill," the officer says. "Why?"

The girl says, "Bill *what?*"

Bill gives his full name.

The girl's classmates cheer.

Now Bill gets it, well enough to strike a pose of defiance, arms akimbo.

Assistant Principal Everest Toole frowns, sensing what's going on—or at least sensing that *something* is going on. He interjects, "Let's get back on track."

The girl, Morgan Jacobson, bound for the University of Pennsylvania in the fall, takes note of the trooper's name; literally, while standing there over the heads of her classmates, she jots it into her phone. Anyone who knows Morgan understands that she has every intention of pursuing justice vigorously.

The chorus of students in my classroom is heaving with collective self-satisfaction after relaying all of this to its teacher. Of course, I'm impressed by such a display of social consciousness; at the same time, I'm uncomfortable with the image of that student grandstanding and at least attempting to humiliate this authority figure. Meanwhile, her fellow students are riding on the thrilling sense of their own collective power, even as they must fear the very same authority that today claimed powers that exceeded those that have been vested in this officer.

At lunch, Dean and Sam, who attended the Mock Crash as well as the subsequent Q&A session, break it all down in the faculty dining room.

Sam says, "Who said the guy in the accident was even Mexican?"

"That's exactly the point!" Dean shouts. "The driver is brown, so he must be a Mexican criminal. Not to mention illegal! This cop is obviously a Trumper."

Sam says, "I don't know. I give the cop the benefit of the doubt that the dude was an undocumented worker."

Dean explodes, "Come on! If he actually *is* an undocumented worker, then it's all the more a demonstration of what's happening in this country, where a cop has become convinced that he's the arm of the law, he's got no regard for the actual *rule* of law but takes his own higher law into his own hands. This is exactly how it goes! First, the authoritative leader gets the police on his side. Then, he takes down the institutions. He preserves the right to bear arms of military-grade weapons, then claims victory when the NFL owners agree to fine players who protest the Anthem, just like Hitler did when he imposed a year-long ban on soccer players who didn't salute. Did you see that article I posted on Facebook?"

Sam says, "Yeah, I saw it. It's not the same thing."

"It's *exactly* the same thing!" Dean says. "So now, in the NFL, players are *permitted* to stay in their locker rooms, which, *gee,* do you think will draw boos? Or *worse,* when they come running onto the field after Beyonce or whoever finishes singing the 'home of the brave'?"

Carolyn says, "Carrie Underwood."

"What?"

Sam laughs.

"Singing the National Anthem," Carolyn says.

"Uh-huh." Dean is still waiting for a proper response to his diatribe, or at least some acknowledgement from Sam.

"Don't worry, Dean," Carolyn says. "Morgan Jacobson is going to get that cop. I guarantee it. That girl is scary." Carolyn pauses. No one disagrees. Carolyn continues, "I would not mess with her. She could be president one day. I hope I'm alive to see it. A woman in the White House, I mean. Right? I mean, come on already."

SEX CRIMES

Because of recent accusations of Kevin Spacey as a molester of minors, I can't bring myself to show the dinner scene from *American Beauty*. For years I've shown movie scenes that use food as a prop to demonstrate how the physical lives of the characters reflect their emotional lives, and this one has always been the most instructionally effective. For nearly two decades, instead of avoiding the scene because of its profanity and vulgarity, I've emphasized those features in our analysis of the craft of screenwriting, pointing out how the protagonist's line "Would somebody please pass me the *fucking* asparagus!" functions as an intensified beat in the trajectory of his struggle to achieve his *conscious* desire (simply to receive the asparagus) and how "Your mother seems to prefer I go through life like a fucking prisoner while she keeps my dick in a mason jar under the sink!" is a manifestation of his *unconscious* desire (to reclaim his masculine authority).

Before I cut the scene from my plans for good, I contemplate the potential value of a philosophical discussion about whether the behavior of an artist in his private life should influence our judgment of his work. I wonder if we can, or even should try to, remain critically objective about, say, a painting, despite the painter's pedophilia, or his tax evasion—and where do we draw the line, anyway? Should I discontinue my effective lesson on Act One of *Good Will Hunting* because convicted sex offender Harvey Weinstein was the film's producer? The truth is I don't know how many of these kids are even hip to the news of the latest allegations or if they know Kevin Spacey from Kevin Costner.

I set aside *American Beauty* and go with *Annie Hall,* not failing to see the irony of my choice; indeed, I'm secretly amused by it, betting that few students will know who Woody Allen is and that no one will call him out as "that guy who married his daughter." For once, I'm grateful for their youth and ignorance. No one says a word. That is, until Annie tells Alvie, "You're what Grammy Hall would call *a real Jew."* There are audible gasps from some, who in this hyper-sensitized age of "micro aggressions" recoil even more strongly than Woody's character does. I failed to anticipate this potential offense, and I brace myself for the backlash. Last year on Halloween when a white kid wore a vintage Julius Erving jersey along with his hair teased out into a magnificent hairdo-dome, I applauded, "Great afro!" and a girl in the corner whispered to her friend, "That's racist," and I froze, my mind racing for a defense in case this accusation took flight—this accusation I assumed had been directed at me, not at the boy pretending to be Dr. J. To my relief, the moment passed, just as this one does, and before long Annie and Alvie are chitchatting and Alvie's unspoken thoughts appear as subtitles on the screen—"I wonder what she looks like naked"—and I'm bracing myself again.

Christopher Finds a Coin

Christopher finds a coin on the floor in Michael's classroom when we pick him up after school. He shows me. "This looks like a dime, but it's not."

"What is it?" I ask.

"I know it's not a dime because there's not a man on it."

Indeed, it is a woman, and he knows from observation that there are no women on American currency.

"It's Canadian," he guesses correctly.

WETBACK

At the start of first period, I show Rodrigo the printed pages of his "Chapter in My Life" assignment. "I hope you don't mind I added a title. I thought it was perfect—right out of your last line," I say.

He peeks, nods, appearing pleased but puzzled by this printed-out presentation of his story.

I explain.

Before bed last night, I figured I'd just take a quick look at his shared Google Doc. If he was working on it, I'd exit before he could notice. But I figured he probably works till closing time at Wendy's, so I wouldn't be caught snooping.

It appeared he was finished. The thing was a grammatical mess. One giant paragraph, a page and a half long, just short of the two-page requirement. Not a lick of punctuation. Dozens of misspellings. But there was a *story* here. Short and bittersweet. His name signed at the end, as if it were a letter.

On a whim—I was curious; I wanted to see what this story would look like polished—I copied and pasted his words into a document of my own and got to work on editing, not changing a word, just plugging in the periods, commas, and quotation marks. Fixing the misspellings. Not so that *I* could see what it looked like revised, but so that *he* could see what it looked like when I presented it to him the next day and asked if he minded if I read it out loud to the class.

And now I'm asking him, "Can I read it?"

His eyebrows float up. "Seriously?"

"No big discussion or anything. I want them to hear it."

He's looking at me. I'm in no hurry. He can see that.

I say, "No one has ever heard this story before. Not in here. No one's ever told it. Not to them. Not with your voice. Your details."

He must be wondering what I've got up my sleeve.

"This is your story."

He nods, politely acknowledging this fact and understanding that I must mean to convey something more profound. I'm not sure I do, or maybe I think that this fact is profound enough in itself: *This is your story*. He must want to know if I know, as he knows, that his story will make no difference in this world, certainly not to the half-asleep crew in here, that it won't *change* anything, or maybe he wants to know if I'm naive enough to think otherwise.

I say, "Sometimes it's good to read a story just to enjoy it. They'll like it."

"Okay," he says.

The class perks up when I announce that I'm about to read Rodrigo's story. One kid lifts his resting chin off his arms; another plucks an earbud from under his hoodie. I explain that this is a great story. Just listen. This is Rodrigo's story. This happened to him, and he wrote it. It's called "Wetback." Hushed snickers. Halfway through, I look up and see Rodrigo beaming back at me, along with his dozen or so classmates at full attention.

Rodrigo's smile gives me a charge, and I decide that today I'm going to read this story to *all* my classes so that they might begin to understand how little they, or we, truly comprehend the plight of the undocumented immigrant and the chasm that divides our experiences.

An instant later, I understand that today I am *not* going to be reading this story to the rest of my classes, or to anyone else after this. The reason for this quick reversal has something to do with the dreadful feeling I imagine I'll have while reading this story *without* Rodrigo in the room. Or the feeling I'll have in the moments *after* I read the story—when it's just the chorus and I staring at each other, all of us aware of the author's absence as our shame rises inside us and we direct it outward, toward action, toward *doing* something already, or at least at some point in the future, because it's not enough just to know about these things—before we get back to the business of the day.

I take my time reading the rest of it, milking the moment, thinking he's safe here, for now, even happy. I realize that, of course, I'm doing all of this for Rodrigo and no one else, so that he might find courage in his own story when this world that he came to for its freedoms doesn't rush to make him feel at home. So that he might rescue himself from his own history—*with* his own history.

One day last summer I was working at this pizza place in Scranton, PA. I remember the customer well.

He said, "Can I get a pizza?"

I said, "What did you say?"

I remember this customer saying, "Can you understand what I'm saying, you wetback?"

Then I was, like, "Really? Well, this wetback makes your pizza. Get outta this store."

And he was, like, "Let me speak to the manager."

I call Bill over. Bill is not just the manager. He's the owner. We call him Dollar Bill because he's rich. Instead of backing me up, he tells me to get outta the store.

I was, like, damn, okay, but the next day I get a call from an unknown number because I deleted the manager's number.

I answer, "Hello, who is this?" and it turns out it's Dollar Bill, and he was, like, "I'm sorry for being an idiot and telling you to leave the store," and, just listening to this poor rich guy begging for me to come back to the store, I was, like, "Nah, I'm not coming back," and he said, "Fine, nobody needs a wetback in their store."

I just laughed. Wetback. *We came here on a bus.*

If the actual story ended here, Rodrigo would get the last word. Instead, who knows how it ends? One thing is for certain: all of us in Rodrigo's little world here—Morgan, the cop, my students, me—will each have our own story, thanks to Rodrigo, who is the hero of *his* story, just as we will be the heroes in the versions *we* have to tell.

CHANGING YOUR MIND

Vana thanks me for cleaning up the kitchen, before she'll return to the bedroom, where she does her doctoral work. "I enjoy it," I say. She chuckles, but I'm not kidding. I tell her how I've come to like these domestic chores. How they give me a sense of accomplishment, not only in the physical, but also in the psychic, effects. She says she's familiar with that sense of calm while washing dishes. I remind her that I've been meditating every morning and lately seizing every opportunity to enter that state of heightened consciousness, of luminous awareness, driving in the car, folding laundry, washing dishes. I recall the first time my psychiatrist friend described how the brain can literally, physically change, or *be changed,* by the subject's altering of his own thoughts and behaviors. That possibility of permanence, or, rather, impermanence, inspired me. "I think I've actually changed my mind," I say.

"How can you tell?" Vana asks.

I shrug, not sure how to prove it—or if proving it matters.

I wonder if she, or anyone, actually recognizes the cooling-out I've undergone. Six months ago, on the night I told her I'd been meditating an hour every morning before anyone else woke up, she told me, "I love you for what you're doing." She seemed genuinely moved by my commitment, as if I were demonstrating an unprecedented level of devotion to our collective well-being.

Now she asks, "How do you know if it's the meditation?"

I say, "How would I know if it's not?"

"Well, if you can just change your mind..." She pauses to contemplate the question she's about to ask. "How do you know who you really are? How do you know what's really *you.*"

"I don't know." I smile. "How do you know what's really *you?*"

She answers with a roll of the eyes, then heads upstairs to do her work.

In a way, our relationship is better than ever because our roles and expectations are so exquisitely defined. Tomorrow after school, I will rush to get the boys to the dentist by 5:30. But first I will stop at Lowe's to pick up a propane tank for the grill as well as biodegradable paper bags to replace the twelve unacceptable plastic bags stuffed with leaves still sitting on the curb, which were rejected by the garbage men, and then I'll transfer the leaves from the plastic to the paper. I'll swing by Whole Foods, pick up Christopher at school, drop off the groceries at home, pick up Michael at day care, drive into the city to the dentist's office, and afterward take the boys to McCrossen's Tavern for dinner in the old neighborhood. All while Vana is home doing her doctoral work. I will bring her a burger and fries.

It is satisfying—*clarifying*—to perform all these tasks for my family without the distraction of my own unmet expectations.

PUNISHING AARON

Eighth period I'm in the hallway waiting to ambush Aaron Jackson before class, figuring that, if I don't talk to him now, I'll miss my chance when he races out of the room at the sound of the last bell. Meanwhile, I'm staring at the clean tile floor, from which the swastika has been removed. At lunch Serenity Davis told me, "We took care of that thing." She'd already passed me before I made the connection.

As I prepare to confront the plagiarist, I'm afraid my Disappointed Voice isn't going to ring true, but no sooner do I say "Aaron, let's talk" than he seems convinced enough. I inform him that I'm willing to forgo the usual protocol of dealing with the administration's discipline policy for plagiarism (there isn't any) and will just give him a zero. And, I add, "I'm afraid I'll have to call your parents." I *am* afraid, actually. Or, rather, I *dread* this task I feel obligated to perform, lest at some point the parents discover and question the mysterious zero and I'm deemed negligent for not reporting the child's dishonorable deed. And so, after school I will make the unpleasant call, hoping for voice mail, but understanding that at some point I must endure the humiliating exchange in which the grownups must affect politeness and measured passions as we discuss the impossibly stupid act of a teenager who, despite his continued efforts to sabotage his future, is literally days from graduating from high school.

Aaron nods, as if to say, *that's fair*, or, *whatever*.

I tell myself this has gone as well as I could have expected. No denials. No smugness.

I tack on for good measure, flaunting my nearly limitless fairness and deference, "So, should I call your mom? Or your dad? Which would you prefer?"

Of course, I know the answer. From time immemorial, nine out of ten students have shared the same preference in situations like this. But there's nothing lost, I figure, and perhaps something to be gained, in giving him this authority.

"Mom, I guess." He shrugs, as if it makes no difference to him.

I give a quick nod, indicating that I've merely registered the answer, not that my personal preference aligns with his. "Okay, we'll go with Mom."

The bell has rung. His classmates are waiting for us. Aaron leads the way back in.

MILLENIAL GIRL

Angie is amazed that I liked her story. "It's great—or, at least, *potentially* it is," I tell her when I return the purportedly final copy she handed in yesterday.

"*Really?* Sorry about the title. Do you like it? I mean, I know it's kind of stealing. But it seemed perfect. I can change it."

"'Millennial Girl.' I *do* like it," I say. "But you need to polish this for tomorrow. I won't count it as late, but I can't accept it like this."

"What's the matter with it?" she asks.

"Your lower-case 'i's?"

"My what?"

I point to the countless uncapitalized first-person pronouns I've circled all over the first page. "Small 'i'?"

"That's a problem?"

For a moment I'm sure she's joking. Then I realize—I can hardly believe it; I'm half-thinking she must be messing with me—she's not kidding. Her expression is one of earnest surprise and genuine interest to learn. We are both equally shocked by the other's reaction.

She mirrors my grin.

"No one has ever said this to you before?"

"No." She has just thrown all of her English teachers under the bus.

"The irony," I say. "Your story is about a girl who hates millennials—her own generation of technology-obsessed slackers—and she writes like she's *texting,* with complete disregard for capitalization and punctuation."

Angie's not the slightest bit insulted by my observation. She still seems to be pondering the initial revelation of the conventionally capitalized "I," growing less skeptical. She says, "Seriously? Like, there's *never* a small 'i'? Like, what about 'i'm'?"

For a second, I give serious consideration to her use of "never," ever hesitant to tell a student "never" or "always" about anything—then shake my head. "No."

Part of Angie's charm is that she's unashamed of what she doesn't know, and if anyone ever makes a dumb-blonde joke—as I've witnessed, most recently when lanky, bespectacled Derek Orlov chuckled at something she said the other day—she will turn to her antagonist with laser eyes and instruct him to kindly fuck off. On a day like today, when she cares enough to pay attention, she shows she really does want to learn, and I'm taking full advantage of this infrequent occurrence. The thing I love most about teaching Level-Two Creative Writing is working with students like Angie in hopes of reinforcing my theory that great storytelling is not reserved for those conventionally identified as the most intelligent.

I point to one of Angie's 'im's. "And you need an apostrophe."

"But I thought apostrophe meant possessive!"

"And contraction. It represents the missing letter or letters. In this case the 'a' in 'am'."

"Oh. Okay. Cool."

Her reaction is one of such simple delight that it seems this is truly the first time she's grasped this aspect of our language. Not that a teacher hasn't taught the concept—every year since first grade?—but that she's processed it, perhaps not accidentally, now in the context of something she cares about.

"So, is five pages long enough?" she asks. "You said at least six."

"Remember the students' Greatest Hits collection? A few of those aren't much longer than yours. Writing a story *that* good in five pages is not easy. But you can do it."

"Yeah, right. All those stories are by Level-One kids."

I keep my mouth shut, for now.

Angie's story is already every bit as good as any Level-One kid's. When I tell her this tomorrow, after she's made the necessary corrections, she'll resist her instinct to call "bullshit" in my face, as her cheeks flush and she smiles.

Mrs. Jackson's Story

After school I call Aaron Jackson's mom and explain how her son copied a Wikipedia page verbatim and submitted it as his own "missing chapter" from the British history book he claimed to have read. She says, "I don't know if he's told you, but it's been hard. His father left us after twenty-four years, and we just found out that he's been having an affair for two years. I had two heart attacks last year and his brother just got arrested and he sees me crying every night, so it's been hard."

I say, "I'm really sorry."

I listen to her life story for a half an hour more, before she thanks me and says, "Well, I'll talk to Aaron, but I can't promise you anything."

No more than I can promise her.

★

Leaving school, I pass Aaron in the hallway outside the main office. I wonder what he's still doing here. Maybe he had a detention. Or he's delaying the showdown he's expecting when he gets home today. Or he just missed the bus.

He makes actual eye contact with me, nods, and even enunciates something close to a greeting, "'t'sup."

I return his nod. *A relationship has been born,* I think. We've been through something real together. He plagiarized, and I treated him fairly. I spoke to his mother, an ordeal that perhaps has won his sympathy. "What's up, Aaron?" I say.

He appears to be fighting off a friendly smile.

AFTER-SCHOOL SCIENCE

In the kitchen I say to Christopher, "Let's have a serious conversation about something."

"Okay," he says, standing alert.

"You know how Mommy has been working so hard every night, studying and writing. She doesn't *have* to do any of it."

"So why *does* she?"

"Well, that's just the point. She does it because she *wants* to. She likes to learn. She keeps discovering what she wants to know more about. We're lucky to have these opportunities..."

I can see in the knowing squint that he's just figured out my agenda. The realization crystallizes: Daddy has allied himself with Mommy. This whole pitch about *liking learning* is prelude to the return to an unfinished conversation Christopher had with Vana in which he refused to pick an after-school science class to complement the usual athletic activities. I've seen his expression when she brings sports into the discussion. He believes it must mean a choice between shooting hoops and staring into microscopes, or at least a fifty-fifty split, which is bad enough.

On Sunday Vana started with, "Come look at this program that I'm going to sign you up for."

"No!"

This went on for days. "You're going to do this," she told him, "so you have to pick. If you don't pick, I'm going to have to pick for you."

"I'm not doing it! Don't sign me up!"

And on and on.

Now, I try, "If you hate it after two sessions, I won't make you go. I'm sure you won't hate it. I'm not making you do the nature camp again next summer. You tried it, you were a good sport about it, but you said you didn't like it enough to do it again. Okay. But you have to pick one of these—the building-engineering one, the digital-animation one, or the robots one."

"No."

I show him the sheet with the dates. "Look, this one's on Mondays. This one's on Tuesdays..."

His eyes widen. He sees that there are eight dates spreading from October into December. "So, it's not every day?"

"No." This has been stated infinitely clearly innumerable times. "The robots one only meets twice in November."

"I want to do the robots one."

"Good. Go tell Mommy."

He runs upstairs. I can hear him in the guest room, where Vana lies on the couch reading.

Then I hear, "Good, honey! I'm so happy."

Score another victory for the parents, who believe they've won again. Meanwhile, for a measly eight afternoons over three months, the son will enjoy learning about robots; on all the other days he'll be in the gym playing basketball.

TEACHER AGES

In Level-Two Creative Writing, I announce today's plan to present out loud, in front of the class, the screenplays they've just completed—nothing formal or especially theatrical, just a read-through, as if we're sitting around a big table, as a Hollywood cast might do, to get familiar with a script. My instruction, not meant as a proposal open for discussion, is met with protest, veritable boos, even genuine offense at what some seem to consider an uncool move on my part; an unannounced, surprise attack. "Is this mandatory?" "What if we refuse?" "You never said we had to do this."

"What is this reaction all about?" I ask. "It's supposed to be fun. I've read many of these scripts, and they're hilarious. Don't you want to share them?" I'm obviously serious, and they know it. I'm holding in my hands a stack of genuinely entertaining screenplays worth hearing, original episodes of *The Simpsons, Family Guy,* and *It's Always Sunny in Philadelphia,* along with original pilots and twisty horror stories. The kids don't seem at all moved by my flattery. I've never had to sell this plan in past years, not even to classes whose scripts I would have preferred *not* to hear performed. But this is a bunch of good writers—I've flattered them about how their work is not only as good as, but in many ways *better* than, that of their Level-One and AP counterparts. But apparently they're shyer than I've realized, or less interested than the quality of their work would suggest, or even burned out, as if this were second semester and only days before graduation. But it's January. Come on, people. Let's do this.

Somehow they can tell that I've already yielded to their pressure, or to their apathy, and that there's really no way to *make* them read their screenplays if they don't want to, and that I should just grade the work (generously) in my own peace and quiet and not make a public spectacle of the scripts, which they wrote under the assumption that, since they were not required to produce them, they would not be required to present them in any way, other than to submit a hard copy to me. Besides, if they don't want to perform their work, why should I care? It's the writing that matters, right? They can see that their less-than-crafty arguments are wearing me down, and after a few minutes of this carrying on I'm actually feeling relieved about scrapping today's plan, though at this point I'm scrambling in my mind for what to do instead—

Just then Natalie blurts from the back row, "Last night I was telling my dad how this is my favorite class. I had him read my screenplay."

"That's nice, thank you," I say. "What'd he think of your screenplay?"

"He liked it. He thought it was funny that last year I had Donaldson for English, and this year I have you. So, my two favorite teachers are, like, the two youngest teachers."

"Hah. That's funny." I'm waiting for the punchline to this silly crack.

She adds, "My two *least* favorite are, like, the oldest—Norris and Spagnol—"

"Okay, let's not go there," I interrupt. "I don't want to know who your..."

Her smile sinks, and for a moment I'm sure she's still messing with me. I smile to let her know I'm actually flattered, grateful, really, that she feels comfortable enough to have some fun with me, pairing me with Donaldson, who was hired last year and who, coincidentally, now teaches in my old classroom.

Natalie's smile returns. "It's true, you two are my favorites."

I nod, seeing now that she's being as earnest as can be. I say, "You realize I might be twenty years older than Donaldson."

"Nuh-uh!" a chorus lets out—mostly from the near side of the room, while the far side seems to be wondering if we've officially ditched the screenplay-reading plan in favor of this aimless rerouting. I'm leaning in the direction of yes, let's pursue this, because, frankly, I like the direction this conversation is going.

"You guys are serious?" I ask. "You think I'm Donaldson's age? How old do you think I am? Or *we* are?"

"Thirty-five?"

"Thirty?"

I announce, "You guys are awesome. I'm giving you all A's!"

"Yay!" the chorus cheers.

Someone asks, "On the screenplays or for the whole course?"

I laugh. "Norris and I are the same age, by the way. He student-taught in the room next to me when I was just starting out."

"Nuh-uh!" Then they all laugh, thinking *I'm* messing with *them* now and liking this game of Truth or Not Truth we've happened upon.

"It's true. I've taught a lot of your teachers. Riken. Cardozo—"

"No way! Cardozo? I thought he was, like, fifty!"

"Hey, I'm forty-eight."

"No way!"

"Yes way."

"No way!" They're all cracking up—not at the truth, but at the lie they think I'm telling, at this game they think we're playing.

"Seriously," I say, obviously not serious, "A's on the midterm for all of you. We can keep talking about this for as long as you want. Flattery is definitely working for you today, whether you're serious or not."

"We're serious!"

"On Monday when you come for the exam, just bring a comic book or something to read, to look busy. Pretend you're working hard and don't tell anyone about our little deal, okay? So, where were we?"

Both sides, students and teacher, are milking this moment of mutual affection for all it's worth, even as we understand that the actual content of our playful banter—their automatic A's in exchange for my long-lost youth—is pure fantasy. For the next ten minutes, they try to guess the other teachers who were once students of mine.

"You taught my aunt!" Abigail offers from the far side of the room. "Remember?"

"Thank you, Abigail," I say. "Incredibly, I do remember."

"But you didn't have my *mom*. She wishes she had you. She says all the girls wanted you back then. You were, like, the hot, young writer guy. Didn't you write a book or something?"

Abigail is entirely at ease sharing this bit of gossip from the past, from a time that predates her existence. The room is silent for a moment, but for a faint giggle or two, as we all seem to wrap our minds around such an abstraction—this notion of their mothers and fathers, once their own young age, sitting at these same desks, staring at the same man in a room just like this one.

Here, time both flies and stands still.

The bell rings. I feel my age again.

I shout, "You guys did a great job today!" as they file out, understanding, as I do, that unfortunately we're finished joking around.

Chapter in My Life

Third period, I crouch down next to Ethan MacDonnell at his desk and say, "This is a hell of a story. I'm sorry you had to go through all that."

"It's okay." He smiles.

Earlier this morning I read Ethan's "Chapter in My Life," five pages on growing up as a punching bag for his brother, Danny, whom I "taught" two years ago, or, rather, who *attended* my Creative Writing class, the semester before he graduated. After collecting his diploma onstage at the ceremony, Danny performed a spectacular fake trip somersault before exiting, one last display of his irrepressible genius.

I say to Ethan, "The part about that night when your brother is standing in your dad's bedroom doorway and then they're fighting downstairs, yelling and screaming, and then there's a sudden noise and then silence, and then you say things changed after that…"

He nods.

"Are you being intentionally mysterious, or is there a way you can let us in on what made that a turning point? He never laid a hand on you after that?"

Ethan shakes his head no.

His big brother, Danny, was destined to become a composer, like, say, Schubert, Danny himself had explained to me in the library one day when I was trying to coax some actual writing out of him, and, *like* Schubert, he didn't need a high-school diploma to achieve such acclaim. Indeed, to Danny, a prerequisite to being truly brilliant was *not* to graduate from high school, and he was doing everything in his power to realize this vision, despite administrators who were doing everything in *their* power to make sure they never had to see him again after June 8th. However, there was little they (or I) could do in the face of his determination to produce absolutely nothing during an entire semester in Creative Writing.

"You write that there had been nights of yelling and fighting before, between your brother and father. Are you intentionally withholding here, about *that* night? It's okay if you are, but as a piece of writing this good, you don't want your reader to think he might have missed something. Remember in *Catcher in the Rye* how Holden tells the story about James Castle, who jumped out the window? He says those boys went into his room and beat him up and did other stuff that's just too disgusting even to tell. He won't tell us the details, but we get it, or we can guess. Or maybe we can't even begin to guess. And that's the point, right? It was horrible enough to make the kid jump to his death. With your story about Danny, it just feels a little incomplete. Maybe you could hint at what's missing, or even just acknowledge that something *is* missing, something too awful or too personal to tell."

In June of Danny's senior year, thanks to the "alternative school," a program designed for students struggling to adapt to the district's conventional offerings, he managed to earn the required English credits in the three-day window before graduation, after I insisted to the alternative-school director that, no, there was definitely not "a little project or something that Danny could do at this point just to pass Creative Writing." He had done literally nothing in my class, and at this point there was nothing he could possibly do to earn enough credit to pass—or to make up for the weeks and months of his determined effort to fail.

Ethan reaches for his laptop. "I know how to finish this."

I want to know what he's got in mind, even as I dread what he might have to add. But I won't blame him if he doesn't finish the story, or if he never shows me how it ends. He's got me in suspense.

SEX TALK

When I pick up Christopher after school, I'm anticipating having the birds-and-the-bees conversation I know from legend and movies. *Son, it's time...* But Christopher is in second grade. It hardly feels time. I try a more casual, indirect approach. "So, how'd you and Mommy get into that conversation about *biology* last night?"

He says, "Huh? I don't remember talking about *biology."*

Last night after Vana tucked Christopher into bed, she said to me, "FYI, Christopher mentioned biology when we were reading tonight, and so I felt compelled to tell him."

"Tell him what about biology?"

"I told him the penis goes into the vagina—"

"You what?!"

"You might want to follow up. In case he has any questions. He didn't want to talk about it with me."

"You're kidding. Why did you—?" I stopped myself. "I wondered what you two were talking about in there. I heard him laughing."

"I told him, 'That's how you and Michael got here,' and he said, 'I never want to get married!'"

Christopher has been ahead of the curve in most things developmentally, and so it's reasonable for Vana to expect him to be out in front on this subject, especially given his anatomically detailed drawings *("What's the problem? It's art! It's a nude!")* and his predilection for bra advertisements *("What's the big deal? It's in the newspaper!").*

In the car I try again: "Okay, well, then— How did you and Mommy get into talking about what you talked about last night?" I knew what was coming next.

"What did we talk about last night?"

Okay. Here goes. "Penises and vaginas?"

"Daddy!!!"

"What? Didn't you?"

"I don't remember."

"How could you forget? I thought we could talk about it."

"Maybe you had a dream," he says.

"Come on, bud. You can talk—"

"No, I don't remember. Or you had a dream. Those are the possibilities."

I nod. I find his eyes in the rearview mirror. "I don't want you to be upset about it."

"Well, you're not doing a very good job."

I hesitate. "So, let's talk about it."

"No."

Long pause. "When you're ready to talk about it, please just tell me."

"Okay, so that will be never."

Last night before bedtime, Vana was drying off after a shower when Christopher walked into our room, sat on the floor in his underwear, and pulled up his pajama bottoms.

Vana said to him, "I think you're getting too old to be watching me get dressed."

"*You're* watching *me!*" he scolded her.

She stood with her towel draped. "I mean, can you leave the bedroom, please?"

Today, when we get home from school, I say to Christopher, "I could go for a fruit shake. How 'bout you?"

"Mm-hm."

In the kitchen I keep quiet in case he has any questions for me, after all. We take turns dropping ingredients into the blender. Ice, OJ, yogurt, banana, strawberries. He pours some shake into a cereal bowl and tests it with a spoon. He carries the bowl toward the living room.

"Where you going?" I ask.

"Do my Legos."

He's into the Lego architecture collection these days. The Arc de Triomphe is taking shape on the floor. Soon it will take its place on his dresser next to the White House and the Great Wall of China.

This whole time I'm watching him, trying to detect some sign that he's mulling over the mysteries of sex. I'm sipping my shake. He returns to the kitchen. I'm waiting for him to broach the topic bravely.

"I almost forgot," he says, refilling his bowl.

I brace myself.

"Can we wash the tie-dye T-shirt we made using mud in science class today?"

Busted

Neil Gillespie unloads this one on us at lunch—an especially sticky situation he's in the midst of untangling. Senior Jimmy Kingsley, soccer phenom on the fast track to the pros and also my star Level-Three student, who doubtless selected Level Three to manage the workload during his yearlong season, is in trouble—possibly serious trouble. Unless he's in no trouble at all. On Saturday he was at a big party at the house of a ninth-grade girl, who happens to be one of Neil's most pathological students. Cops come. Numerous kids get busted for drinking. Turns out the ninth-grade-girl host has made numerous such runs at this operation before: She collects cash from her guests to give to her babysitter, who buys the beer and then hangs around, as if she's there to be a kind of supervisor or protector. Jimmy Kingsley and the ninth-grade girl hosting the party are in her bedroom having sex when the babysitter barges in and tries to stop them. Jimmy punches the babysitter in the face. When the father returns from his business trip and finds out about all this, he wants the babysitter to press charges on Jimmy for assault. But the babysitter refuses, for fear that she will incriminate herself for buying booze and playing madam to a bunch of teenagers. A catch-22, to be sure.

On Girls and Death

For dinner the boys and I go across the street to the Club. A middle-school-aged girl and her father sit a few stools away from us at the bar. The girl is big for her age, athletic, and wears thick-rimmed glasses. She and her father, in matching white shirts and shorts, are faintly perspired, presumably from the squash or tennis they just played. Michael catches eyes with his brother and giggles. The man nods hello to us, and I say, "Hi."

Christopher nibbles at his cheeseburger, distracted by the cop show on the flat-screen TV, specifically by a boy his age sitting in the backseat of a car. The image of a handgun flashes, and we hear the word "kidnap." Christopher literally shivers and closes his eyes. His frightful reaction to such things on TV has become commonplace.

"Turn the channel," he says to me, not to Tom, the bartender, with whom I promptly share the request.

Tom aims the remote and finds a college softball game.

The girl at the bar says, "*Yes!* Softball!"

Christopher groans, "No. *Baseball.*"

I sigh. "We *like* watching softball," I remind him.

It's true. When he spent the day with me at Benfield, he was glued to the gym window after school, mesmerized by the helmeted girls whiffing at pitches hurled by a student he recognized from my second-period AP class. "How does she *do* that?" he asked, as Grace's arm cranked and shot the ball as if from a cannon near her knee.

I ask the girl at the bar if she plays.

She beams. "Yes."

Her father says, "So does her sister." He grins. "We have it the opposite at our house. Your wife is outnumbered three-to-one like me."

I think, *three* to one? Does he have three daughters and assume I have a third son? Then I realize the spouses have been included in the outnumbering.

"I'm Jack." He raises his glass of beer. "This is Olivia."

"I'm Jim. This is Christopher. And Michael."

"Baseball players?"

I nod. "Big fans."

I cough to get my sons' attention, amidst their stifled cackling and luckily inaudible obscenities, muffled by fistfuls of French fries.

"Be polite," I hiss, and at least Christopher manages a "hi."

I shake my head in mock exasperation, Jack smiles, and we slug our beers.

In the parking lot, Michael is talking boobs and vaginas as two older women walk to their nearby cars. Absurdly, I ignore Michael and instead let Christopher have it for laughing at him, for egging him on—and also for being rude to the girl with glasses and to the man who was trying to have a civil conversation. "You're almost eight years old. You need to sit up. Show some respect. Answer the man's questions. Maybe *ask* one. Be a gentleman and say, 'Sure, softball.'" Christopher is understandably stunned by my mini tirade. I say, "You wouldn't talk dirty around Miss Katz—" his much adored first-grade teacher from last year. "Right?"

He shakes his head. This line of thinking seems suddenly to have clicked. He seems to be looking right through me, at an imagined scene in which the lovely Miss Katz would be exposed to this kind of talk and he would want to shield her from it.

"Because you *respect* her. You need to respect girls and women and *all* people."

He nods, and I wonder, doubtfully, at his stoic reaction. He's not crying—until we enter the house and I exit the family room. Then he unloads—not just tears, but real, sad sobs—and I feel shitty for having added to the burden of being big brother to an oblivious, foul-mouthed four-year-old. But I convince myself that I did land on a decent message, so I decide to let it stick, not to retract or redirect.

When I reenter the room a minute later, Christopher is sitting up on the green chair, arms crossed and staring straight ahead at nothing, while Michael, pounding his mitt, asks, "Can we go outside and play baseball?" He waits for an answer.

I nod, okay.

I pat Christopher's chest. "Come on. Let's go."

He lets a few long seconds pass before meeting us in the front yard. He makes the third point of a human triangle, and the three of us quietly throw the ball, one to the next.

"Like this," Christopher says to Michael, demonstrating how to step properly.

Michael observes him faithfully, makes the catch, then steps and throws to me. We keep throwing and catching, around and around, until it's too dark to see.

★

Upstairs, I hear Christopher crying in his bedroom—that real, sad sobbing—and I think, *Again?* I thought we'd moved on.

I find him standing at his night table, arms hanging helplessly at his sides, tears streaming down his cheeks.

I walk toward him and see, in the cloudy bowl by the lamp, his little black betta fish, unmoving, on the bed of blue pebbles.

Jesus. *Now?*

"Aww, buddy, I'm sorry."

I'm on my knees, our arms wrapped around each other. He lays his head on my shoulder and empties his sorrows into the air.

"What happened, Daddy?" Michael asks from the door.

"Fish died," I say.

Michael approaches the bowl and bends to see. "Why everything dies?" he asks. He seems to understand that he has arrived at something profound. "Why-*why...?* Why if it borns, it dies?" he pursues stubbornly, trying this philosophical voice on for size. "Why everything is born dies?"

"I know," I say, and bring Michael into our hug. "I don't know."

Our first death together, I think. Here we are. Mommy is at Penn, not home until tomorrow. I'm staring at the dead fish and wondering what's next.

"You want to sleep in my bed?" I ask.

They both nod vigorously, then race out of the room.

I'm not tired enough to sleep yet, but I pretend to be, situating myself between them on the king-size bed. They cozy up to my shoulders, each in an armpit nook, Michael huffing and sniffling to match the sounds of his brother.

In the morning we hold a funeral in the boys' bathroom, huddled together at the small toilet. I've explained how this water goes through the pipes and eventually reaches the sea, where he would want to go. "Where he came from," Christopher agrees. "Like people buried in the earth."

"That's right," I say, and we reflect on this cycling of the dead. A scoop and a plop, a black feathery thing sinking through white porcelain.

We do our cross—three fingers together, head, belly, shoulder, shoulder, palm on heart—and the boys quietly await my next move. I say, "You were a good fish, Kingdom—" Christopher's clever name for his king betta. "A good first pet."

"You want to...?" I gesture to the toilet handle.

Christopher shakes his head no. I flush.

It's raining. I get a text announcing that all Little League games have been canceled today. I inform Christopher that our team is meeting at the indoor batting cages instead.

He takes this news in stride.

Michael asks, "I come?"

"Of course." I give them both a pack of baseball cards from the box I keep in my sock drawer for desperate situations. They sit on the carpet in my bedroom while I get dressed. Christopher shows Michael how to trade.

"I get one of yours...and you get one of mine."

Christopher takes Michael for all he's worth. Neither of them could be happier with this reciprocal arrangement.

MICHAEL RUNS AWAY

Summer's almost here. Christopher and Michael seem to be feeling the full thrill of anticipation. They are wrestling and giggling on the kitchen floor. Christopher pins Michael and begins kissing him, pressing pursed lips into his brother's face and then on any other exposed skin he can find. Michael's giggling turns to a cackling-screaming.

Christopher sits up to catch his own breath, and in that instant Michael frees himself and rises to his feet. Christopher smiles and sighs, just as Michael pulls his foot back slowly (I can see what he's about to do, and I can't get a word out in time, not that a word could restrain Michael at this point), quickly gets his footing, and lands a hard kick in Christopher's teeth.

Stunned, I barely choke out a "Hey!" before Michael flies out of the kitchen and into living room, after the two of us make brief eye contact. He knows he's done something bad. I hold off on the chase until I examine Christopher's teeth, which appear to be unharmed.

Then I holler, "Michael!" but there's no response. I order Christopher to check his bedroom. I blast through the front screen door to find the porch bare. I circle the house, calling out, "Michael!" When I return to home base, Christopher blasts through the front door and announces, "He's not upstairs!"

"Shit."

I sprint across the street to the Club, eyeballing the line of pine trees that hide the parking lot, then hustle to the pool and pan the grounds, before racing back home. Christopher is on my tail this whole time. He follows me inside. I bolt upstairs, taking two steps at a time. Michael's door is closed. I reach for the doorknob.

Christopher yells, "I knocked already!"

I open the door, and there's Michael, under the covers. I look at Christopher with twisted eyes.

"What?" he says. "I knocked. Nobody answered."

Our fears allayed, Christopher and I approach the bed. Michael tries a smile—a peace offering.

NEIL'S BURDEN

I'm late to lunch. What'd I miss? Turns out a lot. Sam, Dean, and Neil are talking about some Benfield grad who just got put away for thirty years. Arrested for child porn. Neil remembers him all too well. When he was under eighteen, he was busted for drug dealing, sent to other schools, then eventually returned to Benfield. All along it was known in the community that he abused younger girls and sold drugs. "He raped his own sister," Neil says.

Apparently, his sister is a junior now. I finally make the connection, catching the last name. I taught her in ninth grade. I'd always wondered about the way she avoided eye contact.

"Everyone knew it," Neil says.

He doesn't mean me. He means the parents. And local officials.

Sam gets up and walks out. "This is the worst lunch I've ever had. Have a nice day!"

We chuckle at the familiar joke, cracked usually in the midst of political talk that Sam can't bear anymore.

Neil continues: in high school the boy's parents made him live in a van on the driveway, where local kids would assemble. He would prostitute himself online. Once, the police went to charge the older man, who defended himself, "I'm the John—the client. *He's* the prostitute." The kid was never put in prison, but the school district knew all about the case. Turns out his father was the treasurer for the borough of Benfield, and he had connections. Neither the school district nor the parents wanted to attract attention or pay for private schools, so he ended up with a Benfield diploma.

Thanks to Neil's help, after high school he started getting disability for mental illness. He was able to get his own apartment, where middle school kids and Benfield students continued to meet up. When word got back to Neil that our own students were being abused by one of our graduates, he told the administration, who said there was nothing they could do about it, since the illicit conduct wasn't taking place on our property. So Neil called the FBI, who made the arrest in the next twenty-four hours, after watching what was going on in that apartment.

Neil resents bearing the burden of being *technically* an administrator—the one who ends up calling the FBI after the nominal leaders say it's out of their hands, the only one who remains in the building after three o'clock. "And don't even get me started about the summer packages delivered to the main office—*I'm* the one who gets the call, 'Can you come down and sign for this delivery *as administrator* because everybody else is gone?'"

Carolyn chimes in, "The administrators leave before most of the teachers. They cannot possibly be doing their jobs in seven or eight hours. It's impossible. These are ten-to-twelve-hour-a-day jobs."

"Correct," Neil says.

I say, "Keep up the good work, Neil." I mean it. I can't fathom what he deals with on any given day, let alone in a year, or a career. I can't imagine how he endures it all, the sole school psychologist, and I wonder if he's got someone to unload his burdens on, other than his receptive audience in the lunchroom.

He mirrors my smile—and the stiff upper lip.

RYAN CANCELS

Holly Knight, Ryan's English teacher this year, texts me to ask if I've read "Somebody Please Help Edwin." Holly knows that Ryan has shared his writing with me since I taught him as a freshman. I *have* read it, I tell her. I thought it was brilliant—an opinion I keep to myself, lest she press me to explain. My preference is to reserve my critical analysis for Ryan himself—and for Neil Gillespie, who just yesterday told me, "Oh yeah, he's getting a *lot* of help"—as if to reassure me I'm not the only one on the case.

Holly asks, "Is he okay?" as if I possess some expertise on Ryan's state of mind, because of my familiarity with his writing—a delusion I'm happy to indulge.

"I think so," I reply, though I feel more confident than I'm willing to let on. Again, my impressions of Ryan seem like privileged information, not something to be bandied about. Or maybe I'm just afraid to be wrong about him.

Another text comes from Holly—"Is he schizophrenic?"—and I scoff at my colleague's failure to appreciate the liberties Ryan is taking as a fiction writer.

Last year, as a tenth grader, Ryan disappeared for a month. One afternoon in the library, he told me he'd been hospitalized. This struck me as welcome news, a relief, a confirmation that of course something had been up all along; and if that something could be identified, then perhaps it could be treated, and maybe he really was some kind of genius, or at least extremely creative, and maybe he would be The One to go on to become A Writer—if he could conquer his troubles, which remained a mystery, he told me. Depression? Sure, of course. But there was more to it than that. There had to be.

As a freshman, he'd written lengthy papers with flashes of insight, amidst convoluted sentences that might have been inspired by David Foster Wallace or Jonathan Franzen or Jeffrey Eugenides, whose novels I'd seen him hauling around. "I want to be a writer," he'd told me sincerely, more than once, with a kind of heartbreaking foresight, as if already dreading the life he would face if this fate were not borne out—or if it *were* borne out. I'd told him he was certainly reading the right books.

For as long as I've been teaching, people have asked me if there are students I can tell are destined to be writers. Or at least who have "it" in them to be writers. I have hesitated to say yes—not because my best students lack the talent, but because they lack a certain quality that marks the writer, a quality I could never quite pinpoint. On the other hand, some of them have a very pinpoint-able *disqualifying* quality, like a ken for math or science, that they wisely determine will lead them on a path toward professional and financial satisfaction.

Then came Ryan Henry, who as a freshman already appeared to have "it": that need to write despite everything; that sense that if the world conspired to make him go in any other direction, he'd find himself scribbling away, with the full understanding that people out there would never give a damn...but that they *should*, and they *would*, eventually, if they had any sense, if he just kept at it, if life had any meaning.

Indeed, the story he sent me a month ago is an intricate, hilarious, heartbreaking representation of a brilliant mind aware of its own decline, a story about a teenage boy with a crush on a girl, the simplest of premises, taking shape in the most ordinary of settings: biology class, a bus ride home, a Friday-night party. While the boy freezes up at the girl's every friendly gesture, his mind implodes in a chorus of voices, neither encouraging nor discouraging, obsessive scrutinies of the inadequacies of language, rationalizations that spiral into philosophical reveries, deconstructions of the very words used to express them, wave after mental wave sweeping the boy away from the demands of the world around him, all conveyed so enthrallingly that the reader, along with Edwin himself, loses track of the scene, of the *story* taking place, where the girl is standing there waiting for the boy to offer any kind of normal response to whatever she may have said, until, in the end, after the last wave crashes and recedes, he wakes to discover himself surrounded by nothing but infinite white space, "into which, after an endless breath, and without direction, he takes a step—a kind of progress," he writes.

Here is a kid staring his own demons straight in the eye and writing them out—and sharing them with me. Now a junior, he is once again not my classroom student, and yet the prospect of working with Ryan Henry on our own time lights me up. The moment after he vanished into the hallway that afternoon a month ago, I printed out the story and dashed off an email, telling him how excited I was to talk with him about the pages he'd just shared with me, deep down hoping this plan might help his chances of avoiding another extended break this year.

Today I have an appointment with Ryan after school. We're finally going to discuss "Somebody Please Help Edwin." I'm taking a pencil to my marginal notes, sharpening the handwriting to make sure Ryan can make sense of it all after he takes this marked-up copy home with him, not that I'll let him just walk off with the pages before I get a chance to talk to him.

I'm waiting at my desk for him when I finally get an email: "I hate to say this but I can't make it today. It was really important to me, but I forgot I have an appointment in Philly this afternoon."

I see Neil Gillespie in the hallway on my way out. I tell him of the canceled meeting.

Neil grins. "Yup, Tuesday and Thursday, he sees his psychiatrist."

I nod, oblivious. "You have to read the story he sent me," I say. "About a schizophrenic. Fourteen pages, single-spaced. It's amazing."

"I'll bet it is," he says. "You don't know the half of it."

I'm waiting for him to dish, and for a moment it seems he's drawn the line, withholding the scoop. It's only after he makes a face of exaggerated exasperation and rushes off that I realize: he doesn't know the half of it either.

Lost Children

When I pick up Christopher at school, it's already pitch-dark and there's a boy at the curb outside the black iron fence, calling, "Daddy!" The kid is visible between two parked cars. My window is down, and I call out to the kid not to move. My hand out the window freezes him with his toes over the curb. Other cars are lining up behind me, their bright beams lighting up the street, where I dread this kid is about to dart. "Daddy!" The kid is looking right at me, pointing at me. Apparently, I look like his daddy.

"Stay there!" I shout, and open my door, just to make myself, or the car's lit-up interior, more conspicuous to the other drivers. The car behind me begins to make the inevitable move to pass me. I leap out, engine running. The driver behind me stops, seeing the potential disaster, and now, at an angle, plays blocker for me as I go to the boy.

"He forgot me," the boy says.

I ask his name. I hesitate before picking him up, but he's reaching for me. "It's okay, he'll be back," I tell him. I look around, expecting a car to be racing up to the curb. I'm prepared to make some appropriate gesture, of handing over the child, to whoever approaches and claims to be his parent and possibly asks what the hell I'm doing with his kid in my arms.

"Cody," the kid says, or something like it.

"Huh?" I lower my ear for him to speak into.

I imagine the parallel-universe (or crime-show) version of this scene, in which a stranger, not me, pulls up, grabs the kid, and speeds off. Gone. Unsolved mystery.

I wonder if I should put the kid down to move my car: My lights are on, inside and out, the door hanging open. Or should I put the kid in my car and then park it? I eye the school's entrance doors across the playground. I wonder if the kid's daddy is still inside, presumably looking for Cody. I consider going up to the glass doors and announcing through the speaker system to the downstairs caretakers that I'm holding a Cody out here and asking if they know whose son he is. But then I keep imagining the daddy's car roaring up to the curb the moment I step away from here. I stay put.

Minutes pass. I tell the boy that no doubt his father will get home and realize, "Oh my goodness, I forgot Cody," and come right back. But then I think, *there's no way the guy makes it all the way home, or even* leaves *for home in the first place, before realizing he's minus a son.* I ask if he's got a sibling, figuring for sure he does, just making chitchat.

"Landon," he says. "My brudda."

I ask if he sees his car, and he shakes his head. I figure the dad really did split. I reconsider that he could still be inside looking for his kid, in which case he must be frantic by now. Why would he look *outside,* after all? The kid is hardly tall enough to reach a door handle. I ask his last name. Carson? *Cody Carson?* Can this be right? And his big brother *Landon Carson?* When did parents start giving their kids interchangeable first and last names—Smith Jones? Jones Smith?—names that seem designed to ensure that their sons become leading men or professional quarterbacks?

And then, I can see—or, rather, Cody sees, and points at the silhouettes at the door—his father and brother coming out. Landon spots Cody and hardly realizes the gravity of the situation, pointing and giggling at his baby brother, who's had them on a scavenger hunt inside. Dad isn't nearly as delighted as Landon is, though he's clearly relieved to see Cody. They never left for home. Of course. They've been combing the place for him. I'm trying to imagine the father's thought process, as he finally gave up on the indoor search and figured, well, maybe he's outside waiting for us. I'm relieved when the dad smiles at me, maybe even recognizes me, as I recognize him. He takes the boy into his arms and says, "Where'd you go, buddy?"

"You left me," Cody says.

"You thought I left without you? We've been looking for you. We were in the gym and then you were gone." He looks at me and says, "Thank you," but without the sense of horror or relief I would expect, considering the parallel-universe version of what has just transpired, the version in which the dad comes outside and there's no trace of his kid. At what point does he lose his shit? Evidently, he hasn't lost it yet.

Had I been in his shoes, I would have been shouting my kid's name the moment I blasted through those doors. *Christopher!!!*

After another moment, the dad seems to be getting his bearings and makes eye contact with me. The thank yous start coming in rapid succession. He says, "Don't you have to go get your kid?"

I point to my car, which is still running, lighting up the street. "I gotta move my car."

He thanks me again, apparently putting the scene together in his mind, realizing now just how dramatic the whole episode might have been.

He shakes his head. I go to park my car. I do a quick U and park right behind his SUV, where he's buckling his boys into the backseat. Their car was right in front of us, literally right in front of Cody at the curb, the whole time. The kid didn't know his own car from mine or whatever one in which he imagined his father driving away without him.

As I round the front of my car and head inside to pick up Christopher, the dad meets me behind his SUV. He reaches to shake my hand. "George Cody," he says. "Thanks again." He smiles and finally lets out a little "whew" to let me know he understands what shit just missed the fan.

On the way home, I tell Christopher the story.

"Cody is Landon's *last* name," Christopher clarifies. "His little brother must be named Carson." He contemplates the scene for a moment. "It would be like in *Home Alone* when the mom is on the airplane to Paris and realizes 'We forgot Kevin!' only in this case Landon's dad would have gotten home and said, 'We forgot Carson!'"

I recall an incident some years ago in Bethany Beach, when I drove down Atlantic Avenue and spotted a little barefoot blond boy crying in the street. I'd been driving this same car, I remember, and I slowed down, thinking the mother or father couldn't be far; the kid must have been frightened despite his parents having their eye on him, or so I figured. What did I know about kids? Or parents, for that matter. After another moment I stopped, foot on the brake, engine humming, to make sure the kid was okay, but I didn't jump out. It never occurred to me to leave my car running in the middle of the street, even as a toddler was hobbling aimlessly in the opposite lane. No cars were in front of or behind me, and I was relieved after another moment when a man on a bicycle approached on the opposite side and, quite appropriately, stopped next to the boy sobbing shirtless in his swim shorts. A moment later the boy's father appeared, dripping sponge in hand, jogging slightly in flip-flops, having lost sight of him while washing his car on the driveway. The father shook the bicyclist's hand and shot me a thank-you wave, which I didn't deserve. By now my foot was easing off the brake, and it occurred to me that the kid didn't know his own house right behind him, just as "Cody," or Carson, tonight, didn't recognize the car parked right in front of him. These lost boys might as well have been abandoned in another state. God knows they could have been abducted and taken to one. Lost is lost, found is found. The father scooped the kid up and walked past the trees between the street and the driveway, where the hose was running.

I'd always regretted my insufficient response that day.

Tonight, I held that boy in my arms as if he were my own.

HALLOWEEN IN AP

A half dozen AP kids are standing on their desks when I return from the bathroom. Miles, who's waiting to hear from Harvard early-decision, is wearing a Halloween costume I can't quite identify. "O Captain, my Captain," the elevated six stammer, not quite in sync. "Uh-huh," I reply, returning their grins. My first thought is: *You have an essay test today, and you think I'm going to go soft from this ass-kissing?* Then I think: *You've got my number.*

"Are you a piece of notebook paper?" I ask Miles.

Three black construction-paper circles are attached to his white attire, at the shoulder, knee, and ankle.

"A three-hole puncher."

Sue-Lin, standing on the floor, asks, "Can you read us a scary story?"

"Seriously? A scary story?" This kid's off to Princeton or Penn next year and here she is asking me to read to them on Halloween.

Miles cheers, in only barely disguised mockery, "Yay, a scary story!"

Others echo his encouragement. A sucker for an audience, even when I'm the willing victim of a bribe, I quickly consider which stories I may have to read.

They have successfully appealed to my sympathies, and to my vanity, first by imitating the worshipful boys at the end of *Dead Poets Society,* which we watched in conjunction with our reading of Walt Whitman back in September, and now by imploring me to entertain them, as if I were on stage with a guitar, taking requests.

At this point I am seriously thinking about reading them a chapter from my cancer memoir. ("A scary story? You asked for it.") But decades of experience, for better or worse, have led to this momentary hesitation, an impulse of caution in times like this, when I'm suddenly moved to say to hell with today's lesson plans—lest I regret reading aloud some unplanned passage that I've failed to anticipate will offend or traumatize, or lest I regret delaying our progress and falling short of my goals for the marking period.

I say, "We've got this Robert Frost and Dylan Thomas essay to write today, and time's a-wasting."

"Booooo. Scary story!"

I'm considering reading them the chapter from the cancer memoir called "The Bear," about the night twenty years ago when I believed I was going to be mauled to death by a bear in Yellowstone National Park, and then the night twenty years later when I was told my days were numbered because of a tumor lodged in the vein going into my heart.

"I've got a scary story for you," I say, tempted.

"Yaaaay!"

"—which I promise I'll read to you tomorrow." I look at the digital clock above the door. "We better get started on this essay."

A confused mix of groans and muted cheers float for a second, as the few kids still on desktops descend anticlimactically—good soldiers all.

Someone asks if they still have to do the previously scheduled homework for tomorrow, to read and analyze the "The Love Song of J. Alfred Prufrock."

"Tomorrow is scary-story day," I remind them. "T.S. Eliot can wait."

I expect cheers of celebration, or at least gasps of relief, but I hear only the shuffling of obedient hands, in book bags, searching for pencils to do today's work.

Last Night Out

I head to Whole Foods to stock up for the week—eight full bags, a typical haul, barely containable in the large cart. A man in the checkout line says, "Hard to get out of here without spending a few hundred dollars."

I nod. "Two little boys at home."

He says, "They won't be little for long they keep eating like that."

Tonight is the last night out for Vana and me, as her tidal wave of work is growing. Tomorrow I'll hit the ground running with my students, after today's introductions. I pick up Michael and Christopher from school. At home I unload the groceries, including tonight's dinner for the boys and the babysitter, who arrives at six.

Vana and I go to a reputedly hot new spot in Bryn Mawr, some wannabe urban-swank joint tucked in a tiny suburban strip mall twenty miles from Center City. Martini for me. White wine for Vana. "Cheers," I say. Vana hesitates, her attention seized by Roger Federer playing in the US Open on the flat screen above the bar. "He's so elegant," she says, turning to me. I don't mention my preference for Rafael Nadal's punchier style, which she finds crude and unrefined. We clink glasses. All around us, men and women are drinking and laughing, turning their heads and shifting their eyes, as Vana and I are, checking out the scene, all of us drawn toward the mysterious lives of our fellow middle-aged suburbanites.

Three blonde women sit at the adjacent table. They aren't shy, craning and crooking their necks, despite Vana by my side. When Vana excuses herself to use the restroom, I'm bracing myself for company—or an invitation. There's a dark-haired woman at the bar who keeps looking in this direction, and now she's making her way over here and I'm wondering if I know her from somewhere, and I'm relieved, mostly, when she passes my table to join the three blondes at theirs. I imagine that between here and the bathroom Vana has been distracted by dudes on the lookout.

When she returns, we channel our excitement into talk of Michael's nightly milk ritual. We agree that maybe a bottle in an ice pack set on his nightstand might be the way to go. It's too late to break the nighttime milk habit, after all. I suggest a barrel around the neck, like the kind on a St. Bernard. Maybe a little refrigerator to replace the nightstand. We crack up at the thought. We discuss the months ahead. The workload. The interrupted sleep. Vana says she can't be waking up at three a.m. and expect to survive the year. I say I don't mind the wake-ups.

Hours later, Michael is up at one o'clock. I get him milk. I'm wide awake with restless energy. Back in bed, I gaze at Vana in the dark, looking for signs of life. My toes find her leg. She stirs. I say, "Maybe I'll go for a run."

She turns, squinting. "Are you nuts?"

"Just kidding." Moonlight, or just the streetlight, leaks through the blinds. I scan the headlines on my phone. "Federer lost in five sets."

Vana moans, "*Nooo,*" and falls back asleep.

It takes me a while to join her. For now, I'm wishing it were five-thirty already, fired up for the school day, before I doze off again.

The War on Halloween

At lunch everyone is talking about Halloween costumes. Once again, I've arrived mid-conversation. Apparently, there's been a big stink about a boy dressed up as Jesus.

I shrug.

"Postmortem," Dean says.

My eyebrows shoot up.

"Right there in the front row of my classroom. Blood all over." He drags his fingertips across his forehead, down to his ribs, to show the extent of it. "The whole thing is ridiculous. I think all costumes should be banned. They're distracting. First thing in the morning, I'm trying to teach, and Andy's dressed as Frankenstein, Ashley's a French maid. Give me a break. Are we a school, or are we—?"

"You're such a conservative," I tease Dean, who worked religiously for the Bernie Sanders presidential campaign last year and, like the candidate, wouldn't deny accusations of being a socialist. "Ease up."

Dean grins. "I know. I should have kindly asked Jesus to remove his crown of thorns instead of reminding him that hats are a dress-code violation—a claim he took offense to, by the way."

"Hah!" I crow.

"I'm with you, Dean," says Randi Gordon, the veteran special-ed teacher, a self-described Catholic conservative, who was horrified to see the risen, bloody Jesus exiting Dean's classroom and who is delighted that for the first time in memory she's in agreement with Dean, the leftie—the two united in Christ.

"Well, that's a first." Dean returns her smile.

"Post-crucifixion," I say. "Pretty impressive, really."

"He even had the stigmata..." Neil shows the intact palms of his hands and explains that, second period, Jesus' math teacher directed him to go see his guidance counselor, who then sent him to see Neil, the school psychologist. Neil first tried to talk to the kid about good taste and respect for people's religion. They discussed whether he intended to offend anybody—he said he didn't—and then they discussed whether his intentions really mattered. The kid explained that he didn't believe in any of that superstitious stuff, but he had read the Student Handbook last night and he'd followed the dress code to a T. A crown of thorns was not a hat. And even if it were, hats are permitted on Halloween—the principal said so on the announcements yesterday; he just said "no masks."

"He's not even a Believer," Randi says.

"He believes in the Constitution," Dean replies. "I'm proud of him."

"Despite your anti-costume stance," I say.

"Yes." Dean laughs.

Randi takes a step back. "Well, I was offended. I just don't think it's right."

There's only so much Jesus can do to keep these two united.

Dean says, "First period I was discussing the Bill of Rights with this kid. Now he's defending his right to be Jesus."

"And now you want to deprive him of that right," I tease.

"Well, remember," Dean says, "you don't have the right to yell fire in a crowded theater."

Neil says, "He totally knows what he's doing, too. He knows he's being provocative, but he's always trying to make people think, without breaking the rules."

"I can vouch for that," Dean says. "The kid's got a counterpoint for everything, but he *is* interesting."

"I think this kid is my hero," I say.

Neil says he tried to explain the subtler aspects of the situation to Principal Freddy and Assistant Principal Everest, who, devout Catholics themselves, have a less favorable opinion of the student. They barked at Neil about the dangers of a "slippery slope." Neil laughs. "If we let kids dress up like the crucified Jesus, what's next?"

"I honestly don't know," Sam says. "What *would* be next?"

There's a pause as we ponder what this precedent might inspire.

"JFK." Dean makes his fist explode at the back of his head. "Post-assassination."

"Oh, that's gross, Dean." Carolyn laughs, then offers, "Martin Luther King. Gandhi."

"The possibilities are endless," Dean says.

I ask, "Why do these examples seem even more offensive to me than dead Jesus?"

Neil says, "The kid was sent home before second period was over. He's missing the rest of the day. Technically, that's a suspension."

"They didn't want other students to see him." Carolyn grins. "Afraid of copycats."

"The start of a costume craze," I say. "Great men, post-martyrdom."

Carolyn says she tried to warn Freddy, before he put the total kibosh on Jesus, that the slippery slope slides both ways. But none of her arguments held any weight with Freddy, who was shocked to discover, upon calling the boy's parents, that last night they helped assemble their son's outfit, including the cross made of two-by-fours—just as they helped him last year with his Donald Trump getup, which had not gotten him sent home despite the volatile election season. When Freddy admitted to the parents that a *pre*-crucifixion Jesus would have been okay, they countered that their son's Jesus was literally carrying the cross, so the intention here, obviously, was to represent not only the crucified Jesus but also the un-crucified Jesus.

"They actually used the phrase—" Carolyn pauses to be sure she has our attention. "The Stations of the Cross."

I say, "The kid's a performance artist."

Carolyn speculates that this will finally mark the end of Halloween at Benfield.

I recall our recent discussion, in AP Modern Lit, about Andre Serrano's "Piss Christ," the giant photograph of a keychain crucifix submerged in the artist's urine, catapulted to fame in the 1980s by the conservative Southern Senator Jesse Helms, who believed that such junk was not art, or at least not art worthy of government support through the National Endowment for the Arts, which he proposed should be abolished.

Carolyn says, "A few years ago, a kid dressed as Hitler. His friend wore a KKK outfit. *Those* assholes didn't put an end to Halloween, but now *this* could be the end. *Jesus.*"

"I'm all for it," Dean says.

"So much for freedom of speech," I say.

"I'm for my freedom to teach!"

"You're a fascist," I tell him.

"But it will end for the wrong reasons," Carolyn says. "This is not a matter of what's good or bad or offensive. It's a matter of what Freddy can comprehend in a black-and-white way. Hitler, easy. KKK, no argument. But this kid's parents kept asking Freddy for clarification on what the issue with their son really was. You should have seen him in the office. He was sweating, ready to explode. 'Isn't it obvious! Your son was making fun of Jesus! He was making a mockery of Christians!' But that wasn't cutting it with these parents. He was just digging himself into a deeper hole."

"I can't wait for the lawsuit," Neil says. "Did I mention the kid's autistic?"

"You're kidding," I say.

"Not an extreme case, but he's on the spectrum. He said he listened carefully to Freddy's announcement and he'd been sure to follow the rules. So, what was the problem? I honestly couldn't tell him. I didn't know. The blood? No. Even if he was dead, so what? Kids are dressed up as zombies and Dracula."

"You missed a teachable moment." I nudge Dean. "You could have compared the historical Jesus to the scriptural Jesus. Instead, you're stuck on the First Amendment."

"At least I didn't kick him out of class," Dean says.

Lorena, the art teacher, recalls the aborted-baby sculpture in the art show, or *not* in the art show, a few years ago. She was told by an administrator to remove the piece, and she didn't argue with the decision. The parents of the artist complained when they found their child's masterwork missing from the exhibition. Fortunately for Lorena, the girl failed to write up the required description of her sculpture on a notecard, a failure that Lorena cited as the reason for the piece's exclusion. Disqualified on a technicality. Now Lorena admits it wasn't the subject matter that was offensive; it was the girl's lack of talent.

"It was just awful," she says.

Today Lorena is adorned in a crown of roses and delicately applied mascara, her eyebrows united into a convincing unibrow—a spitting image of Frida Kahlo. Lorena sits in her usual upright posture, eating her couscous with a plastic fork. I ask if she is the post-trolley-accident Frida Kahlo, with the iron back brace I remember from the self-portraits.

She grimaces.

I remember the warnings I got decades ago from my college English professors. "I'm afraid you're going to get bored teaching teenagers," one said. "I don't think a high school is going to be a stimulating enough environment." Another said, "You don't want to have to be telling your students to stop throwing chalk while you're trying to teach Chekhov."

How quaint those concerns seem to me now.

Stormy Daniels

I'm leafing through a *Time* magazine when Christopher identifies a tiny headshot of "Stormy Daniels!"

The boys have been calling out her name a lot lately, unprompted, as if the name or her image bubbles up randomly from their subconscious. Yesterday Christopher was singing "Stormy Daniels" to the tune of "Oh, My Darling, Clementine." "Stormy Daniels, Stormy Daniels, Stormy DAAAN-iels..." Last night Michael was spelling words on full sheets of computer paper, one after another, on the floor with a marker, as I recited the letters upon request: "How you spell...robot?"

"R-O..."

"How you spell...Phillies?"

"P..."

"How you spell...Stormy Daniels?"

Sigh. "S-T..."

They were in the room the night of the *Sixty Minutes* interview, a broadcast that immediately followed an Eagles playoff game. At the time, they paid no more attention to her than to Anderson Cooper, even when she got to the part about Donald bending over for a spanking. We might as well have been watching a documentary about the fall of Rome.

Only now does Christopher ask, "Who *is* Stormy Daniels?"

"Did you see the magazine cover?"

I'm stalling, failing to formulate a convincing white lie.

He's checking out the cartoon Donald, who's settled at a large desk with the water level rising and the wind blowing his hair, shaped like a perfect orange Frisbee, nearly off his head.

He asks, "Are they in love or something?"

I realize he's just helped me out. I nod. "They *had* been—for a very brief time." I'm preparing to say more if he presses me, as I recall Atticus Finch providing Scout with the technical definition of rape—"carnal knowledge of a female by force and without consent"—to which she replies, "Well, if that's all it is then why did Calpurnia dry me up when I asked her what it was?"

Like Scout, Christopher shrugs and exits the room.

RANTS

Before lunch I decide to squeeze in grading two more essays. These essays have been inspired by the rant assignment. A rant is a kind of complaint, I tell the students. I remind them of stand-up comedians criticizing society or the government or their spouses, and how even the mild-mannered ones are "complaining," if only about mundane things, like a Seinfeld type, whose disposition is pleasant compared to that of a Lewis Black or a Dave Chappelle. They're all observers of human behaviors that anger, annoy, or at least amuse them. You don't have to be funny, I say. Just vent, see what happens. And if you don't want to be overtly negative, think of the assignment as a diary entry. Start with "Today I..." and then let that first recalled experience remind you of other experiences, and so on. Either way, think of a topic or event that triggers an emotion that leads to other thoughts or events worth telling about. Let your stream of consciousness flow.

In the first essay, Angie starts with "This morning I drove to school." She's happy to be driving herself, alone, and to arrive safely, without event. This recent memory prompts her to recall a morning last year when her mother drove her to school, drunk. Angie hadn't realized it at first. But then there was the heavy foot on the gas and the brake, the shaky wheel; when Angie told her mom to slow down, her mom snapped at her, before crashing into a BMW, whose owner promptly exited his own car and marched toward theirs, asking if Angie's mother was insane. Angie cried in the back seat until the cops came and drove her to school. Angie's father called her classroom and demanded to speak with his daughter on the phone. It wasn't until he questioned the cop's actions that Angie realized how odd it was that she'd been whisked away from the accident scene, crying, while her mother hobbled failingly along the painted line on the side of the road. Angie quickly wraps up the story by saying she's never talked to her mom about it because she knows her mom regrets what happened and so she forgives her.

In my written reply, I compliment Angie's vivid and frightening rendering of the scene. I urge her to push the story a bit further, closer to the core truth, which seems elusive to me, though I predict that to her this advice might seem to be encouraging her to identify a problem that doesn't exist. I gently suggest that, sure, maybe everything is fine now, no hard feelings toward your mom, from you or your dad, indeed you even forgive her, but how did you all get to this point of peace? Was that morning the first time? Was it the last? I steer clear of therapeutic advice, but inevitably it's in there, as I direct her toward the frightful gap between that remembered day and now.

In the second essay, Natalie recalls being eight years old, cowering on the couch while her mother drunkenly searches for a lighter. Her father is working late. Her mother turns towards Natalie, lit cigarette in one hand and Guitar Hero guitar in the other. It's midnight. Natalie is eight. She reminds her mother she has school in the morning. "Play a song with me, baby!" Natalie's reply is a warning, "Daddy's going to kill you." Beer bottles fly across the room. Natalie begs her mother to stop, but she's too drunk to register any of her daughter's pleas. The next day, Natalie comes home from school to find her mother waiting, keys in hand, eager to "run errands." There are four familiar destinations. At each stop, Natalie sits in the car while her mother disappears into an alley or dark house. When the mother returns, she snorts powder, deposits pills into her purse, and cries.

The essays leave me stunned. I walk to lunch, blown away by the real lives I've just entered and returned from, the two essays together suggesting an epidemic of great writing by the eccentric daughters of alcoholic mothers.

★

When I get to the faculty dining room, I enter a spirited conversation well under way. It takes me a minute to realize that the person they're discussing is actually a student at Benfield.

Heidi, or Hayden, is a "trans kid," whose mom is having a hard time—"with the new name," says Lorena, the kid's art teacher. Last period, Lorena tried explaining this fact about the mother to the boy, who had been Heidi until this year. "Your mother's just having a hard time," Lorena told him, "but she's trying." The kid seemed to get it—nodding, Lorena says—willing to play along with the lie that his mother is having a hard time adjusting to the new name, not just the new pronoun.

Dean mentions a different kid, "that blond boy—have you seen him? I mean, I honestly could not tell." He hesitates. "No, I was sure he was a girl."

"But now you're sure he's a boy?" I ask.

Dean laughs nervously. "Yes. He's just, I don't know, pretty, or, I guess, feminine. He let his hair grow to his shoulders."

"It's okay, Dean," I say. "This is a safe space. You can share your feelings."

"No, no!" Dean's face turns beet red. He waits for the laughter to die down. "I'm just curious. He's not, you know, *anything*—is he?"

"I think he's Swedish," says Randi Gordon, who never misses an opportunity to insert her righteous perspective, this time laced with uncharacteristic wit, aimed at Dean, whom she views as her liberal nemesis.

"Hah-hah," Dean says. "Gabriella's the one who ruined it for me. I mean, *Gabe*."

"Ruined what exactly?" I ask, though I think I know where's he's heading with this comment. I know Gabriella—Gabe—who used to bring me her (*his* at the time) poems. Gabe wasn't my student, but he'd heard I was the writing guy; his teacher had read his poem and (unsure how to respond, I'm guessing) encouraged him to share it with Zervanos. The poem made it into *Pegasus* that year, his sophomore year, two years ago. By the end of the year, when the magazine was going to press, *he* had become *she*—back to Gabriella, as she'd been before I'd met her (him at the time). I tracked her down in the hallway and asked her how she wanted to be identified in the publication. She asked if the author could be anonymous. We'd been through this. We prefer not to publish anonymously because too many people would resort to that option. Besides, I suggested to her now, anyone who knows you is going to know this poem is yours, this poem about a boy trapped inside a girl's body, dying to come out.

She beamed. "Let's go with Gabe. I was Gabe when I wrote it, so it should be Gabe."

I nodded. "Sounds good." And it *did* sound good. I was proud of her.

I'd always liked Gabe—and now Gabriella. Looking back, I'm not sure if I ever thought of him as a boy, boyish as he looked—and acted. There had always been something almost *too* boyish about his behavior. Or too much effort behind it. Thumbs in the pants pockets. Neatly parted hair. Big smile for the camera. Deep, earnest head nods of agreement. Something old-fashioned, parodic, out of The Little Rascals or Dennis the Menace. But I don't think I thought of him as a girl, either. I just thought of him/her as a kid, going through a transformative time, as they all are. I remember wanting to say, "Hey, whatever you end up being makes no difference to me." I'd had a hunch the transformation was not complete, and it may still not be.

"You have to watch it with *that* one," Randi warns. "She could turn on you."

"How's that?" I ask.

"Oh, is she ever a manipulator. You have no idea."

"I only know her through her writing." I tell about the monologue she wrote last spring, a full-blown rant that, by its conclusion, revealed itself to be a tirade aimed at her mother, who never came to her rescue during all those horrible bouts with her father, who emotionally terrorized her, while he practically worshipped her big brother, as she saw it. The monologue ended up winning a Philadelphia playwright contest, performed by a local actress on stage in Center City. Gabriella had asked me to attend that production.

"Well, she's a stalker," Randi says. "She wouldn't let up on Cardozo and Shoemaker last year." Cardozo and Shoemaker are the wrestling coach and Adventure Club advisor, respectively. Gabe had joined the wrestling team the year before. Trained hard, wore the singlet, the whole nine yards. Won a match toward the end of the season.

I didn't interrupt to say that I'd never felt stalked whenever Gabe, and now Gabriella, popped into my room with new poems, or when she called out to me in the lobby, "Jimmy Z!", or even when she'd made a little booklet with pictures of her favorite (all male) teachers—a project for her publications class.

"Oh, she's a manipulator, all right," Dean says, sounding like a duped ex who still wants an apology. I don't mention his absence from her favorite-teacher booklet. He tells about a camping trip—and the locker room with boys—and how, when Gabe was nearby, he went behind a stall to undress. "But it's not like I ran and hid. For the most part, I played along. Other guys, and teachers, they stayed right there with her—him. Undressed. The whole thing." Now he feels bitter. "I did the work," he says, "you know? I made the adjustment. And then..." He grins sheepishly as he says this; he knows he sounds like an asshole. "And then *he* goes *she*. I see her in the hallway now, and I think, hey, wait a minute."

"You feel taken advantage of," I console.

Dean knows I'm fucking with him. We obviously had very different experiences. I have no memories that need to be reconciled with the new narrative; for me, the narrative has always been about inner turmoil—crafted into poetry. Dean won't say it, but we all understand something else, too: Gabriella is pretty, and she has, quite evidently now, a girl's body; and, in retrospect, I realize she had one as a sophomore, too, as Gabe, breasts compressed against her chest with an Ace bandage wrapped around a sports bra.

"Now *Quinn*, on the other hand..." Tracy Bean says, relieving Dean of our stares, taking us down another path, "now *she* knew from the earliest age—like, two or three?—that he, or she, was a girl. No doubt about it. Born in the wrong body."

Everyone, including Tracy Bean, must be chewing on the same sympathetic thought about Quinn McAlister, whom we all know at least from the hallways, where she can't be ignored: the wrong body indeed, built like a linebacker, with waxed legs in miniskirts and that large square jaw under bleached shoulder-length hair.

On my walk back to the classroom after lunch, Gabriella happens to walk by me. "Mr. Zervanos, can I start submitting stuff to *Pegasus*? I wrote a ton this summer!"

"Great," I say and carry on, looking forward to seeing her latest work.

SOOTHING MICHAEL

In the kitchen Michael is crying because he can't bend his man's knees—his construction-worker action figure, with stiff joints; and now he can't find the man's shovel and wheelbarrow. Michael gets frustrated when he can't do things that I can apparently do easily. Like bend his man's knees, then put him in the driver's seat of the dump truck—a tight fit.

After dinner, I hear Michael calling "Daddy" from the bathroom upstairs. I am playing UNO with Christopher at the kitchen table.

"Daddy, I pooped!"

"You need my help?"

"Yeah!"

Vana is sitting at the dining-room table, working at her laptop, trying to ignore Christopher, who is singing nonstop while he and I play cards, putting melody to whatever inane phrase I just said moments before. So now, as I head upstairs, the lyrics are, "You need my help?! You need my he he he he he he help, wiping your bu u u u u utt?"

Vana calls out, "Can you please...?"

Upstairs, Michael is pointing proudly at his enormous business, standing like a giant over the tiny plastic potty he has outgrown but still prefers. It occurs to me that maybe he was constipated earlier, thus the grumpiness. I hope he will lighten up now. He empties the contents of the potty into the toilet, hands me the soiled remains, and shuffles, pants around the ankles, into Mommy and Daddy's bedroom. We do all of this with the routine efficiency and camaraderie of veteran middle infielders turning a double play. I wash up and exit.

When I'm halfway downstairs, Michael calls, "Daddy, you forgot to wipe me!" I return to the bathroom, where he remains in position, palms flat on the floor, unmoving, in what appears to be a practiced yoga move.

In a minute Michael is downstairs again, making a whining noise that could kill a cat a mile away. I inform him of this fact, in the midst of his screeching, in a deadpan voice, making a game of pretending to be calm, which is funny to Christopher, who imitates my version of someone on the brink of a nervous breakdown, repeating me verbatim: "Um, Michael, could you please stop making that hideous sound or else I'm going to go up on the roof and throw myself off it?"

Michael screams, "I can't do it!"

I try to divert him from whatever his current frustration is. "You want a bath? Let's take a bath." He loves baths.

"Put it in!" he hollers.

"Put what in where?" I plead. "Please stop screaming."

"Nooo!"

"What do you want me to *do,* Michael? Show me." Now I am racing to bend the man's knees at just the right angle and pressing the wheelbarrow handles into the man's tight grip. Mysteriously, Michael goes quiet. I don't know what I've done, if anything, to satisfy him. I don't care. Mission accomplished. End of the world averted. For now.

Finally, upstairs again, Michael seems content with his dump truck and man and shovel and wheelbarrow, until, in his bedroom, I say, "Arms up"—the first step in getting his clothes off for a bath.

"Don't want a bath!"

I hiss, "What do you want, Michael? What's the problem now?"

I manage to get his pants off. He is nude in the hallway. He throws himself onto the carpet. I am afraid he is about to throw himself down the steps, just as I stupidly threatened to throw myself off the roof. Now I stand in the bathroom and say, "Come on, I'll take a bath."

He is stunned, not sure if he heard me right, or if I'm bluffing.

"You want me to?" I ask. "With you?"

He nods. His face is soaked with tears. He creeps toward me as I unlace my boots. In minutes we are up to our ribs in bubbles. Michael is giggling. I am refilling the rubber crab with bathwater and squirting steady streams at Michael's armpits.

Vana's Volvo

The Volvo's sunroof is open on the driveway. It rained last night. The Volvo is Vana's baby, her dream car, which we bought two years ago, our first car purchased together, for more than we could afford. On the passenger side, I discover pink construction paper melded to the seat. Pink patches and patterns of flowers appear on the leather when I peel off the paper—Michael's art project. I give the cream-colored leather a rub, and it appears that the pink is permanent.

I take a deep breath, denying an impulse to respond to this accident as if it were a tragedy. It is in this moment that I find myself thinking of my student Ryan Henry, consumed by his OCD, imagining him paralyzed at the sight of such a stain, losing himself in the seeming imperfection—or in some perfection I'm unable to see.

Michael is dunking a ball into the Little Tykes hoop on the porch. He leaps past an invisible defender. I feel a profound gratitude for his transparent and uncomplicated happiness. I can't help assuming that Ryan Henry's parents must remember their son in such moments as this and that they hope such memories are evidence of some essential, immutable self that surely must exist, clouded by some temporary condition.

I show Michael the remains of his pink paper project.

"What happened?" He peeks into the car. He's curious but not disappointed.

I want to inform Vana of this misfortune without seeming accusatory. *You left the sunroof open last night...* Not quite. Try the passive voice: *The sunroof was left open last night...* I see this moment as an opportunity to practice the kind of enlightened mindfulness I've been reading about in the book *Happiness.* I want to project the same calmness, compassion, patience, joy—those Zen virtues of love and non-judgment that the Buddhist-monk author deems accessible at all moments and that seem especially incongruous with such moments as this. *Behold, my dear, the pink paper and leather upholstery that are one.*

I say to Michael, "You want to give this to Mommy and tell her the seat is pink now?"

"K." Michael takes the scraps into his hands. I follow him into the kitchen, where Vana is washing a dish. Michael takes Vana's hand and says, "Come."

"What is it?"

"It's pink... The car..."

"What?"

I grab a roll of paper towels from under the sink. I find the Armor All on a shelf in the mud room, just as Vana is already returning from outside, fuming, "Oh my God, I can't even—" She cuts herself off and, in a rush, exits again, this time with a Mr. Clean white sponge.

"Good idea," I say, trailing her.

But Mr. Clean only slightly lightens the stain. I follow up with the Armor All, which does no good. Vana bears down again with the Mr. Clean pad, really muscling her thumb into it, as if to drive the pink particles into the subsurface of the leather forever. I wince.

I say, "I think maybe in time it'll fade. You know, just naturally, with the sunlight—"

"What about an SOS pad?"

"That's just steel wool and soap," I say. She's already inside. I'm right behind her. "You definitely don't want to use steel wool on leather. It doesn't make any sense. And the soap isn't as strong as Mr. Clean."

"What if I try it on just a little part?" She plucks a gray-blue pad from the yellow box under the sink.

I say, "No, I don't think so."

She's determined. "Just a little corner."

I stand in her path. "But why? Just—please explain to me how an SOS pad could possibly be better than Mr. Clean?"

"I can't, but I'm going to find out." She steps around me.

"I really don't see—"

"Why do you keep talking?"

I follow her onto the porch. What am I supposed to do, get between her and the Volvo? Wrestle the thing from her? She's about to make it worse. I know this. But the more certain I am, the more certain she is to challenge my certainty. Permanent damage is inevitable.

"Vana, please. You're upset. Just— Don't get emotional about this and lose all sense— You're gonna—"

At the car, she sneers, "I'm going to try it no matter what you say."

I nod. It's well past the time for me to shut up. "Well, okay." I can't watch. And I don't want to be standing here on the porch when she realizes the damage she—or, the SOS pad—has done.

I go inside. I put away the paper towels and the Armor All.

Vana returns from the driveway, strangely smiling.

"How'd it go?" I try.

She seems curiously at ease. "It's what you said."

"Damaged the leather?"

"Only if you really look."

"Mm."

She returns the box of SOS pads to the cabinet under the sink. I'm standing there nodding, watching her exit the kitchen.

Only if you really look.

Maybe that's the trick, I think. Don't look. Not so critically, anyway. Or look away. Why not? There's only so much you can do. And sometimes there's nothing at all you can do but let nature take its course. Be a mindful, compassionate witness to it all.

Ryan is only a junior. There's still time for us to do the work that remains for us to do together. As if I'm the kid's last chance at conquering his demons—at least through fiction. It's a delusion I choose not to relinquish. *Next year he'll be a senior, and we'll forge on, make up for lost time,* I think, assuming that he signs up for Creative Writing, and that salvation, or at least sanity, lies in telling the stories we have to tell.

After Vana goes upstairs, I gather the Armor All and paper towels and go back outside. The pink is gone, almost completely scrubbed away. Of course, the steel-wool marks and scuffs are here to stay, appearing as a tuft of black hairs embedded into the surface of the cream upholstery. But, I tell myself, from a more enlightened angle, nothing bad has been *added* to the leather, only good removed—or, *moved.* The seeming black hairs were there all along, hidden under the cream surface. These scuffs are merely evidence of the absence of what was once present, of the cream coloring that has been rubbed off, like the pink, the faint remains of which in time will fade from the leather, not ceasing to exist, but simply relocating.

I take a deep breath. The challenge of mindfulness remains. I set the cleaning supplies on the porch. I say nothing. Let go. Begin again. Be here in the present moment. But I know there must be more to it than this. So now what? Michael is back to his slam-dunking. I sweep the porch. I carry the unused firewood from the porch to the roofed pile at the edge of the backyard. I clip shrubs. I take out the trash.

Golf with Dean

Dean Garrett and I are teeing off on the fifteenth hole at Spring Haven Golf Club, just miles from the high school, where we slipped out before the last bell, hoping to squeeze in a round before my kids' aftercare programs close at 6:00. Dean's kids are nearly grown, one in college and one in high school, so he's not on a strict schedule, but with one son in second grade and the other in preschool I have to plan my days to a T.

"I really don't feel like doing Parents' Night tomorrow," I tell Dean.

Parents' Night. The annual pageant at the high school where mothers and fathers file in and out of classrooms to examine their kids' teachers in the flesh, while we teachers sweat through a half-dozen back-to-back presentations of the courses we teach their children—"the most delightful people I could ever hope to spend forty-seven minutes with every day," I tell the parents, who, depending on the class, chuckle at either my sincerity or my wit.

"Christopher's Parents' Night is tomorrow, too," I say, "at the elementary school, and I'd rather go to that."

Dean and I are riding in our cart alongside the fairway of the fifteenth hole. Or is it the sixteenth?

"Vana can't go because she's got classes Thursday nights," I say, "so we have to pay a babysitter eighty bucks to be home with the kids—not for us to go out on a date, but for friggin' Parents' Night."

I don't want to sound bitter. I remind myself that this is *Vana's* time now, these next two years, to devote herself to pursuing her doctorate while working full-time. It's *my* time to devote myself to taking care of the household. This commitment means putting off my own usual pursuits (writing, painting...*sleeping*) or attempting to subsume them in meditation, my recent pursuit, which I had always believed was for people with unfathomable troubles and which, for me, has amounted to listening to a couple of Buddhist audio books and a mindfulness app—during my one hour alone driving to and from school.

"I'm not doing Parents' Night." Dean's grin stretches wide inside his peppery goatee. "I just tell Freddy I've got my own kid's Parents' Night to attend."

"You do? Since when?"

"Back when shit started to hit the fan with Janey. Now I like to go alone."

Dean is divorced now, so he answers to no one, whereas I need Vana's blessing, or at least her cooperation, to participate in activities outside the home or workplace.

"Interesting," I say, thinking about how duty and neglect can become strange bedfellows. "I've actually never been to a Parents' Night—as a parent, I mean. Vana has always gone."

This is Vana's time now. It's a mantra I have on a loop, a reminder that I welcome these arrangements. After all, I've had my time. Time to devote myself to my passions, and to the welcome and unwelcome challenges life has presented, always with Vana's support, especially five years ago, when I got cancer and she had to work full-time while taking care of Christopher. She kept it together through my illness and treatment and the six months it took to regain some sense of normalcy after a year of traumatic events, most notably when the chief vascular surgeon said there was nothing left they could do to save my life, before another surgeon, with a Hail Mary pass, performed a radical operation, removing the impossible-to-reach tumor by excising most of the main vein that goes into the heart and replacing it with a graft made out of pig intestine. All the unrelenting apprehension and terror had taken a toll on Vana. So, two years later, once the boys weren't babies anymore, it made sense when she announced it was time to get her doctorate.

"Just ask Freddy." Dean hits the brakes, and we alight from the cart. "He'll let you. He always says, 'Family first.'"

I nod, impressed. "I'll ask first thing in the morning."

We grab our five-irons and head for the rough.

"Anyway," I say, "sorry I interrupted you back there at the tee. What were we talking about again?"

He mirrors my grin, as if either of us forgets. We're searching for our balls in the tall weeds that border the woods.

"Oh yeah," I say. "Blow jobs."

Dean and I were talking about the sex he's been enjoying in his single life and the sex I've been longing for in my married one.

He whacks at some tall fronds with his five-iron, giving himself ample room to swing. Mercifully he spares me details of his latest pleasures but tells me with a satisfied grin that his new girlfriend is game for anything. He imitates her imploring him to "tell me what you want." Then he says that, despite the tremendous sex, he knows she's not the one.

I hesitate. "The one?"

"I know, I know, there's no *one.*"

He lofts one out of the rough, and for a long moment we both lose it beyond a tangle of branches and the blazing sunlight, before it drops and disappears in the distance, maybe twenty yards from the hole.

"A pitch and putt for birdie," I say. "Well done."

He nods. "I just mean, she's not someone I want to be with for the rest of my life. There are just little things about her that don't do it for me, or won't in the long run."

After a thorough investigation of the rough, I discover I've been lying in the clear, all along, at the edge of the fairway. I take a deep breath and smash my ball with my five-iron, a sensational shot that splits the two giant oaks in the foreground, cutting off the entire bend of the dogleg—an accident I won't admit to—and lands inches from the flag.

"Jesus Christ," Dean says, as I hop into the passenger's seat of the cart and he guns it.

As we walk toward the green—of the *seventeenth,* Dean informs me (much closer to finishing than I realized)—I feel stronger in my marriage, content with our relatively modest bedroom ratings of late. "The grass is always greener," I say.

"Always."

When I arrive at the edge of the green, I discover that my ball indeed landed inches from the hole, leaving an impressive dimple, then spun back and settled into the unkempt rough.

Dean has discovered his ball in a sand trap. Eyeing the grassy lip, he says, "There's no way out of this thing."

I picture him in his small house with bedrooms for his teenage kids, who stay with him half the time, when they aren't with their mother, who lives in the house she and Dean bought and rehabbed together. He says he's been going over there a lot lately, to help her with household chores, lugging boxes, that kind of thing.

"She's so alone," he says, as if neither of us can imagine how she's feeling.

I three-putt and drag my feet to the cart.

After three hacks at the sand, Dean says, "Fuck this," picks up his ball, and leaps over the rake to beat me to the driver's seat.

PARENT-TEACHER GROUP

At lunch today, Carolyn Winters describes how at the PTG meeting last night Principal Freddy joked that nobody better pull a Kaepernick and take a knee during the Pledge of Allegiance. Afterward, one of the four African-American teachers on our staff admonished him for the insulting quip.

"What was his reaction?" I ask.

Dean interrupts, "Wait, *what?* The *National Anthem* at the *PTG meeting?"*

"No, the Pledge of Allegiance," Carolyn says.

"What are they doing the Pledge of Allegiance for at the PTG meeting?"

"Ya got me," Carolyn says. "All district meetings begin with it. Believe me, I hear you. I was on the PTG in Strath Haven, and I guarantee you we never did the Pledge of Allegiance."

Dean remains shocked. "You got all these teachers and parents and administrators in a conference room standing there with their hands over their hearts?"

Sam chimes in about the Pledge in homeroom that morning. "A student refused to stand," he says, stifling a laugh, "and trust me, this kid was not making a political statement. He was just being lazy, probably copying somebody else's homework. So I just told him, 'Um, we stand for the Pledge,' and the kid stood right up. No problem. But then the kid didn't recite it, and after homeroom another kid confronted him and told him something like 'love it or leave it.' And the kid goes..." Sam can't stop laughing. Now we're all laughing with him, even before the punch line. "The kid goes, 'I'm planning on it! After graduation I'm going to *Alaska!*'" Sam nearly falls out of his chair. We're all howling with him.

Carolyn dishes us the latest headlines: "Trump is tweeting again, criticizing the wife of the Green Beret soldier who died in Niger. Oh, he's also taking shots at the Florida congresswoman who was witness to the president's phone call while the two women were in a car together. Now Trump was calling the congresswoman a nut and a liar. Apparently, the wife of the soldier was telling the story this morning on the *Today* show." She scans the article for the next point worthy of sharing.

I say, "Matt Lauer should turn to the camera and say, 'Mr. President, instead of tweeting while you're watching, why don't you call the show right now?'"

Carolyn says, "Oh my God, are you kidding me? What's his name Cuomo on CNN does that all the time." Carolyn puts her hand to her ear like a phone. "He goes, 'Um, Mr. President. I know you're watching. Call me.' And sometimes he does!"

Neil tells us that Freddy gave a girl a ten-day suspension for posting on Facebook that "they" (the administrators on duty at the dance Friday night) "are such idiots" because they failed to find her pot hidden in her deodorant stick. Instead, she was busted for cigarettes she claimed were not hers. She got an automatic three-day suspension for tobacco on the premises, while the kid who admitted to hiding his cigarettes in her bag got one day.

"So three days became ten days because she called Freddy an idiot on Facebook?"

Neil shakes his head in disbelief. "I'm already anticipating the legal backlash. Is she being punished for bullying the administration on social media? Or for the pot she claimed was in her deodorant stick but no one actually saw, much less confiscated as evidence? Nearly all the lawsuits I have to deal with are about the unjust punishment administered by the principal, not about the alleged crime."

I resist the urge to take a knee and bow my head, right there on the cold tile floor.

Why? Because I Love You

Lately Michael has been asking, "Why?"

"Why why why why why?"

When I run out of answers, I've started to say, "Because I love you." Which seems to satisfy him.

"Why it's not a home day today?"

"Because it's a school day."

"Why today is a school day?"

"Because it's Monday."

"Why today is Monday?"

"Michael!"

He grins. "Because you love somebody?"

Sweet, sneaky boy. "Yes." He knew the answer all along.

CANDI

Right before I leave for the day, on a whim I check my email and find a note from Candice MacPherson, aka Candi, who asks about continuing the "independent study in creative writing" she began with me last year—a novel-in-progress called *Lolli,* about a gay high school boy writing letters to an address of unknown inhabitants. Candi's plan, which she exuberantly describes in her email to me, is to give the boy a wasting disease that may or may not do him in before or after the recipient of the letters is revealed near the end of the book and the point of view shifts dramatically to said recipient, who rushes to meet the sender, Lolli, who has finally revealed his identity to him—or her (not yet sure about the details of the recipient's identity, to be determined). It's a great hook, I tell her, the mystery of the recipient and of what he, or she, may do once Lolli reveals his whereabouts.

The chapters, or letters, Candi wrote last year are smart, quirky, funny, and intriguing. Once a week after school, she sat here and wrote for an hour before handing me her iPad to read the finished product, two or three pages that begin "Dear Stranger" (and, as the story progresses, "Dear Friend") and end with Lolli's vocabulary word of the day, some exotic term Candi cleverly uses to express some hidden emotion that her narrator will soon reveal in the form of seeming accident or intellectual discovery—not unlike the author, who I am coming to see, in more and more fascinating ways, is one and the same with her male creation. Lolli. Candi. Of course. The name Lolli is itself the fictional narrator's own clever nom de plume—a mishmash derived from LOL (the abbreviation for Laughing Out Loud, which Lolli frequently employs to disguise, and draw attention to, both his fathomless sorrow and his nonchalance) and its diminutive form, LOLLI, as in lollipop, the preferred candy of his favorite literary character, Lolita, that tragically precocious and vivacious girl whose name he happily and not coincidentally (almost) shares.

What Candi needs to work on this year, I tell her in my reply, is to develop novelistic qualities despite the letter format, to really let Lolli forget he's writing letters, to realize that the letters have always been just an excuse to tell the story he needs to tell, to a reader he imagines he can trust with his life—with his truth.

She asks if Thursday afternoons will work for me again.

I'll be busier this year, I answer, with grocery-shopping duty and Christopher's soccer practice and Vana's monthly excursion to Penn. But we'll make it work.

She responds with a smiley-face emoji and three exclamation points.

I reply to the emoji smile with an actual one she can't see.

Classroom Supplies

On the drive home from school, I stop at the Rite-Aid and buy boxes of tissues for the classroom. And bags of mini candy bars and lollipops for the giant can I reserve for the lit-mag staff. When did I become this teacher who cares so much about providing comforts and treats to my students? When a girl asked today if I had tissues, I felt genuinely bad for her, and disappointed in myself, when I offered her the paper towels I'd snagged as backup from the bathroom.

VANA'S MLK PROJECT

Tonight, after I tuck the boys into bed, Vana asks if maybe later I can assist her with her documentary project, which is due next week. It's the first major project of her doctoral program. For the past week, she's been collecting data, digging up vintage photos and video clips, traversing the campus to interview faculty at St. Joe's—all while working full-time as associate dean of the business school.

An hour later I pause the Yankees-Twins game after the thrilling top of the first inning; incredibly, the Twins lead 3-0 in the wild-card elimination game in New York. I leave the TV and the lights on in the living room and go back upstairs to see if she still wants my help. She sits up in bed with books surrounding her. She sets the laptop on the bedcovers beside her, where I take my position and await her instructions. She explains that she compiled audio clips of Martin Luther King's speech at Saint Joseph's University—then Saint Joseph's College—in October, 1967. She says she needs to whittle all these speeches, including those of the professors she interviewed—nearly two hours of footage—down to three minutes.

Two hours of footage down to three minutes? This is going to take a while. I wonder how the Yankees are faring in the bottom of the first.

I arrange my laptop on the bed, legal pad on my lap, and headphone in one ear, so that I can work alone while Vana reads another in a series of articles in preparation for her upcoming classes. King's speech reveals a man with radical ideas. This is not the "I Have a Dream" speech of 1963, but something charged with a fiercer, more urgent force. He urges massive economic reform and equality, proposals that doubtless contributed to the perception that he was a Communist. He pushes for legislation meant to change the habits of men whose hearts might be unchangeable. He suggests that changing habits might lead to changing hearts; but, in the meantime, we needed laws that would protect a black man like him from being lynched. He was shot down months later, in April.

I listen to the five-minute excerpt of King's speech and, following Vana's instructions, try to determine the essential thirty seconds of it. Then I do the same with the unedited interviews of the professors whom Vana recorded in their offices. The professors—from the History, English, Economics, and Student Life departments—are asked by Vana to reflect on the volatile times in which MLK delivered the speech, considering that, on the fiftieth anniversary of Dr. King's visit, this year is not unlike 1967 in many respects. Vana's working thesis is that universities must take risks in order to influence positive change and that inviting Martin Luther King to speak at St. Joseph's was just such a risk—and an example of the kind of moral and intellectual courage that should define higher education—especially admirable in 1967 at a Jesuit school whose alumni were threatening to withhold their donations if that Commie so much as set foot on their campus. But it was actually the student government, a group of mainstream, if not conservative, students that had done the inviting. This background points to the questions Vana hopes to answer: Have times changed for the worse? Is there reason to be optimistic? Is progress possible?

When she poses this question to the Student Life professor, a long pause follows. Evidently the professor anticipates with foreboding the answer she can't help formulating. She takes a deep breath and says that, at the rate we're going, she's afraid caution will win the day and the university will lose its significance as a setting for dynamic discourse in this country. It's only when opposing ideas collide, she says, that students are challenged and forced to open up, to reckon with their own presuppositions.

I record the times, 1:16, 3:34, 11:45, and on and on, marking the segments that seem final-cut worthy. The result is thirty minutes of footage, which Vana dreads compressing into a three-minute film.

In a flash I think of my lecture notes on the whiteboard in my classroom, from a fiction-writing lesson that identifies the basic elements of a scene or a story. I suggest to Vana that we consider these three related questions to help streamline her documentary:

1: What is the protagonist's conscious desire, i.e., what does he want?

Answer: He wants positive social change.

Okay.

Show King speaking to an audience.

2: How does the protagonist try to get what he wants?

Cut to: King pushing for legislation that will change the habits, if not the hearts, of men.

Great.

And 3: Does the protagonist get what he wants in the end?

Uhh...

Cut to: "I Have a Dream"?

No. Even King himself offers only a hushed echo of the dream at the end of this 1967 speech.

Cut to: Student Life professor saying she's not optimistic?

Yikes. Not a very happy, or even hopeful, ending.

Then it occurs to me that the documentary form is more like a personal essay than a work of fiction and that, as such, MLK is not the protagonist. "*You* are," I say to Vana, who raises her eyebrows in surprise. "You're the first-person narrator. Martin Luther King is just one part of the answer to question number two, just as the professors are part of the answer to that question: How does the protagonist try to get what she wants? Answer? She asks the hard questions and in doing so demonstrates the deeper purpose of her project. Or, no, the deeper purpose is revealed through your actual struggle of making the documentary. This is the protagonist's unconscious desire, what you really wanted all along: to be a living example of the kind of dynamic discourse you hope to influence, or effect, or energize on the university campus. The university as it should be, not a place where students and professors exercise caution for fear of disruption, but a place where students and professors welcome disruption, because it's the only way to learn, and to achieve real change—"

"Oh my God!" Vana interrupts: "You need to be writing this down! Or recording this. Energize...yes."

I laugh.

She says, "I'm serious! This is my voiceover!"

"I can't repeat it, it's lost, I lost the thread..."

"Try. Write."

I set pen to paper, scribbling what I can recall of what I've just said. When I finish, we draw circles and arrows and asterisks to indicate the shape and order the final cut might take.

"Thank you," she says with a kiss.

"This is awesome," I tell her. "Your video is going to be the envy of your cohort."

She sighs. "I'm so tired."

When she turns the light off on the nightstand, I say I'm going downstairs to watch the rest of the game.

"Now? It's past eleven. You're going to fall asleep in five minutes."

"Maybe."

It's pitch-dark downstairs. Lights out in the living room. TV off. Doors locked. Evidently Vana has long since shut down the house for the night. I never noticed her leaving the bedroom, where I was engrossed in the interviews and that obscure MLK speech, which has stirred something in me, something that remains unsettled, an awareness of some dimension of life, of learning, that feels not fully formed, and out of reach—some truth I don't want to come to peace with. It has something to do with the fact that King's "I Have a Dream" speech had been delivered five years before his death—and nearly as long before the St. Joe's speech, in which his allusion to it, "And that is why I still have a dream," sounded tired and pitiable. Or maybe that's just how it sounds to me now, fifty years later.

My laptop is on the coffee table. I meant to do some writing tonight, to stay disciplined with this business of keeping a diary. It will have to wait.

I lie on the couch and turn on the TV. I depress the pause button, and the room comes to life. I fast-forward through the commercials. It isn't long before I am lost once again, in the sights and sounds of bats cracking against baseballs and the Yankees roaring to victory, as if there had never been any doubt that New York would come back.

PARENTS' NIGHT

Before the school day starts, I pop into Freddy's office and ask if, for the first time in my twenty-plus-year career, I might have permission to miss Parents' Night tonight, for the one and only good reason, of course, to attend my own kid's Parents' Night. He mirrors my smile and says, "Family first," as Dean predicted he would.

This morning Christopher told his teacher, Mrs. Deforest, that his mother can't go but his father-the-teacher will be attending instead. I follow up with an email to clarify that I'll be missing my own Parents' Night to attend hers.

She emails back, "Aren't you lucky. You really shouldn't go to so much trouble :)"—a little teacher-to-teacher snark that I welcome.

When I arrive at Christopher's classroom, I have to find my child's desk by recognizing the clues each student wrote on a piece of paper left on his or her desktop. I know I'm not the father of the kid who wrote "I have season tickets to the Sixers."

"I *wish,*" I say to a mother hunting down her daughter's desk.

Finally, I find "My favorite color is silver. I like football."

Christopher's favorite color changes by the week, his favorite sport by the season, so I figure I've arrived.

Mrs. Deforest encourages us to write a note in return on the provided paper with smiling suns at the top. The sharply dressed mom next to me is already at it with the lovely pen she plucked from her handbag. "I forgot my Montblanc," I tell her. I'm sitting in Christopher's little chair, nearly crouching. "I'm going with the green

Crayola instead." She laughs. I dig out a box of crayons from inside the desk, whose top opens on hinges. In my note I resist commenting on the incredible disorder I found inside it. Instead, I tell him how proud of him I am and leave the note poised atop the clutter, a note that will doubtless slip into the maw of disarray inside the desk.

While the rest of the parents file in and, with dwindling options, take their children's seats, I imagine the thrilling newness of everything through Christopher's eyes, marveling at life from new angles.

Mrs. Deforest asks us to sign a paper giving her permission to post photos of our kids on Twitter. After an awkward moment, a father asks if it's a private or public account.

"Um, public?" She laughs nervously. "Sorry, I'm new to Twitter."

A mother asks, "The purpose is to share with parents, right?"

The parents grow restless, while Mrs. Deforest seems to be fighting off a cold sweat, deflecting questions hurled her way.

I feel delightedly indifferent about the matter, recognizing my shared allegiances, to the collective grievances of the parents and the noble intentions of the instructor. I can see that the Twitter plan is dead in the water, even if Mrs. Deforest hasn't accepted this fact yet, and that the outcome of this collision of interests will be just fine—everything is going to be okay, I want to tell them all.

The dialogue carries on awhile, until Mrs. Deforest says, "I'll look into it, the privacy option and whatever."

Afterward, in the hallway, I linger near a small circle of parents still debating the issue. I'm betting Mrs. Deforest has already canceled her Twitter account and trashed the permission forms. I decide I won't give it another thought, and I wave goodnight.

Outside on the sidewalk, I catch up with Bill McBride, the father of Christopher's classmate Joey, whom I know from Little League.

He stands patiently in the white glow of a streetlight, as if he's been waiting for me.

We shake hands. "I was trying to catch the end of that Twitter shitstorm," I say. "Did you sign that paper?"

"No way, I know better." He smiles and pats the flap pocket of his corduroy sport coat. "I've got it with all the other papers we got. My ex-wife is in technology, and she would flip."

"My wife would flip too, but I signed it like a blind mule."

He laughs. "Anyway, it'll never happen. She's a good teacher. Probably had an eleventh-hour brainstorm this afternoon and just didn't think it through."

Bill is lean and silver-haired, only a year or two older than I am, but I always feel humbled in his sage presence, which emits a kind of stoic affability.

"I hope she doesn't think we're all out here talking about her," I say.

"I'm *sure* she knows we're all out here talking about her, but I also think she was probably embarrassed for five minutes and moved on."

I nod, pleased by Bill's level-headed wisdom.

He says, "You want to grab a beer? Joey's with his mom tonight."

"I'd love to, but I gotta get back. Babysitter, the whole thing. Vana's at Penn till Saturday."

"I thought of you the other day. I read a long article in *The Atlantic* about how the iPhone is destroying a generation of minds, and it made me think of what you were saying that night at the pub—you know, about this generation."

I confess that I can't remember whatever unstudied theory I imparted last time over burgers and beers. I do remember describing Michael in front of the iPad, on YouTube, watching some five-year-old internet phenom playing with trucks, and I remember saying how Michael preferred that virtual world to the one in which I was imploring him to play with actual trucks outside by himself, or even with Daddy.

Bill shakes his head. "It's really an addiction. Joey's out of control."

I nod, sympathetically. Last season Joey threw a fit every time a teammate made an error, which was at least twice an inning. As a hitter, he'd showed a promising swing, until his rate of contact dwindled inexplicably in the opening games. His parents waved to me from foul territory after another strikeout-and-tantrum, in hopes I might work some encouraging magic. "You seem to have a way with him," they said, as they headed back to their fold-out chairs while I squatted with Joey and said nothing in particular. But I wasn't his mom or dad, a fact that seemed to make all the difference to Joey. "Do you like ice cream or Legos better?" he asked me. He pulled at some grass, and before I could answer, he raced back to the bench. His parents shook their heads in awe. I shrugged, happy to let them believe I had a special gift.

That night at the pub, Bill and I chatted about writing, movies, our shared fondness for Tim O'Brien's fiction, his military service as an officer in Iraq, and the years he lived in Milwaukee, with his wife and infant son, before moving East. Bill had been a lieutenant because of his time in ROTC at Notre Dame, where he'd earned a degree in engineering and architecture. He told me about the old Milwaukee dump they moved out of and about the new house that he'd taken months to design and build and that his wife, with the heightened senses of a mother with a newborn, insisted smelled moldy. And so, after just days in the new one, they moved back into the old one, just before it would have sold—another source of tension. They sold the new one. The mold was, of course, illusory, Bill said, an excuse of some kind, another way for her to make her case that he just didn't think things through.

"I should have seen it coming," he said. "Or I should have acted more decisively when I saw it coming. I knew it was coming. Why I didn't do something earlier, I don't know. That's sort of my problem. Or it's certainly her problem with me." I watched his pained expression as he seemed to study an image he was conjuring in the space between us. "I always thought of marriage as a kind of crucible, you know? You stay in there, and you grind it out." He looked up at me, as if from the dust.

I nodded, offering him my silence, which he seemed to appreciate. He nodded back. We reached for our beers and saluted. We took long slugs.

Their marriage lasted long enough for the family to move back to the Philadelphia area, where she'd grown up and where her parents live nearby.

"I miss Milwaukee," he said. "I miss the dream of my own business, which was thriving there. Now I'm working for the government. Solid, predictable work. But I miss the Midwest, where I grew up. Chicago area. But there's Joey now."

I smiled—a little stiffly, to convey the sense of fellowship I felt—just as I'm smiling now, on the sidewalk outside the elementary school.

Bill says, "We should get the boys together to play."

What a fine line there is, I think, *between our two lives as fathers.* And what a fine line there is between the lives we're living now—any of us, all of us—and the altered lives we might be living a year from now. Bill said that night at the pub, "If you would have ever told me I'd be divorced, living alone in Philadelphia, and working for the government, I would have told you you're fucking crazy."

Driving home in the dark night, passing under the streetlights, I feel Vana's absence. I experience it completely—she's there; I'm here—and I understand just how fully these two years are going to require me to give of myself and expect so little from her. Recently, she asked me, with books spread out around her on the living-room couch, if I was jealous, not of the homework but of her doing something so gratifying and adventurous as attending graduate school in our forties with two young sons, and I answered honestly, no, I was happy for her, and I was happy for me, too, to be so singularly focused on taking care of the family. It was something of a relief, actually, a reprieve from the demands I put on myself to accomplish personal goals, tangible achievements, when life affords enough free time, as it did before the kids were born, as it did even just months ago when I was sharing parent duties.

The babysitter says that Christopher is sound asleep already and that Michael is a bit restless but in bed. "He had his milk," she says.

After she leaves, I hear footfalls overhead. I tiptoe up the steps to find four-year-old Michael at the distant windows in my bedroom, on tiptoe himself, looking over the windowsill at the sounds of the night. I realize he must believe he's home alone right now, with his sleeping brother, seeing that the babysitter has just driven off. Christopher would be screaming bloody murder if the roles were reversed, if he thought he'd just been abandoned. Meanwhile, Michael appears to be pondering the stars. *Twinkle twinkle.* How different the view of the world is for him. How different even our shared experiences. *How I wonder what you are.*

He hears me breathing, turns, beaming, and runs across the carpet and into my arms. Simply delighted, not relieved. He joins me downstairs, drinks another bottle of milk at the kitchen table while I pack lunches.

Vana calls my cell phone and Michael answers it, so it's Michael she sees on FaceTime.

"Hey, you!" She laughs, walking on the street in West Philly. The night is illuminated all around her. "Why aren't you in bed, kookie? Where's Daddy?"

Michael laughs, thrilled, I imagine, at the impossible thought of being on his own here—and thrilled, even more so, at the thought of being perceived (by his mommy) as being on his own here, if only for a moment.

I laugh, too, off-screen, and linger out of view awhile, letting them wonder at the strange sight of each other alone, far away yet so close, before I enter the frame.

SEX ED

"What?" I've come in late again at lunch. Did I just hear correctly? "Someone had sex in the stairwell?"

Carolyn provides the abbreviated update. Asperger kid. Not autistic, but "very much on the spectrum." He also sent dick pics to freshmen girls.

"No."

"Yes. But not *pics. Videos.* Of him jerking off."

"Get out. Who is this?" I ask, as if he could be my student and I wouldn't already know who they're talking about. Someone says his name. Eddie Bolinger. My stomach sinks. He *is* my student. Level-Two Creative Writing. I cannot un-see the image that has sprung instantly to mind. I can't help confirming, "Eddie Bolinger is having sex in the stairwell? I mean, he's having sex *anywhere?"* I hesitate. "Who's having sex with *him?"*

"Exactly," Carolyn says, "He's a total innocent. He doesn't understand. Everest should have called the head psychologist immediately. This has all happened in the last few months. The parents of the girls were calling administration for days, and Everest didn't answer their calls. Finally, Freddy took the call. After that, the kid's punishment changed from zero to nine days suspension. The girls' parents are suing. Eddie's parents are not lawyered up." Carolyn sympathizes deeply with Eddie, who "does not deserve to be on Megan's List for the rest of his life! He'll be ruined!"

"I'm sorry," Dean says. "If he did that to *my* daughter, I'd want him nailed."

Carolyn hisses, "All this happened over a month ago, *Dean.* Since then, guess what? The kid turned eighteen. *Then* the girls came forward to report him. They literally waited until he turned eighteen to turn him in. Is that not evil? They *planned* the delay. You have to wonder if they goaded him into the sexting in the first place? These are *mean girls!* And the mothers! The one girl claims that Eddie stalked her when she was driving with her mom *months ago.* The mom called me and said that if this ever happens again, we're going to *do* something. Even *then* the girl hadn't mentioned the sexting. Not until his birthday!"

Dean still hasn't developed any sympathy for the kid. "Remember Blowjob Alley?"

"Who is Blowjob Allie?" I ask.

Dean bursts out laughing, nearly spitting his milk. "Not a *girl.*"

He wipes his mouth. "Blowjob *Alley,* in the *stacks,* in the *library.* Last year, that was the spot. Eddie and his little freshman girlfriend. It was, like, their *thing.*"

"Blowjob Allie." I shake my head. "You've got to admit that's a good nickname. Blowjob Allie and *Sex Ed.*"

Dean laughs again, this time nearly spitting out his salad. "That's good. Sex Ed. How has someone not thought of that yet?" He wipes his nose. "Six aisles thirty feet long, completely visible from the open table area. We're not talking basement archives here. Supposedly this had been going on a long time before they finally got busted. The kid's having sex like a porn star. Sorry..." Dean shakes his head. "But he is *not* innocent."

"He's innocent," Carolyn says. "He's a child."

Pretty Women

Such good boys, I think. Or is this sense of calmness in the house too good to be true? I can't remember the last time it's been this quiet, each of us independently occupied, for this long. Christopher has been quiet downstairs for a while now. No complaining about the sudden termination of our UNO game earlier, cut short when Michael called me up to his bedroom to help him find his favorite rugby shirt, which I finally found in the laundry room on the third floor—washed, dry, and ready to wear, fortunately.

After Michael prepared his outfit for school tomorrow, he exited his bedroom and headed pleasantly downstairs, to join his brother, I assume. I get my own clothes ready for work, enjoying this extended moment of peace, pleased that the boys are of an age now when they can play quietly together. Or independently. I picture Christopher assembling Legos at the dining-room table or leafing through a *Sports Illustrated* on the couch; Michael lying on the floor nearby with truck in hand, inspecting the wheels turning, his ear to the floor. Meanwhile, Vana is doing her nightly reading behind the closed guest-room door.

"Bath tonight?" I call out to Christopher, or Michael, whoever might be interested.

No answer.

When I go downstairs, the coast is clear in the kitchen. And in the living room. The basement door is open, and the light is on.

Christopher rarely ventures into the basement alone, which I assume he did before Michael found him there. I wonder what they're doing down there. I find Christopher standing with Vana's phone. Nearby, Michael is lying in a pile of toys on the carpet, uninterested in whatever his big brother is doing. I ask Christopher what he's up to.

"Checking something—Tom," he says.

"Tom? What do you mean, Tom?" I grab the phone, and on the screen are pictures of Tom Brady, Thomas the Train, and Tom the cat of Tom & Jerry. I'm not buying it. I press the back arrow and there's a screenful of beautiful women, models' headshots, and in the search band are the words "pretty ladies boobs." I take a deep breath and back-arrow again. "pretty ladies boobs on the beach." I think, *this kid is in second grade. Seven years old. Isn't it too early for this?*

Months ago, I asked my dad if it seemed young for Christopher to be getting erections, not that the kid called them that. "Why does my penis get like a stick?" he'd asked me. I'd asked him, "When does it usually happen?" He grinned. I said, "You can tell me." "Sometimes when I think about pretty ladies. Or if I see boobs, like on TV."

I was trying to remember, when did *I* start with all of this? The first *Playboy?* Not second grade. Not that early. No way. I am resisting the feeling of being impressed, not just by my son's precociousness but by his excellent taste, as I continue scrolling down with my index finger. Faster, faster. I back-arrow again. "pretty ladies boobs bras."

"Jesus, buddy," I say.

"What?"

Back arrow. "pretty pretty pretty pretty pretty." *Still innocent,* I think—he's got literally the universe at his fingertips and he's searching for "pretty woman," and just like that there is the movie-poster image with Julia Roberts in knee-high black boots and a pink top. Back arrow one last time: ESPN.com. I picture him an hour ago in the kitchen, where he first found Mommy's phone. "Siri, what time is the Eagles game tonight?" 8:30 game time. It was only 7:30.

An hour to kill till then. Daddy and Michael were upstairs searching for some lost shirt, he must have figured; Mommy was busy doing work. The wheels were spinning, calculations being made. He raced to the basement, musing, pretty, pretty, pretty, pretty....

Now there is 4% battery left. I am still scrolling. Christopher is still waiting for my reaction. My God, Selma Hayek.

"What are you doing?" he asks me.

I say, "You've been busy down here, pal." I close the pages. Then I wonder, *Why am I covering for him?* I start for the stairs. "Let's go put on PJs."

"Are you going to tell Mommy?"

"No. Let's go. Eagles game soon. I've gotta put Michael to bed."

I'm covering for *us.* And also sparing Vana the anxiety, I tell myself. I plug in Vana's phone to charge, back on the shelf in the kitchen, where it belongs.

After I get Michael to bed, Christopher is finishing his homework, twenty minutes of reading silently, in the guest room with Mommy on the couch. He tells me not to start the Eagles game without him. "At 8:42 I'll be down," he says. He is timing it. Twenty minutes is the required time. He won't read a second more than he has to. At 8:42 he promptly descends the steps, and we turn on the TV.

We watch the game for about a half hour until Mommy leans over the banister: "I don't understand what's going on here... It's after nine o'clock."

I say, "He's eating a banana."

He holds up the stub of banana—the evidence.

I say, "As soon as he's done, we're coming up."

The peel sits on the coffee table.

As Vana ascends, Christopher raises his eyebrows at me. I return the silent gesture. We are partners in crime.

Minutes later I say, "Okay, let's go."

"Aww," he tries.

But I'm already up.

At the steps he remembers: "Wait! My tooth!"

Luckily, he remembered. I would have forgotten—again. He points to the top shelf in the kitchen, where Mommy put it earlier, delicately placed in the center of a white paper napkin, after he lost it playing "Ready Set Hike" with Michael in the living room in the blur of pre-dinner activity. He walks it carefully upstairs on the napkin, like a jewel on a pillow. He places it perfectly centered under the pillow on his bed. I study its placement and picture my arm slinking under there in a few hours, after the Eagles game, exchanging the tooth for cash.

"I wonder if the tooth fairy will give me six bucks," he says. "For my sixth tooth."

I play dumb. "I guess we'll see." My sweet, innocent boy.

Phucking Philly

Freddy Whetts makes a surprise announcement about our students' unfortunate behavior—vulgar chants and cheers—at last night's district playoff basketball game. Apparently the entire "Bull Pen," our self-appointed student fan-gang, was escorted out of the gym, and, he reports (the old story): "Non-guilty students suffered consequences for the actions of a few."

This news makes me realize: *There was a district playoff game last night? On the same day school was canceled because of the Eagles Super Bowl parade?* I've heard that many of our students took a train into the city to join the celebration. Apparently, the diehards made it back to the burbs in time for the basketball game.

Freddy has not mentioned whether the basketball team won the game, but I assume so when he announces that he expects better behavior from the Bull Pen "next time."

I'm puzzled by his explicit reference to the "Bull Pen," this perennially replenished group of students, who must feel both elevated by the principal's recognition of them and also diminished by his comfortable usage of this nickname that once held the air of top-secrecy, or at least of badassery.

Dean texts me in my classroom: "What happened at the basketball game?"

He must know I have no idea. Like him, I was home yesterday, watching the parade on TV, happy enough to have a day off but fearing we'd end up paying for it with a tacked-on day at the end of the year.

I spent most of my day with one eye on the TV and the other on my laptop, as I drafted queries to new agents and fielded rejections from others, one in particular whose "no" came like a blow to the kidneys, an agent who a year ago had raised my hopes with shrewd feedback and the invitation to revise and resubmit. Today I'd made it my goal to lose myself, and to rekindle my dashed hopes, in a blur of countless fresh proposals emailed into the ether.

The parade was slow to get going, flatbed trucks and trailers filled with players and personnel putt-putting along Broad Street from South Philly toward City Hall, soaking in the cheers of adoring fans lining the sidewalks. Some of the players took to the streets on foot, high-fiving fans at the curb, most conspicuously the team's mammoth, bearded All-Pro center, Jason Kelce, strutting in full Mummer's regalia, glistening in green sequins. Once the parade reached the Ben Franklin Parkway, the sun was shining bright and the crowd was in all-out worship mode. Newscasters elevated on scaffolding swooned at their own good fortune to be witness to, with bird's-eye view, such a long-awaited moment.

On the hallowed Art Museum steps, immortalized by that iconic loser, Rocky Balboa, whose bronze statue rests, arms tirelessly raised, in the grass below, one Eagle after another stepped up to the microphone and gave a brief, levelheaded, at times inspiring speech, most notably Nick Foles, backup quarterback, Super Bowl MVP, and recently anointed saint of the city, who spoke of persistence and overcoming failure in order to reach one's potential greatness—a message I took stock in, happy to see Philadelphia, at long last, shed its inferiority complex, just as Rocky did in the sequels, first becoming heavyweight champion and ultimately defeating the Russian superhuman and saving us all from self-destruction.

But my enthusiasm was crushed when Kelce took the mic and, after some harmless bluster, led the sea of fans in a cheer that, he said, he'd proudly crafted for this occasion: "Nobody likes us and we don't care! We're Philly, fucking Philly, fucking Philly, *fuck you!*"

So much for repairing the city's ageless chip on the shoulder. I thought of my students in that sea of worshippers, so close had they all been to becoming a new generation of well-adjusted Philadelphians, a people as expectant of success as New Yorkers and Los Angelenos. But no. We're too afraid we might lose that underdog hunger. And then what? Who would we be? So instead of *hurrah,* we were back to *fuck you,* the crowd's anger revived. Rocky (of the first movie) would live in our hearts for eternity as if those sequels never happened. He is our hero who goes blind in battle, who was only in it to prove he was tough enough to go the distance. His indifference to loss (Apollo Creed says, "Ain't gonna be no rematch"; Rocky says, "Don't want one.") is transcendent victory, and our mythology. This is the bronzed Rocky we idolize. Not the juiced-up version who's a lock to take down the next monster twice his size, the Herculean version who goes on to defeat greater and greater foes and who, ironically, in this absurdly unrealistic evolution, further immortalizes that earliest version of himself, becoming, at least to Philadelphians, as real as Joe Frazier.

As the fans on the Parkway were catching their breath after Kelce dropped the mic, all the newscasters were yucking it up, hah-hah, saying how, "Salty language notwithstanding, he really nailed it," "Everyone here is an underdog," "No one respected us or expected us to win," "That's who we really are."

I thought, *Okay, but forever? Don't we ever get to move on from all that?*

"Philadelphians will never forget this epic performance," the commentators said.

I'm afraid this is true.

In his announcement to the student body, Freddy Whetts states, "Inappropriate behavior and offensive language will not be tolerated."

I reply to Dean's text: "A million Eagles fans cheering fuck you on the Parkway yesterday and kids are supposed to understand what's appropriate?"

"Good point," he replies, though given his brevity I suspect I've rained on his parade.

At lunch, after several of us bemoan yesterday's school cancellation, dreading that we'll have to make up the day at the end of the year, Sam regales us with the wonders of the downtown festivities, starting with breakfast at his wife's office overlooking Broad Street and culminating in that "epic performance" by Jason Kelce. "Oh, man, we were all going nuts! He nailed it! That's who we are!"

Phucking Philly.

SIXERS GAME

Christopher tells his buddy Parker how huge Joel Embiid is in real life. They're in his bedroom, tossing a ball into the hoop hooked onto the door.

Last night my brother-in-law gave me two floor-level tickets to the Sixers game. Christopher and I were in the third row. We were mesmerized by the size and speed of the players just out of arm's reach, by the loud sounds of the huffing and squeaking.

Christopher tells Parker about the dancers who performed at half-time. And then the highlight of the night: "After the game, my dad and I saw this one lady in *a fishnet bodysuit"* (the term I offered when, at the time, he asked, *What is she wearing?).* He clarifies for Parker's sake: "You could see right through to her boobs and butt."

I imagine Parker's skeptical eyebrows rising, Christopher's head nodding.

Christopher's voice drops. "Sometimes when I think of stuff that's inappropriate (the term he attaches to all things of the flesh), my penis gets straight. Does that happen to you?"

Inaudible whispers.

Is this normal conversation at age seven?

I wonder if Parker is wondering what the hell his friend is talking about—my son, whose question Parker will perhaps repeat to his parents tonight at the dinner table. *Does that happen to you?*

I've been standing in the hallway with a pile of folded laundry in my arms.

"Oh, it's my dad."

The door opens. I smile.

"Daddy, I just told Parker about the inappropriate lady we saw last night. In the fishnet bodysuit, remember?"

I nod. "Did you tell him about the game?"

KIM JONG UN

At lunch Dean recognizes my leftovers from the new Greek joint we like in downtown Benfield.

"Chicken souvlaki," I say.

Last night at the dinner table Christopher asked if our house-cleaner, Karolina, is from there.

"From where?" I asked.

"Chicken Souvlakia." He grinned.

Clever kid. Czechoslovakia.

"That's right," I said. "Chicken Souvlakia."

Dean shares his printed copy of Kim Jong Un's full statement in reply to Trump's UN speech. Kim promises to retaliate with full force, having been left no choice. He calls Trump a "dotard," a term new to all of us.

I do my English teacher duty and quote from the Webster's Dictionary app on my iPhone: "DOH-terd." As in dotage, old age. Now I get it. Kim called Trump an old fart who's losing his mind.

"Doh-TURD," Tracy says.

"I've learned something from Kim Jong Un," I say, "a new word, of all things, which is more than I can say about Trump."

"It doesn't take away from the fact that he's fucking nuts," Carolyn says. I'm not sure which nut she's referring to, until she adds, "And starved a million of his own people."

"Trump's got *that* on him," I say. "For now."

After dinner tonight, Christopher and I, along with my brother, John, watch the Phils on TV. We ate grilled steaks, and now we're eating ice cream in the family room. Christopher spots an Asian face on the opponent's team and says, "We don't like him, the North Korean." Uncle John glances at me with skewed eyes.

"Christopher," I say, "just because we don't like the *leader* of North Korea doesn't mean we don't like North Koreans." *This is how it starts,* I think. Stereotypes, racism. "In fact," I add, "we sympathize with those people, because their leader mistreats them and keeps them isolated from the rest of the world. They don't even know how bad they have it. They're deprived of information, to keep Kim powerful. You understand?"

Christopher doesn't hesitate. "We don't want people not to like us just because Trump is our president."

John and I swap impressed glances.

"You got it," I say, as if we aren't responsible for Trump—as opposed to the North Koreans, who didn't vote their asshole into office.

Christopher spoons his ice cream, eyes on the baseball.

ANGRY GIRLS

Sealing up his Tupperware, Dean tells the story of a girl who was offended by his comments in class. He says he simply mentioned to the kids that "the NFL protests dominated the headlines this weekend, so you probably didn't hear about the health bill or even about the devastation from Hurricane Maria in Puerto Rico."

After class Alicia, a Chilean girl, lectured him about the significance of the American flag and how for eight years she stood "for Obama's flag." Dean says the girl has never before said one word in class.

Randi Gordon jumps in, "Oh, you'll be hearing more from *her.*" She goes on to explain that, apparently, the girl believes she's victimized by everyone. Last year she accused girls of bullying her. Not only in school, but also on Twitter and Facebook. She accused them of leaving cruel notes in her locker and spray-painting her house with threats of rape. Her parents installed home cameras in hopes of catching the vandals. Turns out the administration got video of her in the school hallway putting a note in her own locker. When the cops accused her, saying they had video proof, she confessed to all of it. Even to the fake Twitter account and Facebook page, with the sole purpose of posting horrible things about her(self).

"Wait..." Only then does it occur to me: "*Whose* locker?"

"Her own, of course."

"Of course. But why would you actually go through the act of putting the note through the slots of your own locked locker? If you wrote the note, why not just take it to the office and *lie,* and say, 'I just found this note in my locker'?"

"She draws the line at lying to your face," Dean jokes.

"No, she doesn't," Neil says.

I laugh. "Seems like half the thrill for this girl is playing the abuser, not just the victim."

"It gets worse," Neil says. After ten days of suspension and fines, she returns to school and complains that she was being bullied again. Or, to be clear, she was being *ignored*—by the same girls, "her friends," she said, whom she'd accused of bullying her. Neil had to explain to her, "They aren't your friends anymore. You destroyed those relationships. Now the girl's parents are angry with the school for punishing her." Neil's face turns red. His smile stretches wide whenever he's flabbergasted by the details of his own stories of kids and their parents.

"What's the *real* story here?" I ask.

Neil grins. "There's always a story behind a story like this one, right?" Turns out Mom divorced a rich guy in Chile, then moved here for another rich American guy. Alicia has a German last name and father. A descendant of Nazis who moved to Chile after the war.

I ask if the parents realize that their daughter's behavior is all about *them,* clearly (in my expert psychoanalytic opinion); it's about the attention the girl gets or doesn't get from them.

Neil chuckles. More recently, he says, she claimed to be coughing up blood and refused to see American doctors. Only Chilean doctors, she insisted. So, the parents flew back to Chile with her. The doctors found nothing, of course, because the whole story was a lie.

"She accused me of invading her privacy," Neil says, of telling teachers about the bullying she endured, or *didn't* endure, as it were.

He reminded her of the detailed emails she'd sent all her teachers informing them of the terrible time she was having, in case they noticed her distressed affect. "Personality disorder." Neil shakes his head. "A genuine criminal mind. Narcissistic. Everything comes back to *her*. She actually manufactures situations to come back to her. At anyone's expense."

"Watch out, Dean," I say. "No taking a knee during the Pledge of Allegiance."

Dean laughs.

"She's a four-year work in progress," Neil says.

After a moment, I ask Neil how my old student Summer Lane is doing. Last year, as a ninth grader, after she returned from "the hospital" that winter, Summer Lane wrote a story about her depression and her time in rehab. She described how, months earlier, we'd been right in the middle of reading *Romeo and Juliet* when she excused herself from class to use the bathroom, where she swallowed a bottle of aspirin.

Something in her written version has never quite added up for me: What about her book bag? Surely, she hadn't taken it with her on a routine trip to the bathroom. I would have noticed that. On the other hand, I would have remembered a book bag left behind on the floor or someone returning for it after class. It goes without saying that she hadn't come and gone empty-handed—apart from that bottle of pills.

Today Neil fills me in on details he's since gathered. Turns out there were a lot of girls in the bathroom at the time of Summer's arrival, so it must have been at the *start* of lunch, *after* English class. Not exactly looking for privacy. The girls in the bathroom asked her what was wrong. The ambulance came. She didn't return for a month.

"So, she didn't actually leave during our reading of *Romeo and Juliet*."

Neil shakes his head. "No."

I feel relieved, somehow off the hook—along with Shakespeare.

"It's not just the suicide attempt," he says. "It's the forbidden love, too. Forbidden to see her girlfriend."

"Oh no. I had no idea."

"Neither did her parents. Her father is relentless. Even after the suicide attempt. *Total Benfield,*" Neil says—as in, total Benfield County, meaning total white, working-class, religious, right-wing... "And we're talking *Nether* Benfield. South of the tracks. You know what I'm saying?"

I shake my head, not in shared exasperation, but in genuine ignorance. In moments like this, when I hear such descriptions of the district where I've been teaching for more than twenty years, I'm grateful for my conveniently detached relationship with this community, from which I've always lived a thirty-minute drive away. For better or worse, I don't know one family or neighborhood from the next. In my classroom, each kid starts fresh.

"Does her father think it's a phase?" I ask. "Some kind of rebellion?"

"She hates him beyond words."

I say, "It's no wonder so many gay kids kill themselves. It's not just the bullying in school by other kids. It's also the parents who make them feel worthless."

Neil nods.

"Speaking of bullies, how about the balls on that bull!" Tracy cracks, a Hail Mary to lighten the mood. She's referring to the new bronze statue erected this week just outside the school entrance, a gift from last year's graduating class. "All the kids are talking about it," Tracy says.

Dean explains, "Kids with their parents last night were on their way into the Academic Excellence Dinner..." He laughs. "I was right behind this one kid saying, 'Dad, you have to look!' And then the dad—" Dean can hardly contain himself. "The dad looked and goes, 'Oh Jesus!'"

Tracy says, "Did you see the box sitting there next to it? The students are having a contest to name it."

"Why?" I ask. "Does it need a name? Like Billy the Bull?"

"How many puns on balls can you come up with?" Neil asks.

Tracy says, "I think they're high."

"The kids?" Neil asks.

"No, the balls! I mean, they're, like, right below the asshole."

"Like hemorrhoids," I say.

"Yes!" Tracy says. "They look like hemorrhoids!"

"How about *that* for the name?" I say. "Hemorrhoids the Bull. Picture the T-shirts."

Dean says, "We could sell those rubber nuts people hang from trailer hitches. In the school store. Make a fortune. Start a scholarship."

The bell rings. Time for class.

CAR WASH

After picking the boys up from school, I stop for gas and then pull around back for a car wash. As we're approaching the entrance to the cinder-block tunnel, Michael tells Christopher to smell his finger. I watch in the rearview mirror as Christopher whiffs without hesitation and then screams, "Poop!"

I bark, "Hey!"

Michael cackles, that deep belly laugh that's hard not to love.

"Michael! Stop it! That's disgusting!"

"Ass-gusting!" he repeats, and they're both roaring in their strap-in booster seats back there.

Michael's hand inches towards Christopher's face, and Christopher, laughing and nearly retching, fights with the window button, which I've locked with the master button up front. I do him the favor of lowering his window, toward which he pretends to hurl himself, despite the safety belt.

"Hey!" I repeat.

Michael's laugh peaks and his hand disappears behind him.

I holler, "Michael! Knock it off!"

He thrusts his finger at his brother.

Their joy knows no limit.

I'll show them.

"Do you guys want to get out and walk home?"

I'm surprised, actually, when this threat doesn't do the job.

We're approaching the kiosk to pay.

Michael's hand disappears again.

I whip around. "Are you seriously sticking your finger—? Michael!"

You've never heard laughter like this.

I've lost track of my mission. It has become some kind of primal battle I don't understand. I open my door and lift a foot out. We're staring at the shadowy maw of sudsy machinery. "I'm clearing out, you vermin! You're on your own!" and in a flash they're screaming bloody murder, and just for a moment I can't tell if these are real screams of terror, not pretend terror, and I try quickly and desperately to correct my mistake. "It's okay, I'm kidding!" My two boys are strapped inside a machine, convinced they are about to enter an even bigger machine, alone, into oblivion. "It was a joke! *Vermin?* When have I ever called you *vermin?* Are you listening?"

"Don't leave! Don't leave!" It's not just Michael. It's both of them. Jesus. Their fear is as deep and spontaneous as the pleasure they were experiencing moments ago, the pleasure that I have vanquished like a real-live monster. Michael cries, "I promise I won't stick my finger in my butt!"

This is rock-bottom, I think. For all three of us, really. Just a poor performance all around.

"It's okay," I assure them, as we're enveloped by soap and water.

When we get home, we play Wiffle ball in the front yard, when Christopher spots the Amazon Prime delivery truck and announces, with pure delight, "My cup! Is that my cup?! My cup is here!" Michael is mesmerized, mystified. For a moment I have no idea what Christopher is talking about either, but, sure enough, it's his cup, and now I remember ordering it, after his last game when he decided that he wanted to play catcher after all and learned that he needed a parent's permission and the proper protective equipment. He slips into the house and in seconds rushes back out, displaying his black leather baseball glove and flipping me a hardball. "I have my cup on!"

Michael howls with pleasure when Christopher punches his groin to prove it. "Pitch to me!"

Vana comes outside onto the porch, no doubt drawn by all the excitement. "What's going on out here?" she asks.

You have no idea, I think.

Somebody Please Help Edwin

"What's the latest with Ryan?" I ask Neil Gillespie in the hallway. "I never see him."

"You might not see him for a while."

"Don't even tell me..."

He nods.

I shake my head. "Not schizophrenia." I may owe an apology to my colleague Holly Knight, who had predicted such a diagnosis.

"No, not schizophrenia. His parents want him to go to an institution. Gone for a month last year. This year it might be eight weeks or more. But Ryan's resisting. He wants to stay here."

"What's the matter with him?" I have no idea.

"Psychosis *and* OCD."

"What?"

"Flip a coin. If you treat the psychosis, you get intensified OCD. If you treat the OCD, you get the psychosis. They've been treating the OCD for years. It's the psychosis that's new." Neil explains that the treated psychosis has intensified the OCD, resulting in eating disorders, anxiety, rigid behavior, and attitude. On the other hand, when being treated for the OCD, he's manic, erratic, obsessive. "Adolescence certainly isn't helping matters, nor is his father, who asks, 'How's he going to go to college, get a job, live on his own?'"

All I can think to say is, "You have to read the story he wrote." I tell him about it, with a sense of regret mixed with shame, not that I failed to see that the story's pain was Ryan's, but that I believed that as long as Ryan had the ability to render his pain so artfully on the page, then he couldn't be defeated by it. Indeed, I believed his writing was evidence that he was defeating it. I tell Neil how this latest fictional work reminds me of Ryan's writing freshman year, but only in the most positive ways. All that sweetness he feared he'd lost to age was now mixed with sorrow, laced with a wit that must have been his secret weapon. Those serpentine sentences. Those flashes of brilliance. Extragalactic confusion shot through with a newfound lucidity, qualities I imagined in a young David Foster Wallace, who would go on to write masterpieces that one day a young Ryan Henry would read, before hanging himself at age forty-six; I thought Ryan's brain might be going through some kind of adolescent explosion that would expand and settle into creative genius, and he would thrive—any darker fate be damned.

Neil says he'll keep me updated, and splits. I stand there alone in the hallway, thinking of Ryan's mother, who called me several times his freshman year. She said she'd managed, despite Ryan's protestations, to get her hands on some of his writings. She asked if I thought he was actually good. She said she couldn't tell. I admitted that I couldn't tell for sure, either. That the writing could seem a bit complicated. She was worried about him. I said I was too. She didn't want to say what I believed we were both thinking, that he might be some kind of genius and, no thanks to this gift, that he might also be prematurely losing his mind. I said I was genuinely interested to see how he would develop in the next four years, how he might pull together all this intellectual energy and channel it, express it in, say, a more coherent way.

Then, all of a sudden, he was a junior, and he'd done it. He was a writer. I believed it. Something had clicked in his brain.

Debutante Ball

At lunch Dean tells us about his daughter going to a debutante ball along with her friends from the Main Line private school where her classmates come from families that live in houses that look like Oprah's or Pablo Escobar's. Dean describes the photographs of boys in white ties and girls in floor-length gowns and gloves, another cost he didn't count on when he pulled his daughter from public school after tenth grade for mixing with the wrong crowd. The party was actually a debut for boys, Dean clarifies, so the girls were their escorts. Dean hopes his daughter won't grow disappointed with the life he can provide for her in their small row home, not to mention the tuition he can hardly afford on his salary; he also hopes she won't turn despondent when she doesn't win an athletic scholarship to Harvard or Yale for field hockey.

Dean switches the subject to one of his morning classes, during which he was showing a documentary on a tribe that practices cannibalism and that, having certain standards, labels corpses and body parts to be sure they don't eat their own. Suddenly there was a shriek in the hallway, and his students, after a moment, laughed in relief, having feared the worst for the girl, who went on screaming. Now the class was mortified all over again when Dean investigated the hallway scene and discovered Randi Gordon, the veteran Special-Ed teacher, struggling to calm the girl, who began fiercely swinging her arms.

"I have a question," Dean says, directing his attention to Neil Gillespie and the guidance counselors. "I don't mean to be insensitive," he says, then gently adds, "but why is this kid here? In this school?"

"Her right to a free education," Carolyn says.

"This teacher was at risk," Dean says. "I wasn't about to get involved, considering the legal implications if someone got hurt, myself included. I mean, they literally created a padded room this year for these kids. When did we become the school for the severely disabled?"

Neil says, "*This year*—when the district decided they didn't want to spend the money anymore to send them to the proper institution."

"It's not right," Dean says. "Special-Ed teachers didn't sign up for this. And, frankly, I didn't either. It's like a psych ward sometimes."

"We don't have a choice," Carolyn says. "By law, we have to serve these students."

Dean shakes his head. "It's not right for the kid, either. I mean, are that girl's needs really being met?"

MOVIE PROJECT

Another state-mandated test day. This time it's the Keystone Exams, and I'm proctoring. I've never been one to complain about mandatory testing, not because I'm an advocate for it, but because it means a block of three hours for me to read and grade student work. But this year it seems that testing has taken over, or at least taken over the month of May. For six days, the eleventh graders must arrive at the usual time, 7:30, while the rest of the student body gets a three-hour delay. That means homeroom at 10:30. First period is now fourth period. After homeroom the ninth graders go straight to lunch.

The Keystones come after a day of PSATs and in the midst of two solid weeks of AP testing—in subjects ranging from English and Chemistry to Music Composition and Chinese—a schedule that, for the high achievers, means missing several whole days of classes, and that, for teachers, means class attendance is scant. Not to mention that this afternoon I'm assigned to proctor the AP Physics exam, while a substitute teacher (whom they won't let proctor state tests) covers my English classes. Go figure. It's mid-May, and "regular" school seems to have ended six weeks early. Some students have missed my class ten times because of all this testing. When they return, they say, "I had AP tests. What'd I miss?"

For two decades, during the last month of the class, my AP students have (while doing countless other things) written and produced screenplays, in groups, drafting and revising their scripts and then filming, acting in, and editing their own movies, which we then watch together in the classroom during the last week of the semester. The movie project coincides with and complements our other more traditional "literary" work, reading J.D. Salinger and writing an essay on a book that's been adapted to film, aka the "movie-book paper." In past years they would all be "shooting" their movies by now, meeting deadlines throughout the four-week production schedule.

This year, the few who are in attendance during this extensive testing period groan when I ask how their movies are coming along. "We haven't been able to meet as a group..." There's one kid who's been sitting alone most days, apologizing to me for not having an idea yet. "I'm brainstorming," she tells me. Deadlines have become obsolete. Princeton-bound Paul shows up, says, "Hi. I've been out for two weeks. Can I get a copy of *Franny and Zooey*?" I've hardly noticed his absence in a room with so many empty desks.

I don't want to disappoint any future Stephen Spielberg by cancelling the movie project, but I don't want to spend Memorial Day Weekend fielding emails from the few remaining concerned students whose movie-group partners all bailed and went to the beach, nor do I want to spend two days of class time in the last week of school watching dreadful, unedited video footage of what you wouldn't exactly call "movies," based on what you wouldn't exactly call "screenplays."

In private, I ask Logan, the inevitable choice for English Department Award Winner, "What do you think about cancelling the movie project?"

She gives an Oscar-worthy performance, pretending to contemplate my question for a long and serious moment, before replying, "Um, I think that would be a good idea." She shows me a stiff upper lip, to indicate, nearly convincingly, that she shares my regret.

That settles it. "Okay." Still, I must know: "What's the status of your screenplay? I'd hate for all that work to have been in vain."

"Um." She faux-winces. "We sort of have an outline, sort of?"

I nod. "And how's your movie-book paper coming along?"

"Yeah." She smiles, understanding now that my expectations, even of her, have hit rock-bottom. "Um, I've *started?*"

"It's okay," I say.

I don't want to know the answers to these questions from the rest of the class. When I announce my decision to cancel the movie project, despite whatever work they may have already invested in the screenplay and with the understanding that some of them might have been looking forward to this assignment, whose reputation precedes it—The Zervanos Movie Project, a tradition immortalized and chronicled in a cabinet in the back of the room by stacks of VHS tapes and DVDs (and, in recent years, downloaded videos from thumb drives and saved links to YouTube)—the collective reaction is neither disappointment nor jubilance. They are fried. Numb. They might have reacted with the same seeming indifference had I assigned an *additional* project.

I appreciate the few sighs I hear, expressions I interpret as sympathy, offered for the loss I'm apparently suffering all by myself. One student suggests that, while we're at it, we should go ahead and cancel the movie-book paper as well. I shake my head. "You're pushing it." He grins and shrugs.

I'm tempted to grant the wish, but I think they understand that I must keep up the act that I know what's good for them. *Eat your spinach.*

MICHAEL READING

At bedtime, after potty and bath and snack and brushing teeth, I read the Phillies book with Michael. He's got this one down pat. I point, and he recites by rote, "Chuck Klein, Robin Roberts, Mike Schmidt... Jim Bunning threw a perfect game in 1964... Cole Hamels, 2008 World Series Champions..."

He gets frustrated and says, "I want to read."

I'm not sure what he means. I say, "We *are* reading."

He clarifies, "Why *I* can't read?"

I take this as a good sign, evidence he's ripe for the teaching. I don't remember such a moment with Christopher, a moment when he recognized he wasn't reading, but wanted to be. I remember only those moments early on when he *was* reading.

"You can read," I try, but Michael is not easy to patronize.

He won't read the next page. So, I start. "Cleats, batting gloves..."

"Nooo! I do it." I turn to the trophy page. He puts his finger to the words. "Gold Glove, MVP..." He pauses. "What's that spell?" He points emphatically at the letters. *"Read,"* he implores.

"World Series."

"How you *read* that? I want to."

"Okay," I say. "That's great. Let's—" I grab the alphabet book from the shelf and jump back into bed.

"Here." I open to the first page. "A is for..."

"Awesome."

I trace my finger under the letters as he pronounces them. *Awesome.*

"B is for..."

"Bounce."

I bounce from letter to letter. Still, he knows my finger doesn't make this reading. He could be recalling these words with his eyes closed.

"C is for..."

"Catch."

I say, "Hold on. Look." *DOG.* "Each letter makes a sound. What sound does D make?"

"Duh."

"Good! O?"

"Oh."

"Well, yes— But here it's 'awww.' Dawww... How about G? What sound does G—?"

"Juh."

"Sometimes." Reading is hard. "Here it's guh."

"Guh."

"Yes. So now, all together."

As thrilled as I am to see Michael reading, or sounding out letters, I can't help blaming myself for what seems to be his slow development, at least compared to that of his brother, who was singing the alphabet at one-and-a-half, sounding out words on a page soon after that, and reciting *Goodnight Moon* and *Where the Wild Things Are* by age two—thanks, no doubt, to undiluted attention from his parents, who joined him watching *Sesame Street,* whereas now his parents retreat from the living room to avoid whatever trash Christopher is exposing to his little brother.

Michael knows *SpongeBob SquarePants, Barbie's Dreamhouse,* and *Henry Danger.* He's not familiar with the basic pedagogical techniques that Daddy is now borrowing from *Sesame Street.* "Duh. Aw. Guh. Dog."

Michael cackles, not only at the silliness of the sounds but also at the joyful recognition of the concept clicking.

We work through every broken-down syllable of "underground" and "vicious" and "yoga" and, picking up the pace, "zuh, ih, puh...*zip.*"

Long after lullabies and lights out, I find him sitting up in bed with the lamp on and the Phillies book in his lap.

"What are you doing?" I ask him. "It's past ten o'clock, time for sleep."

"I'm reading," he beams. "Mm. Ike... *Mike* Schmidt!"

"Ahh, you got it."

He tosses the book to the floor and lies down again, fidgeting with pleasure, ready for me to turn the lights off for good.

Returning Stories

Today in AP Modern Lit, I'm handing back my students' graded short stories. Thanks to mandated state exams for underclassmen, and the benefits of being an assistant proctor, I've had the pleasure of sitting in a quiet corner for six consecutive uninterrupted three-hour mornings immersed in their work, while they've doubtless been enjoying these delayed school-day openings for seniors. They appear well-rested, energized, anticipating what I've got in store—or is it just spring fever?—as I stand at the front of the room with a pile of paper in my hands.

"I've got your stories," I announce.

They seem surprised. So soon? They're excited. This is a big deal, for them and me. We've been at this for a month. The assignment is worth 200 points, as big as it gets. I gesture to the poster I made on a whim earlier this year and hung overhead on the front wall, which until then I'd always kept blank, like a page: At the center of a black circle, like a bullseye, or like the first mark of a pen on paper, are the words "YOUR STORY STARTS HERE." I remind them that they spent weeks writing this story, first outlining, then hitting incremental deadlines, first a page, then two pages, four pages, six, until they had a full draft, some complete at the minimum-required six, some reaching sixteen or more. Not that longer is better, I emphasize. What matters here is the quality of the story. The goal, as the printed assignment not-so-facetiously stated, was to write "the best thing you've ever dreamed of writing." That line got chuckles at the time, but "there's no doubt in my mind," I say now, "that many of you met that challenge." I tell them how wonderful it was to see them working so diligently along the way, many coming to meet with me during lunch or after school, swapping pages with each other in class, receiving and giving feedback, all while reading a dozen or so contemporary short stories that I assigned and we discussed in the context of their own works in progress, with a focus on the author's craft, talking about point of view, narrative voice, story structure, sentimentality, how to avoid it, when to risk it—

"Is that *all* of them?" Sydney, sitting front-center, interrupts. Her blue eyes brighten, magnified behind thick lenses.

I smile. "Yes, of course it's all of them."

There's handwringing, giant sighs, and even mock salivation. They want me to stop talking already and just hand back the stories. But first I must tell them that I spend anywhere from a half-hour to an hour, and sometimes more, with each story; that I try, in my feedback, "which you'll find in the margins along the way and in one usually full-page summation at the end," to articulate what I think is working well and what I think could help make the story work better; that I have no choice but to read and think and respond this way, with an eye toward revision, or else the whole enterprise seems pointless, because "I want you to learn from this ongoing exchange, even if it turns out you have no intention of revising, which I have never discussed openly with you, until now, because I wanted you to think of your final submission as in fact final, so it would be as good as you could possibly make it, but it's not final until you decide it's final, and even then you might find yourself returning to it, still itching to make changes, and if that happens, even if it's next week or next month or next year, I'll be happy to see a revision—"

"*Okayy...*" Sydney is clenching the corners of her desk with white-knuckled fists. Her glasses slip down her nose. "Sorry." A finger presses the red frames back against her face. She grins nervously. "I just want to see..."

"You did great," I tell her.

"Really?"

I look up at the class. They are a vision of polite patience, eighteen pairs of elbows on desks, chins and eyes up. "Everyone, please take the time now to read my comments, and then I'll come around and we can chat. This is the plan for the whole period."

Sydney's is on top. I hand it to her ceremoniously and repeat that it was terrific. It really was. *Is.* She beams. She's a blusher. I understand why this assignment was so precious to her. She has more than hinted to me that the story's subject is, regrettably, inspired by her life. "I want to make this good," she confided to me numerous times, suggesting there was something profoundly, inexplicably personal at stake in the actual writing of the story, lingering with me to chat for a minute after class, never letting me read what she'd written so far but wanting to discuss sophisticated matters of narrative distance and handling of time. I understood, as I believe *she* understood, that she was working through something significant, toward something that might provide unique satisfaction, perhaps even a kind of sickening pleasure that can come from writing fiction, or so I may have led her to believe. And yet, as fulfilling as that personal experience may have been for Sydney, getting my response today is apparently a momentous occasion, and I feel suddenly as anxious as she appears to be, cautiously optimistic that my praise will please her and that my advice for revision will excite her, not demoralize her or seem to indicate that I missed the point of her story or, worse, her pain.

I stand in the corner, effectively invisible, watching them all page through their stories, some squinting to read my sharp-penciled notes on the opening pages, some cutting to the chase and reading the duller-penciled synopsis on the back page, where the grade is usually squeezed into a corner where I've finally come to a close. I keep an eye out for confused expressions or satisfied sighs, signals that I'm needed for clarification or welcome for follow-up. As their noses inch closer to the words I've written, there's the thrilling sense of shared energy, all of it spent yet somehow rekindled now, all those inked expressions and now my penciled ones, communing.

This was an unusually good batch of stories, many of them moving and, I suspect, autobiographical, so I'm not expecting anyone to be disappointed by a grade or a criticism, but I am especially eager to see how my feedback will be received by the three girls who wrote the best stories, each of them, curiously, about a teenage daughter in a strained relationship with her father. In the front row, Sydney's strawberry ponytail lies stock-still on her back as she burrows into her story, and I anticipate my cue that she's ready to talk to me about it.

But first, Rebecca Anderson sits up straight at her desk. I wait for the deep breath she takes to expire completely before I approach. As I squat next to her, she's smiling and nodding, as I am, both of us now sharing in the secret knowledge that her story was, is, as I've written, extraordinary, utterly original, one of the best I've ever read in my twenty years here. "Really," I tell her. She says, "I worked so hard on this." How brilliant, I say, these thirteen pages made up nearly exclusively of dialogue, a scene of a father and a daughter in a car, on the familiar drive from his house to hers, where she lives with her mother. "You captured something so incredibly specific, so precisely, and yet it's so universal that I'm sure girls your age, and probably boys, too, would relate to this, recognize themselves and their parents." "Thanks," Rebecca says.

In my note I suggested only that she tweak the ending, those closing lines, to sharpen the arc of the story, of the character, to distinguish *this* drive home from all the others, to capture how *this* experience has altered her uniquely. Rebecca looks at me from under lowered eyebrows, her smile turning to a mischievous grin, one that suggests

I know better (or I *should* know better), and says, "My father is incapable of change."

I return her grin. I can't resist: "But how about *you?*"

Her grin stretches wider. *Touché,* Mr. Zervanos. "I'll think about it."

I get it: this story is a veritable transcript. Anything more would be more than the truth and therefore not the truth. "Maybe you're right," I try. "Maybe they've said enough, these two." I try to read her face, and I tell myself she's open to what I dare to say next. "But maybe let the girl sit there a moment longer at the end, just looking at him. You don't have to change anything—I mean with actual dialogue or action—but maybe use her imagination. Let her fantasize about how this scene might go differently, if only he could be that version of a father she really needs him to be, and *then* when she says 'Bye' and gets out of the car, it won't be just bitterness that we're left with, that *she's* left with, as if she's protecting herself from the pain he's caused her, but something bitter*sweet.* She'll seem different, stronger, I think, because she faced that real wish she has, and the disappointment that comes with it, of her own unmet needs, and maybe she can finally let it all go. Or maybe she realizes it's impossible to let go. But at least she's being honest with herself."

Rebecca's expression has turned unreadable, or impassive, which is readable enough. It is certainly absent delight. *I've finally gone too far,* I think. We've entered sacred territory, that white space that follows the story's final punctuation, an area that perhaps the writer meant to have chained off, to keep to herself, a secret not yet ready for public consumption or teacher consumption or even ink on the page, a secret she perhaps hadn't realized yet herself, but that's what a good story does, whether she approves of this reality or not: It points to the truth, over which even the author has no control and to which she cannot deprive the careful reader access. Rebecca has already, in a way, achieved the ending that I have just described to her, and I have elected to spell it out to her for reasons I don't fully understand myself, but reasons I want to believe are rooted in my most virtuous instincts. And yet, how relieved I am when I see the first hint of that sly smile of hers.

We sigh and nod. I ask her if she'll read her story aloud to the class, not today but next week sometime.

"I'm flattered, but no way." She's smiling full bore.

It's not uncommon that the writers of the best stories are the students whose voices have gone practically unheard throughout the semester, as is the case here with Rebecca Anderson. Sometimes they seize this invitation with a kind of vengeful thrill that frees them from their bashful prison, like Sylvia Plath's phoenix rising from the ashes, even as they feign reluctance ("Do I *have* to?"), walking to the lectern, shooting one last sheepish glance at me, their willing scapegoat, before owning the floor for the next twenty minutes.

I say, "If this were first semester, I'd be begging you to submit it to *Pegasus*"—the literary magazine, whose deadline has long passed. Her smile suggests I wouldn't have needed to beg her for that. So it's just the reading aloud in front of the class that has her hesitating. I suppose that's not so surprising. "Think about it," I say.

I check the clock. Only ten minutes left till the bell. So much for making my rounds. I'll try to get to the rest of the students tomorrow or at least by the end of the week.

When I stand up—blood rushing to the head, back aching—there's Hailey, ready to talk, and I'm happy just to listen. "I'm definitely going to revise," she says. She agrees that the second half of the story kind of got away from her and she'll consider my advice to let the boy's family be a little more attentive than she has represented them so that after the boy is outed as gay by his sister at the dinner table and then locks himself in his bedroom for three days, maybe they can at least knock on the door and say a few words to him. Even bullish dad might at least give the door a kick and tell the kid to get his ass to work or something, before the boy writes his epic apologia and hangs himself. She asks, "Was his suicide too predictable, you think?"

"Let's see what happens when you revise."

"Cool."

I know I'm rushing now, but I really want to talk to Chloe Wilson, whose story was perhaps second-best to Rebecca Anderson's. But I'm hesitant to put Chloe on the spot. She's a star athlete, who leaves it all on the field, or, in her case, on the track—and, in the case of her short story, on the page. Her story was so evidently personal, and yet it was a paragon of learned craft techniques. A part of me thinks I should just leave it at that. Chloe is a no-nonsense, pragmatic high achiever, off to Dartmouth on a full scholarship, planning to become a doctor like both of her parents. She's never struck me as one who cares to dig too deep, or even to belabor a point. This quality in a student, or anyone, is often refreshing. My students know I respect their privacy, and I encourage them to exploit their freedom in this assignment, without fear that I'm going to assume anything about them personally or, I joke, that I'm going to rat them out to the counselors or school psychologists or, worse, to their parents. As blatantly autobiographical as Chloe's story appears to be—at least with the superficial details: overachieving track star, bound for Ivy League, buzzing around suburban hills in her fast car—I don't want to presume that the character's *interior* life reflects the author's. But given the story's grim ending, I don't want to risk presuming it doesn't.

Other kids are chatting and getting restless as the end of the period nears. Ordinarily Chloe would be one of those kids, packed up and ready, chatting with her friends, laughing about who knows what. But today she's sitting at her desk, still idly fingering the pages of her graded story. I decide to go over to my desk, at the side of the room, and after a moment call her over, in a tone suggesting that some random question just occurred to me. She's smiling as she approaches, pleasantly curious about what inconsequential thing I might have to say to her. I choose my words carefully. I want to keep things light while conveying how impressively I think she captured the stressful emotional life that her character keeps hidden from the world.

"I loved your story," I start. "That was clear, I hope, in my comments."

She nods. "Yeah. Thanks."

"So. I don't assume anything, but I also don't want to be insensitive to the *possibility* that certain elements of a student's story might be inspired by real life, and sometimes when I'm responding so objectively, in my notes, it doesn't escape my mind that maybe my criticism comes off as impersonal, or, I don't know, maybe worse, *too* personal."

She's cool as a cucumber, as I suspected she'd be. She says, "I loved the feedback and the idea for the ending. It was kind of a copout, I agree, having the girl drive off the road in the end."

"I can't blame you, considering the stories we read for class. Another death wish fulfilled, right?"

"Exactly."

"I think your instincts are right," I say, "to take the girl to the brink, so stressed from pressure from her father to succeed, in track and in the classroom, but then let her turn back toward home in the end. She doesn't have to kill herself to make this a powerful story. I'm not sure I even buy that she *would*..."

"I didn't want it to be a cheesy happy ending."

"It's not, it wouldn't be, a happy ending, and it's anything but cheesy, because, let's face it, it's no picnic going home, right?"

She smiles. There's the spark of recognition I love. The shared connection, between reader and writer, teacher and student—fiction and life. "No," she says.

"But this girl has proven herself, in the story, I mean, to be tough, resilient, open with her feelings in a healthy way—as she does in that great scene with the brother by the reservoir. That's my favorite scene."

She grins. "That scene never happened. I shared it with my older brother, and he liked it."

"Your *older* brother? How many brothers do you have?"

"Three."

"Ahh. There's only one in the story. That's good work, Wilson." I mirror her grin. "Effective compression. See, that's fiction, right?"

"I've never liked English," she says. "Not one assignment. Until this one. I loved writing it."

"I'm so glad," I say. My heart swells. The bell rings. "I loved reading it."

She turns to collect her things at her desk as her classmates begin to head out.

Amidst this minor commotion, Sydney steps before me, smiling pleasantly, hoodie zipped, backpack straps secured over the shoulders, but I can see she's in no hurry.

"Hi." I sit up straight, arms crossed on the desktop.

"Thank you for all your feedback." She glances at others leaving casually, entering the stream of students passing by in the hallway.

I lean forward to narrow the gap between us.

"I've never written about this before, but I've always wanted to," she says. Then she tacks on, "My father, I mean."

The cat is out of the bag.

I gently reply, "I'm sorry it's as close to personal as I feared it might be."

At once she turns red and chuckles. "There's the embarrassing truth! It's true!"

And just as I'm about to ask the crucial question, she assures me, "Except my brother didn't commit suicide. He's fine." She laughs. She goes on to tell me how he joined the army. How he was a skinny weakling and now he's a muscular soldier.

I say I remember her brother, fondly, from class. I say how all of this surprises me. "Your brother was quiet. Calm guy. Really *nice*."

She gives me another one of her ironic knowing grins, now clearly signaling to me not just that she knows, but that she knows *I* know—

only I *don't* know—that this seeming contradiction is perfectly sensible, that her brother would bulk up, toughen up, "not just to beat up our father," she says, but "to *defend* us."

I'm moved, even slightly ashamed by this added insight into her brother's motivation, which seems obvious enough to me now, but, honestly, I missed it. No matter how tuned in I might feel to the student's actual experience, and no matter how effectively she may have captured in her story what it was like to grow up with an abusive father, of course I can never understand her pain. But Sydney doesn't expect me to. She wouldn't *want* me to know such a thing. She has welcomed me into her most secret and sacred world, her deepest truth, a truth she enhanced by her own invention in an attempt to render, or even immortalize, in a way that might prove satisfying—not just to herself but also to the reader—her family's agony. She has expressed to me her genuine gratitude for helping her to find the way to articulate that agony. I feel the bond I believe she wants me to know she feels too, a real transfer of energy here between student and teacher, a precious exchange neither of us will soon forget.

Sydney says, "He doesn't live with us anymore. I just wanted to write about what a piece of shit he was."

I'm stunned by this blunt admission, as we say our goodbyes and she turns for the door. I shouldn't be so surprised. Of course, the story is only the tip of the iceberg—for all of us.

One after another, my students have exited the room, their secrets with them.

I'll talk to the rest of them tomorrow, I think, as if I'll ever really get to them all.

Embarrassed and Sad

"What's the matter?" I ask Christopher in the car on the way home from school.

"I don't want to tell you. You'll get mean."

"No way. You want to tell Mommy?"

He shakes his head. "She'll put me in my room for an hour."

No one has ever put him in his room for an hour, but now's not the time to debate this claim. "All right. When you're ready. Was there a fight?"

"No."

"Bad words?"

"No. Dr. D. came into our classroom because it was loud. And I smiled. Then he took me into the hallway."

"Why'd you smile?"

He shrugs. "Because he's so big and scary."

"Sounds like a reason to cry, not to smile."

"I almost did cry. He asked me questions, and then I had to go to the office until lunch."

"What questions did he ask you?"

"He said, 'Why are you smiling?' And 'Do you think something is funny?'"

"What'd you say?"

"I said, 'I don't know' and 'No.'"

"When we get home, you're going to write an apology."

"Do I have to?"

"Yes. You'll feel better."

"I *already* feel better."

"Did you say you're sorry?"

"No. I didn't have time after he asked me all those questions."

"So why *were* you smiling? You do it when *I* get angry, too, and then you cover your mouth. That used to make me even angrier, but now I know you can't help it and you really don't want to be smiling, so I don't get angry. So? How did you feel today when you were smiling?"

He hesitates. "Can I say how I was feeling when he took me into the hallway?"

"Sure."

"Embarrassed and sad."

"Okay. I think it will be a perfect letter. Just say those two things."

"Nooo!"

Soon after we get home I find him at the kitchen table, writing. *I am sorry I smiled at you. I smile when I get nervous and emberresed.*

He asks, "Is this good so far?"

I stroke his hair with my fingers. "Very."

MAN IN THE MIRROR

I enter the building late again. 7:32. I'm hightailing it through the hallway, tuning in to the morning announcements over the intercom—Freddy Whetts delivering some kind of salutation for the weekend. "After a week of disruption..." He offers a brief recap, recalling the superintendent's Sunday-night message about a student's online threat of mass murder, a threat made dubious by the fact that the post was a direct quote of song lyrics by some obscure death-metal band; Monday, student attendance was decimated; for the next few days, cop cars were parked outside the school; and kids were being (both falsely and rightly) accused, increasingly harsh accusations and counter-accusations exchanged online...

Ever the finder of silver linings, Freddy says it occurred to him last night that 1,250 kids out of 1,251 did *not* do what one kid did last weekend, in a moment of poor judgment. He goes on to say that we should all be committed to kindness. And forgiveness. I'm impressed by the direction of his remarks. He says we must forgive those who have made foolish mistakes, not condemn them, as they, too, are part of our community. Two other students had reposted the song lyrics, as a kind of protest against punishing a student for posting song lyrics, and got busted for making the same threats. A forgivable sin, to be sure.

I'm passing the office, where I can see, through giant windows, Freddy speaking into the microphone. For a moment, I'm inclined to stop walking and just listen, right there in the hallway, out of respect for this articulate and moving speech.

He pauses and says that if *he* were to post song lyrics online, he would post Michael Jackson.

Oh no, I think. *Don't do that.* I keep walking, but now I'm bracing myself, dreading this unfortunate turn toward the personal.

He proceeds to recite, with great solemnity, the words from "The Man in the Mirror." "If you want to make the world a better place, take a look at yourself and then make a change..."

As he reads on, I imagine myself, not for the first time, in a scene from a high-school black comedy going to the extremes, or an after-school special unashamed of its cheesy sentimentality. Until the Michael Jackson lyrics, I was thinking I ought to march right into the main office and shake Freddy's hand or at least email him to say, "Good speech." But now I think I'll just go into my classroom and try to forget about all of it, including those kids and their plagiarized death threats.

BIG BOY

At dinner we're all sitting at the kitchen table when Michael goes batshit because the iPad has stopped working. I say, "We don't need this here now, anyway." I shelve it, and he flails out of his seat and onto the floor. I watch him without a word. I return to my spaghetti. I say to Vana, "Sorry, I know this is hard for you, but we've got to see this one through."

Michael is on his feet, wailing, "I'm a big boy!" He's panning the kitchen, casing the place. I quickly remove the vase from the table. He's looking for shit to swipe from surfaces. I remove the knives from the cutting board. With all his might, he picks up the footstool, like a small refrigerator or a keg, and he's about to hurl it; I grab it, and him, but not before the corner of the stool marks the side of the cabinet. Collateral damage. Instead, he hurls himself at the floor and proceeds to writhe like a wounded cub. I'm just about to remind Vana of what our old pediatrician used to say when we were trying to sleep-train Christopher: "Nobody has ever cried to death." Suddenly I'm not so sure, as Michael seems to be hyperventilating. I wonder about the earliest signs of mental illness. I wonder, *Do I fetch the iPad for Michael, to end this insanity? No. Tough love,* I tell myself, sensing that Vana is losing faith. I can't blame her. But at this point returning the iPad will obviously worsen the problem long-term, though the short-term benefits are becoming increasingly attractive.

He inches toward me. I'm not sure if he's about to punch or nuzzle. He sets his hand on my thigh, rests his head on my arm. I scoop him into my lap.

"I love you," I say. "Big boy." He calms down. He fits into my arm perfectly. He's been finding this position a lot lately. I repeat what I've been saying, "You can have the iPad *after* you finish your dinner." I lower the bar: "Three bites." I make a forkful and he sweetly takes it. Tears are still falling, but there's no heaving. He's finding his breath. He takes another bite, chews, then opens his mouth. I'm thinking he doesn't know three bites from ten, or he's just hungry, and happy that this alone is his prerequisite for using the iPad. I scoop another ten bites in there before he shakes his head. Full. The plate is nearly clean. After a long pause he says, "Daddy, can I use the iPad now in the living room?"

"Yes."

He goes.

Vana says, "That was amazing."

I return her smile, as if I've been confident of this outcome all along.

(Not So) Fresh Start

Today I bring to school my new red stool and green clock I picked up at a cool store in Bethany Beach, Delaware, last week, a couple things to spice up the classroom, and to help keep the spirit of summer alive, until June if possible. Since moving into this classroom a few years ago, I've kept it minimalist but stylish. I open the windows and adjust the blinds for maximum sunlight and the panoramic view of the front lawn, blue skies, trees, and flagpole.

A few years ago, I persuaded Principal Steve Ponce to let me move into this D Wing room when an English colleague retired—the year after I'd been out sick for seven months. I told Steve that I was ready for a change, that the old room reminded me of that year I'd rather forget. I needed a new setting, preferably in the rancher-style D-Wing where there was no second floor and the atmosphere was quiet, less stressful—fresh digs, where I didn't have to stare out the windows at the rear entrance of the cafeteria and kitchen, and listen to the food trucks backing up and idling during delivery and the garbage trucks emptying the dumpsters and the buses chugging by at the end of the day. Not to mention the Chinese class upstairs, with all its mysterious banging, as if every day marked the start of the Chinese New Year, which apparently was celebrated by the ritualistic slamming of desk legs onto the hard tile floor.

Despite missing the spaciousness of that old B-Wing room with its friendly proximity to my longtime pals Sam and Dean in the adjacent rooms, I am glad for the change, even now, five years later. I can disappear into the D-Wing, which envious teachers see as the newly constructed Ivy League suites, set off from the rest of the school. Some tease that it's the geriatric wing, though this tag refers more to the easygoing lifestyle than to the ages of the teachers here—or so we veterans tell ourselves. I have adorned the back shelf of my classroom with plants, one of which I've repotted twice since purchasing it twenty years ago—a rubber plant, whose leaves, less than a foot long then, now nip the ceiling. By winter, those leaves at the top will begin a downward curve that by spring will appear to be circling back toward the overcrowded soil in its gigantic plastic pot. Next to this giant plant, which is older than my students, are pretzel cans filled with assorted candy, lollipops, and bubble gum, and a bag of mixed nuts, next to an espresso machine and small coffee maker that doubles as a water heater for tea. I want my room to be a kind of respite not just for me but also for my old B-Wing pals. This year, I believe, is going to require a lot of caffeine, and so I'm planning on having plenty of company; or, rather, this year is going to require a lot of company, and so I'm planning on having plenty of caffeine.

This morning, as per administrative instructions, the teachers who are assigned to each group of twenty or so freshmen play the YouTube instructional videos demonstrating how best to utilize the Chromebook and the various apps provided by the school district. In the remaining hour and a half, with the help of a pair of seniors, the teachers present a detailed overview of Benfield's extracurricular opportunities. Apparently, Logan Nichols—who will be my star student second semester in AP Modern Lit, and who will be accepted early-admission to Penn in a few months, and who is an editor for the lit mag, and who will be a shoo-in for English department award-winner—is a participant, if not leader or captain or, in more than one case, founder, of most of the activities available to students.

"So, in band we..." she explains to the eager-eyed freshmen. Logan laughs, as if modestly. "Yes, I'm in band, *too.* I'm not much of a sportsman, though, so Joshua can tell you about sports."

Joshua blushes. "Sports are fun." After a beat, getting into the spirit of his role, he encourages, "Play sports."

After their presentation, I learn that the football team, on which Joshua plays, has started their season 0-2 and has been outscored 70-7. Logan tells me she is applying to Penn early-decision. She has also been working on her common application, for Washington and Lee, Tufts...(I get lost in the list of impressive schools whose offers she'll decline)...and Pitt and Maryland as backups. I wonder when she has time to eat—or, seriously, if she is eating enough—for a moment concerned that she might be newly anorexic, though it wouldn't surprise me if she is just conscientious about a healthy diet and is maybe even writing a cookbook for teens. She is president of Student Council, captain of the band, an editor of the lit mag, a member of all the academic honor societies—"except math," she confessed moments ago to the freshmen—"math isn't my thing."

Logan takes a seat on the radiator next to me and says, "I can't wait to have you second semester." Instantly, I feel both flattered and challenged to raise my game to a new level, happy to have first semester to rehearse. The freshmen busy themselves silently at their desks, disguising their dread by fumbling with their Chromebooks, testing their passwords to access their schedules, no doubt having already come to the conclusion that no matter how successful they might be in the next four years, their achievements will fall far short of Logan Nichols's.

At 1:06, after returning from the Country Deli with Dean, we decide to have a coffee in my room. Since today is Freshman Orientation Day, Dean and I are free from assigned duties for the moment. I brew my fourth cup of Café de Cuba today. I make a mental note to order more capsules of this new featured flavor from Nespresso, wondering what else, if anything, I still need to do to prepare for my first day with students. Copies have been made. Assignments posted. Calendars revised. Dean sips his espresso, sitting in a chair next to me at my huge desk—three tables arranged at an angle in the corner—updating his AP U.S. History syllabus, changing the word "iPad" to "Chromebook," the brand-new device that every student will be receiving this year. Such are the preparations of the veteran teacher—an updating of terminology.

Lacks Self-Control

Vana and I have a conference call with Christopher's teacher. He threw a bead in art class. Joey said Christopher's chin looked like a butt, and Christopher said, "You're annoying and stupid." Christopher has trouble raising his hand in class. He calls out his answers before others get a chance. At times he lacks self-control. We all agree this is something to work on.

At home after school, Christopher is upset because the bracelet he made in art class came apart. He mopes on the couch. He knows his parents talked with his teacher today.

I say, "Cubs are on."

"I don't care." He looks at the Lego catalogue.

I turn on the Cubs game. Rain delay.

He says, "Turn it down!"

I'm interrupting his catalogue reading. I turn off the TV.

While I'm making dinner, I bring him a cookie.

He takes the cookie, suspicious, until I raise a cookie myself, as if to toast. Cheers.

"Yay." He takes a bite, I smile, and now we both feel better.

Before bath time, Vana announces that she will now show her finished MLK documentary on the TV in the living room, mirroring it from her iPhone. She is proud and excited to debut her first film to her family, to our sons, who will appreciate her various talents and her chosen subject for this project.

Christopher climbs onto the green chair. Michael squeezes in beside him.

"I can't focus," Christopher says. He squirms and turns away as if resisting torture.

"You can sit here and watch this for three minutes," I say. "Mommy's been working on it all week."

"Can you please...?" Vana aims the remote.

MLK appears on the screen above the mantel.

"I want to watch the Cubs," Christopher says.

I inform him that the game has been postponed till tomorrow.

Michael slugs Christopher in the arm. Christopher returns a firm backhand.

"Forget it." Vana hits the power button, and the light in the room fades.

Later, I'm washing dishes when I hear a strange dripping sound coming from somewhere behind me. I tiptoe out of the kitchen and discover a steady stream of water falling from the opening in the stairwell onto the living-room floor, where a puddle grows. I run upstairs to find the bathroom flooded, an inch of water, a veritable lake narrowing to a river at the door and forming a waterfall between two banisters. Christopher is still making waves in the tub when I holler, "What the hell are you doing? What are you *doing?!*"

Vana roars, "What is the *matter* with you? What are you *thinking?*" She emerges from our bedroom. She dashes downstairs with towels. Christopher is already crying before the real shouting starts. It's as if he's been manufacturing this domestic disaster all day, inclined to create, for the convenience of all of us, a mess that can be addressed immediately, a crime with real evidence, to justify the punishment he feels he deserves for deeds we were not witness to in school today. Now we can mop it up and move on.

HEART RATE

I've just finished reading Matthieu Ricard's *Happiness* when Vana says, "My heart is racing," and braces herself at the kitchen counter. I set my book on the table as she takes her pulse. "One-twenty." No panic attacks since before the doctoral program started in August. She takes one of her mother's metoprolol, and in twenty minutes her heart rate decreases to sixty. Last summer my psychiatrist friend suggested metoprolol to Vana as an anti-anxiety treatment, after she had tried a couple common meds in tiny doses. Now comes talk of the imminent dissertation. A ten-page lit review on four books due tomorrow.

I take a sip of warm Coke from the can I've been nursing while reading. I ask what's on her mind.

She chokes up. "Just—whether I can do this program."

"Really?"

"I mean, maybe if I weren't doing this program, then I wouldn't be having these issues."

"But the panic attacks went away when you *started* the program, because you were enjoying it—not worrying about it. Not anticipating it."

"I know. I *do* enjoy it. I don't understand."

She says she's got five pages on "How I Learn" due by midnight tonight. She's been writing about sensory experience, like smell, she explains to me, and how she associates certain scents with past events and learned ideas. The aroma of lavender puts her in the backyard of her *yiayia*'s house in Lamia, Greece, where, as a child on summer vacations, she napped in the hot late afternoons.

For me, the smell of Coke, paper money, and freshly cut grass—such common scents—transport me back to my grandparents' house, after I've mowed the lawn, a colossal chore for a twelve-year-old pushing a Toro. I'm transported to the family room, where I'm guzzling from a green glass bottle I've plucked from the wooden case in the garage and receiving the twenty-dollar bill my *papou* hands me from his leather wallet, which is as enormous as the hamburgers he serves at his restaurant, where in a few years I'll be working as a busboy, while keeping the gig as lawn boy. All of this in a whiff...

Something has caught Vana's attention in the *Times* splayed on the kitchen table. She seems to have relaxed and begins to read. On the adjacent page is a full-page ad for Woody Allen's latest, *Wonder Wheel.* Going to see a movie would be fun. Together. In a theater. A simple memory as remote as the scent of popcorn. I keep this bittersweet fantasy to myself, leaving Vana to her moment of peace, before she has to get back to work.

Untethered Soul

I'm reading the *The Untethered Soul* while drinking my coffee at the kitchen table. It used to be I'd write, not read, at five in the morning. But now I don't kid myself. With Michael still waking up twice a night for his milk ("Moke, Daddy!" and, five minutes later, "Cover me!"), I don't have what it takes to wake up earlier than I have to, much less write anything decent. Earlier in the school year I decided that instead of writing I would devote the first half-hour of the day to "meditation and push-ups," a plan that remains marked in the 5:30 slot on my iPhone calendar from now until June 22. I've managed to convince myself that I'm meditating when I take deep breaths while maintaining good posture, especially if I'm doing these things while reading *The Untethered Soul,* which my sister recommended after reading it for her book group led by her yoga instructor. As for the push-ups, I promise myself I'll do a few later in the day.

In the chapter I'm reading, the author talks about how negative thoughts have the incredible power of pulling you down if you let them, if you don't learn how to prevent them from taking over your life. He describes how you must not resist negative thoughts but instead let them flow through you; you can't suppress them because sooner or later they'll return with a vengeance. You must refocus always on the moment. Don't let your mind rule your thinking—or is it, don't let your thinking rule your mind? Find your seat of consciousness and play witness to your ever-busy brain, just as you witness actual physical objects in your environment. Negative thoughts and emotions infect those around you, and you manifest this interplay in your life. Resist it. Or, rather, welcome it and then let it go. Ascend, always in a state of letting the energy flow through you, so that you are present in your life. So that you don't miss the moment because your head is stuck in a thought. People miss not only the moment but the hour. The week. The year.

Through the ceiling I hear Michael waking and walking across the floor to the bathroom. I put my book down to listen. He flushes. Returns to his bed. Sings. *"Bruder... The engine. And windows..."* It is an ode to his toys, specifically to his new Bruder-brand truck and construction-worker figure, whom he is apparently serenading in bed. *"You have a chainsaw and yellow hat..."* I resist the urge to greet him, and instead I give him this time to unwind and me this time to witness, to experience a little of that joyful-living-in-the-present-moment consciousness. Will he sing himself back to sleep? Should I race upstairs with a fresh cup of milk before he gets thirsty and starts with that loathsome screaming? It's silent for a moment. Then I hear footsteps. I think it must be Christopher. The toilet lid falls. No, it's Michael again. Now he's on the stairs, crooning again. *"Please shine down on me."* He's changed his tune. Maybe he's seen the light down here. I join in, la-la-la-ing, a duet. Cautiously he descends to find me at the table.

"Truck," he observes, spotting an ad in yesterday's *Times.* "I want to come see." He climbs the bench at the kitchen table. Then he's right by my side, where I'd like him to stay. "My daddy." He puts his head on my shoulder. "What's that?" A photograph of an urban park.

"Sculpture, fountain," I say.

He says, "We saw a sculpture in Philly-delphia."

"Yes. Time to make my lunch."

He watches. He goes for the iPad on the nearby countertop. "iPad working?" He knows to ask; we tell him "it's not working" when we've decided he's had enough—or *we've* had enough. "I want to watch *Jack Jack Play.*" Gazillions of YouTube videos feature a boy named Jack Jack playing with Bruder-brand toy trucks, nonstop, in varying locations. Michael has turned into a sleepwalking obsessive, besotted with his latest rituals even in his dreams.

When I head upstairs to take a shower, I get him back to bed. An hour later, when I arrive at school, my phone buzzes as I enter the copy room. Michael is wailing on the other end, and for a moment I think he's managed to make this call on his own, about to impart some terrible news about himself or his brother or mother. Before I can formulate a theory, Vana says, "Sorry to bother you. He was looking at Naples pictures on my phone. He saw you, you know..."

I puzzle over this, then realize, oh, *those* Naples pictures—months after chemotherapy, a trip to Florida, when I was still bald and bloated. Michael's crying is coming full bore at this point. "*Daddy!*"

I say, "It's okay, Michael. Daddy shaved his head." In the photos of me by the pool, there's also the fresh scar, like a bronze zipper down the sternum, laid bare in the sunlight. I try, "I love you, I love you, I love you," but it doesn't seem that he's going to be stopping anytime soon. "I love you. I love you— Is anyone else *there?! Hello? Vana?*"

"*Yes,*" Vana says, sounding remote. "Sorry. Have a nice day." And they're gone.

After school, when I pick up Michael from day care, I don't mention the morning phone call or whatever horrors may have preceded it. His teacher says he had a fine day. When we get home, Michael suddenly remembers it all, those memories of the morning triggered perhaps by the kitchen setting or by his desire to find the iPad, which, I don't know, maybe reminds him of Vana's phone and the photos it stored from six years ago.

He's stammering, "Daddy, why, why, why—?", as if he's trying to conjure up this morning's fading concern. "Why—*yesterday...*" (his word for any time *before* the present moment; he's referring to this morning, finding his way back...) "I was looking at Mommy's *phome,* and pictures, and why, why, why—you look like *a boy,* why you have *no hair?*"

"Because he had cancer," Christopher pronounces.

Before I can shoot him a stern look, I realize his blunt explanation isn't registering with Michael any better or worse than "I shaved my head." But then Michael senses there's something ominous to the story. In the pictures, my face is slightly puffed-up, lingering effects of prednisone or symptoms of swelling related to poor circulation due to surgery. "Like a *boy,*" he repeats, with almost tender confusion. He's right to wonder about this unnatural appearance of mine, which preceded his arrival by two years, his eventual existence contingent on my survival.

Now here we are, and he's the boy, I'm the daddy, health and hair restored. Let's keep it that way.

GOTTA PEE

At 1:00 I'm proctoring the Physics exam in the Anatomy classroom. Once again, I'm happily reading students' short stories while a roomful of kids scratch away at their test booklets. I'm hunkered down at the big desk in the front of the room when all of a sudden I've gotta pee. Fortunately, Carolyn Winters and Tracy Bean, the guidance counselors in charge of the AP tests, are so scrupulously organized that they have included in the Exam Folder, along with the roster and instructions, a short list of phone numbers in case of emergency, both their office and cell numbers. They have made it emphatic and clear, first in their oral presentations in the library last week and then here in their typed-up instructions, that they are *on-call in case of emergencies,* or if we just have questions or need a break, that we must follow protocol to the letter, and that we must not repeat any disasters like last year's. From the classroom phone I call all four numbers—straight to voice mail. With my iPhone I text them both: please come and relieve me pronto. No response.

And now, seriously, I really have got to go to the bathroom, which is located right across the hallway, and it's one of those doorless entrances, which makes it all the more tantalizing just to sneak away for a minute. The students' heads are all down; they'd never notice my brief absence. But last year a proctor committed a seemingly minor infraction, misreading the clock and gypping the kids of two minutes of test time, and the whole batch got canceled; a makeup exam was administered at a later date. That proctor, a hired sub for the day, was a pariah not only to those students, who had to suffer through three more hours of testing, but also to the administrators, who determined that from now on only the current AP teachers, considering their own personal interest in seeing the best possible results, would be proctoring the AP exams. And so, right now, I'm pacing in front of the class, sweating it big time, growing paranoid that two of my AP Modern Lit students, Logan and Emma, are onto me; they're smart enough to conclude that something's not right with Zervanos up there, hobbling and tightening his jaw as if—

Fuck! What the fuck am I going to do? This is getting seriously serious. I can't leave the room. The hallways are empty. Minutes upon minutes have passed and not a soul in sight. This must be a record time for an empty hallway! What bad luck! Not one teacher or security guard or even student. The bathroom is *right there,* so close I can smell the deodorant pucks in the urinals.

Still nothing from Carolyn or Tracy. I'm hovering in the classroom doorway, with my head in the hallway, ready to hiss for anyone's attention. And then, like a mirage, history teacher Jeff Cardozo appears in the distance. *Please keep walking this way, Jeff. Jeff!* I'm waving to him. I can't tell if he sees me. If he does, he must be wondering what the hell my problem is. I pray he doesn't turn into the stairwell or dip into the mailroom. Finally, he's almost here, he's here, thank God, and I explain quickly, almost within loud whispering distance, and then, "I have to go," and he gets it, no problem. I go, and it's ecstatic relief. It doesn't take long. And yet, it's the greatest of favors Jeff has done for me.

"Thank you so much," I say. "I don't know what I would have done—" He laughs. "Honestly." I'm delirious with relief. "Thank you." I reenter the classroom, iPhone in hand, pretending to have just resolved some very urgent business that required me to call for backup. Just then a text comes in, from Tracy. *Sorry, Jim, just got this. Everything all right?*

QUICKIE

I've just showered and gotten dressed for school when I hear Vana, from under covers, say, "I just had a sexy dream." It's one of her few cues.

I don't bother to check my watch, which I've just fastened.

"Me too," I lie, stripping. "Are you still...?"

"Aren't you running late?"—a moot question this year, as the answer is always yes. Only today I'm proctoring the PSATs and so I actually *really do* have to be at work on time.

I get under the covers. "I've gotta take my opportunities when I get them."

"That's such a turn-on," she says.

I smile. "Romance, baby."

"What if some little person walks in?"

"This'll only take a minute."

A minute later, the toilet seat claps down in the bathroom. Michael is standing there peeing, his back to us. The door to our room is wide open.

Vana and I are silent, holding in our laughter.

She whispers, "We need a vacation."

"I'll settle for a date."

"Did you forget tonight?"

"Your work event? That counts?"

I'm up and getting dressed again when Michael enters and says, "What's that smell?"

Vana and I swap horrified glances, nearly bursting out laughing.

Before I rush off, Vana says, "Babysitter's coming at six, right after work, so try to hurry downtown."

Michael asks, "Where you going?"

I say, "I'll be there by six-fifteen."

Vana says, "Don't speed."

Michael says, "I want to come."

"Slow and steady," I tell him.

THE WAY OF THE CRAFT

I'm in Tampa, Florida, for the AWP Conference, where thousands of writers, teachers, students, and wannabes of all kinds congregate annually to catch lectures and readings and to wander proudly or enviously through the colossal book fair and, for some, to bask in the glory of their recent publications and seeming fame and, for others, to wonder painfully about how much better their lives would be if only they could publish a short story in a literary journal, or if only they could publish their collection with a small press in the South or the Midwest or the North Pole, or if only they could land not just an actual contract but a big-advance two-book deal with Random House or Knopf, or if, after three critically acclaimed books and one that actually sold a hundred thousand, they could win a Pulitzer or at least a Guggenheim, or if, after all the awards and the bestsellers translated into dozens of languages and adapted to films, they could finally be rightly considered, not just by literary critics and scholars but by everyday readers, to be one of the best writers of not only *this* generation but of *any* generation, on a par not necessarily with Shakespeare, or even a Chekhov, Twain, or Tolstoy, but with, say, a Salman Rushdie or a Margaret Atwood, if a bit less prolific—certainly no less deserving to be the keynote speaker than the hack they've got this year, that sellout whose mugshot is displayed on every poster on every wall and column around every corner in every building in this place...

Doubtless, most of us waste untold energy indulging such corrosive thinking—and tempting dreams.

I wake up to the hotel fire alarm at six a.m.

My perennial conference buddy, Jeff Byers, is already sitting up against a pile of pillows, texting away in his bed.

I snooze.

Jeff showers, then announces he's heading to the lobby to find coffee and a quiet corner to grade papers. I can't help comparing our jobs, always curious and usually delighted to discover that his work as a professor at an elite liberal arts college in Baltimore is distinguished almost exclusively by the age of his students, not by their ability; indeed, I'm often encouraged by evidence (or by Jeff's outright lamenting) that my high-school students in the Philadelphia suburbs are at least as capable as his collegiate charges, not least because they are not yet jaded, still eager to learn, to do well, if only to do well enough to get accepted to a decent college like the one where he teaches.

Apparently, there are no panels or presentations we're in a hurry to get to this morning. For more than a decade I have unofficially, and lazily, given Byers the job of determining our itinerary for these three-day excursions we've been taking together.

I grumble that I'll meet him downstairs in a while. Alone in the room, I peek at the half-stack of papers he's left behind on the desk. Handwritten reflections on notebook paper, some bearing the torn perforations from a spiral binding, a few lines of cursive or a paragraph that reaches halfway down the page, rushed thoughts that seem like anything my high-school students might write on any given day.

Later, over coffee and scones, Jeff's friend Susan, who teaches at another Baltimore-area college, tells us of a student's ten-page essay she stopped reading this morning after two pages. It was a re-write of a draft she read last week, on Ireland motifs and imagery in the poetry of William Butler Yeats. Susan recalls the student saying how "poetry fills her soul. Her paper is a list of allusions to Ireland. One of the poems is *called* 'I Am Of Ireland.' I told her she has no thesis. 'Ireland imagery in Yeats' is *not* a thesis." Susan sighs. "I wonder sometimes if my school should be graduating people like this. Or if I should be teaching them." She pauses again, as if she ever really had a doubt. "But this diploma will change her life. She's over fifty. She's never going to be a writer. She works at a day care, and this will increase her pay. I actually really love this woman."

"I can't read another one of these right now." Jeff tosses his pen onto the table and shoves the stack of papers into his bag.

We're all silent for a moment, complicit in the shame we feel for judging the students who disappoint us in a way that makes us feel we're somehow less than what we are because we're not teaching at Yale. But, of course, what we do, teaching literature and creative writing, is about something larger than the aspirations we're conscious of. Whether the student is fifteen, twenty-five, or fifty, we are devotees, on a kind of mission, not to convert, but to be purveyors to any who will heed our good message, of the Way of the Craft—or to anyone who needs the English credits to graduate.

As we swig our coffees, I check out the advance reader copy of Jeff's first novel, about a boy growing up in New York City, which I read in draft form last summer, hoping to offer some useful feedback. It's thrilling to see this book he's been working on for a decade coming to fruition. He tells me that, after having sent out eighty queries, he's won the attention of an agent who, not coincidentally, has a young son growing up in New York City, as does the newly appointed editor-in-chief who selected Jeff's book to be the company's first publication under her management. In her letter, which graces the first page of this advance copy, she describes how the novel drew her into the familiar landscape of New York City as seen through the eyes of a growing boy, like her own son, whose private world she has always felt separated from and craved access to. I ponder these personal connections, feeling at once encouraged and dismayed that the still-unpublished books I've written may or may not ever come across the desks of these powerful guardians at the gate who, should they see themselves in my work, might offer me passage.

"It's a lottery," Jeff reminds me. "It'll happen." *For you,* he means. "Let's not forget, the one agent who said yes to me was also the one who my very charming and well-published friend connected me with." I'm not sure if this furthers his case about the lottery or undermines it, but I take his point. He says, "You've just got to keep playing."

Playing.

That's it.

One of the reasons I come to this conference every year, aside from hanging out with Jeff, is to discover the reason I came to the conference. This year, the reason seems to be to rediscover the very simple truth that Jeff has unwittingly just led me to: I need to keep *playing,* or, rather, to *start* playing again, the way I *used* to play, decades ago, when I set out to be a writer—or even before that, when there was *only* play, with no endgame in mind. And so, I've come full circle, remembering this simple truth, perhaps not for the last time.

Jeff suggests we hit the panel on point of view. The room is packed. The three of us stand outside the open conference-room doors, trying to catch a glimpse of the presenters, as if it's the Beatles onstage up there, or Jesus, whose words might make all the difference in our lives. Jeff shakes his head, and we split. We end up at a panel on revision, where there's plenty of seating available. Jeff and I sit on each side of Susan. Before long, we're exchanging rueful glances, quietly strategizing a discreet exit. We sit tight, the three of us side by side, paying attention only to the phones each of us holds in our laps, texting emojis of ourselves being tortured—as shameless and caustic as our students.

Not soon enough, we're outside drinking mimosas under overcast skies, sitting with Jeff's very charming and well-published friend who led him to his agent. Considering the weather back home, we couldn't be happier, sipping our tropical-ish drinks and aiming our faces at the haze. Jeff's friend asks me how it's going with the agent hunt. I tell her of my recent disappointments, of one agent in particular whose initial enthusiasm had me fantasizing about fame and fortune and then whose eventual rejection had me scrounging for kernels of hope. Jeff's friend is impressed by the interest I've managed to elicit. "Those are super top agents," she says, then recalls, "Oh my God, I just remembered, *she* was the first agent that rejected me, like, twenty years ago!" I sigh, hoping my path might at some point continue in the way hers has since then.

She announces she'd better get going to the lecture she's giving on plot. It will be a packed house, no doubt.

Jeff and I decide to check out the panel discussion featuring celebrity authors Jeffrey Eugenides, Lorrie Moore, and Dana Spiotta. We sit in the back of a packed dim hall that seats thousands, glancing back and forth between the three glowing figures on the distant stage and the giant screens showing them in close-up. Eugenides is one of my favorites. He reads the opening pages of a work in progress—another masterwork, I conclude. I like to think of him as "the other Greek writer." I also like to tell myself that, not unlike me, he's written four books, albeit published and to great acclaim. Yes, these writers are superstars, and just like us. The stage is not so far from where we sit.

WONDER WOMAN V. SPIDER-MAN

Before bedtime Christopher is drawing pictures of football players on sheets of computer paper on the dining-room floor. I'm sitting with him while Vana puts Michael to bed.

Christopher asks me, "Do you know why I don't want to watch Wonder Woman?"

"I have no idea," I say.

"Because of guns. I don't want nightmares."

"You watched Spiderman," I remind him.

"There's no guns in Spiderman. The only part that scared me is when Peter Parker gets stuck under those rocks when the building falls on him. That part gave me a nightmare, remember?" He pauses. "When Mommy's at Penn, can we watch that again?"

I nod. Okay. He's testing something, maybe my trust in his courage.

"Or maybe just baseball," he says.

Dominica on Retirement

In the copy room, I pause to chat with Dominica Shortt, gym teacher and most senior of the staff. She looks distressed. Her grown son just got a job teaching, she says. She is happy for him, but now she wishes she had retired last year. "This is forty-two years for me," she says. She was planning on retiring after forty-one, but then she figured she'd stick it out another year—increase her pension a few bucks; save a few on health care. But after the past few days of agonizing in-service, she says she just can't take the grind anymore.

"These days go on forever," she says.

I remind her, "Come Tuesday, when the kids come back, you'll forget all about it."

Dean Garrett enters. He catches on quickly. "Happens every year. Once you close that door and start teaching, you'll remember why you're here."

Dean has already told me he's in no hurry to retire. *What else am I going to do?* is how he looks at it.

"Seven more years for me," I say, "thirty and out."

Dominica frowns. "You're retiring after thirty?" She says this not with approbation but with skepticism, which concerns me.

"I'll be fifty-five," I say. "Ned Robbins told me it makes no financial sense for me to stay a day longer. We'll switch to Vana's health insurance."

Ned Robbins is the finance guru of the teachers' union.

Dominica shakes her head. "I don't know. I'd check again. I think the magic numbers are thirty-five and sixty, not thirty and fifty-five."

I insist unconfidently, "Ned swore he was right..."

A few years ago, I practically forced Ned to swear on his pension that he had his facts straight, so thrilled was I to discover that the two magic numbers for retirement (the required minimum number of years of teaching, and one's age) fell on the same year for me. I'll admit it did seem too good (too soon and too young) to be true: 30 and 55. But that's why I pressed him on the matter. "It's true," he said, his grin tinged with envy. He was pushing sixty himself, but he started teaching later in life and so still had a few to go to get the maximum pension. Ever since that day we talked, I've been counting the years. Eight more. Seven more.

But now, if Dominica is right, the prospect of retiring at sixty has me feeling hunched over and weak in the knees. For years I've been holding on to visions of me in a college classroom, holding forth in a creative-writing workshop, maybe a three-hour seminar once a week, attending to the needs of a mere dozen twenty-somethings, while managing to convince myself I'm still young. At sixty, no such delusions will be possible. I am nauseated with the feeling that I may soon outgrow this high-school gig. In the hallway on the walk back to my room I don't delay. I call Ned Robbins on my cell phone. He doesn't answer. I leave him a message. I don't disguise the fact that what I need to discuss with him is a matter of great urgency and import.

Middle East Peace

At bedtime Michael is wearing his Phillies hat, Phillies jersey, and batting gloves.

"Batting gloves to bed?" I ask.

He nods.

Mommy would not approve, but Mommy will be home late again, after a business dinner, and so I'm not about to argue with Michael if this getup will help expedite the goodnight routine. Meanwhile, Nana is staying with us for a few days, and tonight she's having dinner with a local friend and promised to be out late. I'm taking full advantage of the distraction-free house. Tonight, it's early to bed. Daddy cannot wait to have some alone time.

After last night's successful crash course in sounding out the letters, Michael is fired up to read. First "the Phillies book," he says, as he props himself against his pillow. He stares at the cover.

"Ready?" I ask.

He nods.

"Okay…" I start, "Phillies—"

"No, no, I do it. I read. Phillies, exstabished 1883." Of course, he's still remembering what words go with what pictures. He goes on, "Pride and chadition: Mascot: Phillie Phanatic."

I point to the long-legged pitcher from the 2008 World Series.

"Cole Hamels."

I ask, "Who pitched a perfect game in 1964?"

He points. "Jim Bunning."

I find this hilarious, this four-year-old naming players whose photographs exist only in black and white.

"Gloh-ver Clevand Alazander."

"Good!"

He smiles momentarily.

When we finish the book, he confesses, "I can't read! I want to read. How you read?"

I say, "Remember last night? Mm-ike...Mike Schmidt? The letters together make words. You make the words with the sounds of the letters. Look." I point to the next picture and drag my finger under each letter. "Guh—Ll—uh—vuh: GLOVE."

"No, no." He blocks my finger. "I want to." He points to the next word, not exactly sounding it out, but close enough: "Bee—Aay—El—El. BALL!" He beams. "I reading!"

"Yes, you are!" I cheer, and it's lights out. I tug the covers up to the brim of his hat. He slips his gloved hands under the pillow. He's still smiling when he closes his eyes.

It's not even 8:30 yet, and I'm about to pull off the impossible—or the extremely rare: both kids asleep with an hour left before I start dozing off and becoming useless. I might actually get some writing done tonight!

When I enter Christopher's room to say goodnight, he's reading his own baseball book. He's expecting me to lie down next to him now, not just to tuck him in, so I do, figuring two minutes of reading together is a better bet than insisting that "time's up." He shows me highlights from the last ten or so pages: the evolution of the uniform—old flannel jerseys with zippers, the White Sox wearing shorts, the Astros in technicolor orange. We review the "flamethrowers"—Nolan Ryan, who threw over 100 mph; Aroldis Chapman, who throws 105!

He stops abruptly.

"You want to read me something?" I ask.

"No." He sets his book on the night table and flips onto his belly, eyes closed. "I'm tired."

"Good boy." I check my watch. This is going better than I'd hoped. I turn off the lamp and say goodnight.

He says, "I don't know what to dream about."

"Baseball, of course."

"No, I always do that." As if we're flipping through the channels.

"Okay, how about being an awesome painter?"

"Okay."

Okay? That's it? I'm free to go?

"I love you," he says.

"I love *you!*"

I hustle out, but softly, disguising my enthusiasm. It's 8:31 when I slide into bed and set the MacBook on my lap.

Just then I hear the front door opening downstairs. *Shit.* Vana, home early. I cringe at the sound of creaking hinges, shushing her telepathically.

But Michael is already thumping out of bed. "Mommy!"

I get up to find them hugging on the stairs.

"You want me to put you to bed?" Vana asks him.

Vana sees me, and we swap sour smiles, sharing the same regret. She whispers to me, "Oops, sorry."

I whisper, "I was just about to text you to take your time..."

Michael says, "Sing me lullabies."

"Okay," she says. Then to me, "From now on, we'll—"

"Mommy!" It's Christopher.

Vana makes a quick U-turn to say goodnight to Christopher, who is suddenly bawling.

What the—?!

From the hallway I can hardly make out his words of distress.

"Dead.... Guns.... Nana showed me. It's her fault."

I recall the earlier scene in the kitchen while my mother-in-law was cooking dinner. Christopher was regaling me with what he'd picked up from the news today—home on a Tuesday because it was Election Day—while Nana was flipping from CNN to MSNBC. Christopher's globe had been sitting on the windowsill in the living room, brought down from his bedroom, so I'd asked if they'd been doing geography.

Nana said, "No, we were doing a history lesson, of Israel and the Middle East. He was seeing what was going on, on the news. We talked about how Jerusalem is being recognized as the capital now."

Christopher said, "It was Tel Aviv." Then he announced, "It said over fifty people got shot." He seemed enthralled and proud to be part of the conversation.

"Don't tell Mommy," I joked.

"Oh, come on," Nana said. "Give me a break."

"She wants to keep them innocent," I teased, as if I don't feel the same way.

"She doesn't want them to get scared. But he's asking questions. He's old enough to learn about these things."

"I completely agree," I said.

A kid can learn about the world and still keep his innocence, right?

I've made my way back to my laptop on the bed when Vana enters. "Can you please help in there? He's crying about Israel. Apparently, my mom showed him the news and he's thinking about the fifty people who got shot."

I play oblivious and make my way to Christopher. Vana returns to Michael, who's been waiting patiently in his room.

I tell Christopher that they've been fighting over there since before Jesus. "It's a busy, busy place with so many different kinds of people, of religions and countries, and so they fight, over land and ideas and God, since forever, and who knows, maybe they'll go on fighting forever—" I stop short of adding: *No thanks to Ivanka Trump congratulating Israel for moving the American Embassy to Jerusalem as if it's a Trump hotel.* I hear Vana singing faintly to Michael.

I go on, "It's okay to feel scared—it's scary—but let yourself feel other feelings, too, like sadness for those people who died and their families and friends who are really sad right now, and remember that many of those people are courageous and brave for protesting and standing up for what they believe..."

He seems calmed. I'm feeling pretty good about that little pep talk, with a sneaky lesson mixed in.

He says, "It's Nana's fault."

"It's no one's fault. These things happen in the world, and you're learning about them."

"Well," he says, "I didn't know before Nana showed me the news, and now I do know."

"Would you rather not know what you know? The other emotion to remember is empathy. It means understanding what others are going through, while you're lucky to live here, where we're safe." I pause, testing. "Feel better?"

He nods. I cover his ear with the bed sheet folded back over the comforter. Mommy has returned to the bedroom doorway. I'm not sure how long she's been standing there behind me. I'm relieved when she smiles. I take her place in the doorway when she sits on the bed and begins to sing: *Row, row, row your boat gently down the stream, merrily, merrily, merrily, merrily, life is but a dream.* I realize for the first time in my life the profundity of this song.

Run Hide Fight

Another in-service day. In the library the nurse gives a presentation on administering the EpiPen to a student having an extreme allergic reaction. Assistant Principal Serenity Davis demonstrates, pretending to stab herself in the thigh. Her arm rises and thrusts down numerous times like a psycho killer's. She gets laughs from the front rows, but from the back row it's hard to appreciate the full effect.

Next, Assistant Principal Everest Toole goes over safety for the year. He announces that an evacuation drill will take place this fall, the full-blown fleeing-from-the-site drill. Taking buses to the local community college. Something we've never done before.

Over his shoulder, Dean mutters to me, "There goes a day."

"Ever think we'd be talking about this shit twenty years ago?"

Dean shakes his head, rolls his eyes.

"We have to do this," Everest announces, "so that we know what to do if we ever really have to do it."

On my right, Neil grins. "If this ever really happens, this place will be like roaches flying out of here, to the mall, into the woods. Forget it."

Everest reviews various techniques of barricading the classroom door. First, he emphasizes that doors must be closed at all times. Then he says, "Now let's shift gears a little bit. What is your plan for an intruder? You need a plan." He hesitates, as if to give us time to formulate one. Then, indicating with his fingers—one, two, three—he says: "Escape. Lockdown. Defend. Or... Run. Hide. Fight. Remember?"

Last year we had an in-service day devoted to the new protocol. We got the full low-down from a local FBI guy with a fake fluorescent-orange gun he used in a mock demonstration with a volunteer who failed to stop him from using it. He showed us shocking videos that were produced by the Department of Homeland Security and featured actors playing office workers running for their lives, hiding in a break room, attacking the mock intruder with a chair and a coffee pot. Now I wonder what the new teachers are thinking, having just heard for the first time, "Run. Hide. Fight," and being told to have a plan to barricade themselves in if running and hiding is no longer an option.

"Think it through. Right now," Everest says. "What's the first thing you're going to do in your specific classroom. With what would you blockade your door?" I'm thinking, *the doors open outward, so what's the use of a blockade?* "You better lock your door. That's the first and most important thing to do. If the intruder somehow gets your door open, you don't want him getting any farther. Filing cabinets, desks, whatever it takes."

I have no filing cabinets. One of my great accomplishments of the past five years is going virtually paperless, as I've been encouraged by administration to do, so that my students, with their iPads and laptops and phones, need only go to my school-district website to access class materials—and save the district thousands of dollars on paper. My classroom is a twenty-first-century minimalist wonder: whiteboards instead of blackboards, erasable markers instead of chalk, a standing lamp where a filing cabinet used to sit, potted plants on the uncluttered surfaces of the back counter, every student supplied with a Chromebook. The downside is that there are no obvious weapons for self-defense, and, as for a barricade, there is only my very heavy, old wooden desk that will require the strength of me and five students to push over to the door. Since the door opens *out,* the desk will serve only to provide a perch from which the intruder can take better aim. I could instruct my students to hurl their iPhones at the intruder, while I get ready to swing the golf club that I keep handy to unlatch the giant windows on the far wall.

Everest goes on, "If you manage to get out of your classrooms to run, make sure you have a second, backup door in mind. We took the handles off the insides of some of the doors because intruders chain-lock doors so people can't get out. For the drill, we'll be locking a door so that some classes will have to improvise."

The staff seems to be taking all of this in stride, despite the horrific images Everest is successfully conjuring for us. We all trust and like Everest. He taught history for fifteen years here before he was slyly wooed into a "temporary Assistant Principal" position, which, after the pay increase and flattery, he later accepted as permanent. Everest is the safety guy now. No one would ever question his seriousness. A decade ago, he'd lost his daughter, eight years old at the time, to sudden cardiac arrest. Everest and his wife started a non-profit in the girl's honor, a run/walk that raises tens of thousands of dollars annually to educate parents and purchase defibrillators for public parks and schools where kids play. After I moved into the classroom next to his, Everest and I had a few long talks in which he confided to me that his father had been extremely tough and, ultimately, absent. He was explaining to me why he was such a strong caretaker, as a father, husband, uncle, teacher. He's had to fill the role his father vacated, making up for what he was deprived of as a son. The administration knew who they were recruiting when they sacrificed a great history teacher. Everest means business. I used to listen through the wall to his rapturous lectures on philosophy—on truth and honor and free will—and so I lamented his decision to stop teaching. At the time, he'd promised me he wouldn't "turn to the dark side." But they got him for good.

Now, Tyler Rose, a Benfield alumnus, has taken Everest's old room. Tyler struts and smiles, as if he's nodding hello with every step. He coaches the boys' lacrosse and golf teams. He plays techno or house music or whatever it is—not just during his prep periods but sometimes during class, as background music while the kids are "working." In the hallway, boys walk by and call out, "Yo, T-Ro!" and girls pop in to say, "Hi, Mr. Rose, we miss your class!"

Teaching next to Tyler is not unlike teaching next to Sam D'Ambrosio, who was my neighbor in my old classroom. Back then, in the rear of the building by the cafeteria, when the delivery trucks weren't distracting me and my students, Sam's apparent stand-up comedy routine next door would elicit a steady stream of laughter that drove through the wall. When he wasn't telling jokes, he might have been playing his guitar and singing. I always felt sorry for my students—as I sometimes do now, with Tyler Rose as my neighbor—or at least I wondered if they shared my feeling, which always reminds me of the opening scene of Woody Allen's *Stardust Memories,* where Woody's character looks out the window of his train car to see, in the window of the car on the neighboring tracks, a gorgeous Sharon Stone beaming in a tiara, waving to him; as the trains roll out in opposite directions, Woody realizes he's on the wrong train, surrounded by old strangers in mourning clothes, before he tries to claw his way out of that locked car.

As Everest wraps up his presentation, I text Dean: Country Deli for lunch today.

From his seat five rows ahead, Dean turns to me, surprised and not surprised that I should want to return to this old teacher dive. He smiles, understands. I've surrendered to the inevitability of all that comes with this job. The only way through it is together.

DAY OF ATONEMENT

Today we're off for Yom Kippur. I'm home with Christopher. Last night, we discussed how a second grader might like to spend the day with his daddy. Following Vana's instruction, Christopher got a piece of paper and a pencil crayon and began to make a schedule for us: Wake up 7:15. Baseball 8:15-9:30.

"What should we do next?" he asked.

"TV," I said. "You need your screen time."

"Hey!" he laughed, beginning to sense sarcasm.

"Okay, maybe just a rest, before the next thing."

Christopher scrawled *Tennis 10:00.*

Vana said, "You guys can use the microscope."

Christopher hesitated. Then agreed: *Sientz.*

"Good, honey," Vana said.

Then lunch. *McDonald's.*

He said, "Remember we made that cardboard house with the box? Let's do that again."

"Sure."

He wrote *Art.* Then *Pick up Michael.*

Meanwhile, Michael had begun to pick up on the incongruity: his brother was planning fun and games at home, while it sounded like business as usual for him. He said, "I don't want to go to school. Not a school day." He was adamant. I okayed him for now as I usually do, figuring by morning he would be going with the flow, getting ready for school, following instructions, as Mommy got ready for work.

I stayed up until one a.m., on holiday, watching the news and eating the entire pint of Ben & Jerry's Americone Dream, a gluttonous display I kept secret—not just from Vana, who would be disgusted, but also from Christopher, who would be furious that I deprived him of even a spoonful—tucking the folded empty container deep into the recycling bin.

In the morning I'm pouring my coffee when Christopher says, "Come on, we're wasting time." He has already eaten his cereal. I pour myself a bowl. He watches me eat for a minute. "It's 8:30!" I go upstairs to change into shorts and a T-shirt. Back downstairs I slip into my Birkenstocks as he races into the kitchen, in peak frustration now, laced up in his fluorescent orange cleats. "Can we please play baseball now?"

In the front yard, I vary my pitches, pleased with the hook I'm developing. These plastic balls have circular holes on the entire surface, unlike the classic brand-name Wiffle balls with elongated holes on one side, to promote curving. Michael is playing in the dirt with his trucks, dressed for school, while Mommy finishes getting ready for work. Every few minutes he calls out to me, "Not a school day?" and I do my best to divert his attention from the question and its apparent answer, at least for his brother and me.

"It's Yom Kippur," I try, mistakenly figuring he might drop the subject.

"What's Yom Kippur?"

"It's the Day of Atonement."

"What's the..."

When Vana steps onto the porch, I anticipate the meltdown, just as Michael sees his lunch box in her hand. "Nooo!"

Vana sweetly lies, "Your brother is going to school *later,*" and tries to whisk Michael into the Volvo. Michael is bawling.

I realize I've already made the decision. "It's okay," I say, "he can stay."

Vana looks at me wide-eyed. Puzzled then impressed. "Really?" She goes inside to put the lunch box in the fridge. When she returns, I'm hugging Michael, who is breathing calmly now. I hug Vana. "You're a good daddy," she says.

Michael returns to the dirt, tossing it from the dump truck into the trees. "Look, smoke!"

Christopher and I cancel tennis. We find our cardboard supply in the basement, a storage/moving box, perfect for the foundation; a Philadelphia Brewing Company case/box; and two six-pack containers, Heineken and Corona. Before long Michael comes in and asks, "Watcha doing, guys?" He grabs his bucket of markers. Christopher tells him no, but then, seeing that his pens are harmless, lets him doodle on the roof. I rip duct tape that Christopher uses to create an A-frame roof and reinforce doors and windows he carves out with the scissors.

For lunch we go to our old neighborhood in the city. I drive by our townhouse and explain to Michael that this is where we used to live. Christopher says, "I remember that really nice guy that lived upstairs. Do you remember his name?"

"Larry," I say, disguising the grief I feel for our old neighbor, Larry Brightman, who used to help fix things and give advice on home repairs and improvements that weren't necessary but interesting—hanging the bike on hooks, turning off the water before going away, vacuuming the vents. I've shielded Christopher from the truth about Larry, the fact that he moved to the suburbs, like us, not long before we did; that he'd gotten another cancer diagnosis and didn't think he was up for the treatment again; that he'd been sparring with the old townhouse neighbors about noise and air pollution from the tools and chemicals he used to make commercial signs and God knows what else and that they'd threatened a lawsuit against him; or that one day, not long after he'd moved into his suburban house, he shot himself. I remember his gun, for which he had a license and which he carried when making deliveries in the city, always on his bicycle, never in his SUV with the Vietnam Vet sticker on the back windshield. I remember his broken heart after a recent girlfriend had called it quits. No other woman would ever measure up, he told me. Many times, I wondered if I might hear a shot overhead and then a thump. I believe he probably considered this option, but, being such a nice guy, he didn't want to horrify us, especially Christopher, to whom he dropped balls down from the balcony and whose birthday party he entertained with magic tricks. Later I wondered if he'd bought the house in the suburbs as a suitable place to kill himself, where he could control the environment and not make a fuss or a mess for his downstairs neighbors or traumatize their little boy.

At Vetri Pizza a block away, Michael stands on his chair and dances to Jay-Z rapping about OJ Simpson, his loose fists meeting at the chest and arms stretching out in smooth rhythm. We chow a long, thin pizza brought out on a wooden spatula, then soft vanilla ice cream, before heading to the Rodin Museum, where Michael gazes at *The Thinker* from his stroller, just as Christopher used to do on our neighborhood jaunts. Now Christopher pushes Michael. We circle the Burghers of Calais. "Look at that guy's butt," Michael says. Then, more thoughtfully, "Why do this guy have a key?" I read the plaque that tells the story, refreshing my own memory of the city leaders called on to sacrifice themselves to save the citizens, only to be saved by the queen, who feared bad fortune for her unborn child.

Michael reaches for the figures in one of the *Doors of Hell* and observes, "They're falling," sensing something ominous. Christopher points at the other door and says, "Look, Michael. Boobs."

Inside, Michael runs from sculpture to sculpture, calling, "Look, guys." He is drawn toward the figures kissing. He spots one after another kissing couple. The lady on watch warns me about the boys touching the sculptures. Michael runs for *The Kiss* and literally kisses the marble base of it, like an icon at church. Christopher follows suit. I see the guard's anxious bulging eyes.

I smile and say, "You didn't just see that."

She says, "It's so cute and great that he's so interested. I think we have a future Michelangelo here. But he really can't be touching these, especially the marble."

After a few more minutes of me chasing Michael from one statue to another, we stop in the gift shop, buy colored pencils, and head out—off to the car wash on Spring Garden Street.

"I don't want to be scary," Michael says, recalling the drive-through car wash near our house. I explain that this one we watch through a big window. He walks down the hallway, mesmerized, as the car gets doused with suds.

He falls asleep on the way home.

After dinner Michael runs in circles carrying the plastic bathroom trashcan in his arms like a football. Christopher screams in mock horror for no apparent reason as he works busily on his cardboard house, securing the Corona-and-Heineken-six-pack-container additions with duct tape. Minutes later Michael rushes at the house, meaning business.

Christopher screams, "No!" only this time in real horror as Michael slams his fist into the side of the house, resulting in exactly no damage. Still, Christopher is livid, screaming at Michael to get away, then launching into "You…ffucking man!" at which point I intervene, tell Christopher to go to his room, and hold Michael, who is smiling and shuffling like a boxer, until the coast is clear.

When Christopher climbs the stairs, he hollers, "Michael, I wish you were dead!"

I am shocked, and then after a moment's thought not quite so shocked. I figured sooner or later a kid is going to experiment with hearing this sentiment stated out loud, especially the older sibling to the younger sibling, who robbed him of his parents' undivided attention. I block Michael, who still believes this is all part of the game he imagines we're playing.

I tell him, "You have to leave Christopher alone because he's upset. It's not okay to punch his house."

Michael listens and goes to his room. I tell him to play with his toys and I'll be back shortly to read with him. I go into Christopher's room and sit on the bed, where Christopher has tucked himself under covers. I say, "Sit up and look me in the eyes. If you're big and tough enough to talk like that, then you're big and tough enough to sit up and have a man-to-man conversation. No fingers in the mouth."

He lowers his fingers.

"No wandering eyes."

He looks at me.

"How do you feel?"

He doesn't look happy.

"Not good, right?"

He shakes his head.

I say, "Those kinds of things you can't un-say. For now, Michael is young enough he won't remember or make much of it. But he's getting older. And you don't feel that way. We say things like that just to hurt the other person, because we want to hurt them, but that's going too far. So is using the f-word."

Ffucking man. I'm fascinated with this verbal construction I've heard from both of them. They apparently understand F— as an adjective but don't have (yet) a suitable vulgarity to replace "man"—like asshole or dickhead—so they bite into that F an extra beat, gearing up for the next word, searching for something new and cruel that doesn't come. So, for now it's just "fucking man."

I ask, "Do you think I've ever called my brother that? Or you think my brother ever called me that?"

Christopher shakes his head. (I'm thinking this over myself, pleased to believe that he's right.)

"How about the other thing, that terrible thing, that you shouted from the top of the stairs? Do you think we've ever said *that* to each other?"

He shakes his head.

I remind him that ten minutes earlier it was *he,* Christopher, who was instructing *Michael* how to play a game in which the little brother pretended to be chased by a maniac wielding a plastic trashcan that might as well have been a chainsaw. "*You* decided that the game was over, or that the rules had changed, but Michael didn't know that. He thought it was his turn to play the maniac. Game on. And then you flip a switch."

"I told him *no,*" Christopher says.

"Sure, but earlier he was screaming 'No!' too. That was the game, running and screaming 'No!' and climbing onto the furniture or running into the kitchen to hide behind me, screaming 'Daddy, Daddy!' He was just playing the game *you* taught him."

Christopher hesitates. He takes a deep breath and says, "You never teach him. He gets to do anything, and you never teach him."

"What do you mean?"

"He hit my house, but you didn't tell him that wasn't okay. And I had to go to my room."

I nod. "You're right. That wasn't fair. I was just trying to stop the fighting before it started. But after you went to your room, I told him."

After a long pause, Christopher says, "When I was four and five and six and I was bad, you would use that word, and that's how I know it."

Ffffucking! I can picture myself losing my cool, red-faced and furious. *Now, he's just playing the game you taught him.* "I know, it's terrible. I shouldn't say it. It's never *at* anyone, though, like, 'You're a…' It's just a frustrated expression, like 'Ugh!' But I hope I don't say it too often. I try not to."

"Yeah," he says, "maybe you say it like two times a year."

"Okay, wow, I'll take that. Twice a year."

Thank you, I think. He's being generous. It doesn't escape me that he stopped counting when he was six ("When I was four and five and six…"), implying that I haven't said that word since he turned seven. Then I remember, I really have tried to stop.

"Tell you what," I say, "if you say it only two times a year, I can live with that."

"But you'll still be mad when I say it? Those two times?"

"Let's just both try, okay? And never say that other thing."

"What other thing?"

"About wishing, you know…"

He nods. "Oh. Okay."

LBJ

I tease Dean and Sam with this text:

I forgot to tell you that today in my level 3 class we were reading *The Things They Carried* and there was a reference to LBJ and I asked who's LBJ and one guessed Lebron James. He was serious and no one but me laughed. Then I said LBJ is the president at the time, 1968. Crickets. I said he's the guy who followed JFK. Nada. I said he's the one before Nixon. Tumbleweeds. I say "Lyndon…" I'm shitting myself. "Baines…???" Finally one of them belts out "Johnson!" Hats off to the History department, gentlemen.

JESUS SUSPENDED

At lunch the kid who dressed up as Jesus for Halloween on Tuesday is across the hall in the so-called Marble Room, meeting with his parents and administrators about the suspension he served. Technically, it *was* a suspension, Neil reminds us, since he had been forced to leave school for the rest of the day, deprived of his rightful education. His parents are not happy about how their son has been treated.

Meanwhile, Neil tells us, this morning a Special-Ed kid wiped his own feces all over the bathroom walls and videoed and photographed himself doing it, and was showing students his work when one of them said, "What the fuck is your problem? That's fucking disgusting." That's when the vandal's teacher intervened and discovered what he'd done. She sent him to the principal's office. Freddy sent him back.

I spell out the obvious: "Jesus gets suspended, but *this* kid gets sent back to class."

"He's special ed, is why," Neil says, insinuating that this should *not* be an excuse. "He's in all regular-ed classes—low-level classes but still. He knows it's wrong to wipe his shit all over the bathroom walls. And Kalvin had to clean it up." Kalvin is the veteran janitor. Apparently cleaning up students' literal shit is a privilege that comes with seniority.

"Oh, that's just wrong," Carolyn chimes in.

I make a nasally announcement on my imaginary loudspeaker: "Kalvin Moss, please report to the A-Wing bathroom."

Neil says, "What, you think they'd make the *kid* clean it up? No way. They're shitting themselves right now about whether they came down too hard on him."

Date Night

Tonight, Vana has a business-school fundraising event at the Barnes Museum in our old neighborhood downtown. We've decided to make a date of it since we don't get out much these days. The plan is buffet and cocktails with colleagues in the outdoor courtyard. I pick up both kids on the way home, where I'm eager for the babysitter to arrive after she finishes her day as a teacher at the same pre-school Michael attends. The moment I've got chicken fingers and fries on the table for the boys and the babysitter enters the front door, I race into the city as it starts to rain.

Along the river I hit traffic backed up miles from the Parkway. It's past 6:30 now and the rain is drumming down. I'm afraid our date will be a bust. I'm already strategizing backup plans. McCrossen's, our old neighborhood tavern, is right up the street. By the time I park and find my way to the courtyard, the caterers are packing up bottles behind the makeshift outdoor bar. Umbrellas are open over empty picnic tables, and the buffet table sits ignored behind glass doors in the well-lit room beyond the patio.

Vana appears out of shadows, looking smashing in a dark slim suit and heels. It appears we have this place to ourselves. "It started at five," she says. She checks her watch. Nearly seven now. "Almost everybody's gone." The rain is a light drizzle. "Let me introduce you." She leads me to a table under an overhanging roof where her boss sits with an older man from Florida who is the head of the Association of American Business Schools. We talk sports, Tampa Bay nightlife, a conference I'll be attending there this winter.

"Come get a plate," Vana says. I follow her inside. It's a nice spread, or apparently it had *been* one, but now there's little left. "It went fast," Vana says. "People started leaving when it started to rain."

Outside, I get a bottle of Amstel Light from the bar, and we stand in the misty air.

"Want to go to McCrossen's?" I suggest.

"No. I just want to go home after this."

"Come on. Let's go somewhere. Date night, remember?"

"I'm not saying I want to go home *yet.*" She glances inside. "Wait here."

I sit at a table under a large umbrella, and in seconds Vana returns with a waitress, who sets a small plate before me and displays a tray of appetizers. I take two. "Take more," she says. I do. In minutes she's back with another tray. Vana smiles. Her boss and the man from Florida have gone. Vana and I sit under the large umbrella. She sips her drink. I feast on appetizers. The waitress returns every few minutes with a tray of new offerings.

The rain picks up again, but we're protected. The women clearing the bar offer us another drink before leaving. Then it's just the two of us alone, a curtain of light rain falling inches from our faces.

"Date night." Vana grins.

"We couldn't have planned this better."

We linger over drinks and snacks. The waitress surprises us with two small complimentary umbrellas. "For when you're ready," she says.

The rain keeps falling.

Vana flashes me puckered lips. "Romance, baby."

I take her hand. The rain dances and sings.

Teacher Dive

At the Country Deli, Dean advises Leonard Hughes, our young, optimistic union president, on negotiation strategies and other contract-related matters. Salaries. Healthcare. The proposed block scheduling versus the current eight-period day. Online course options and the potential decrease in demand for traditional classroom teachers. The whole unpredictable future of public education. The whole unpredictable future of *everything*.

I don't say much. I've had enough. Enough contract talk. Enough in-service. I'm ready to teach. In my mind I'm already in Bethany Beach, where I'm headed for the long Labor Day weekend after work today, before the students arrive on Tuesday.

Back at Benfield after lunch, I pull up to the curb instead of parking in the usual spot.

Dean grins. "You're dropping us off?"

I nod. "I gotta go. I'm ready for Tuesday. I've been ready for Tuesday since Tuesday."

Leonard is sitting in the back, between two kid safety seats. "It's 12:30. You're really leaving now?"

"I can't go back in there and pretend to have work to do. Enough pretending. I have to go."

"I'm impressed," Dean says. "Enjoy."

Leonard, in a predicament as union president and witness to my flagrant breach of contract, says, "I don't see anything."

And I am off. There is no traffic. I listen to the news on satellite radio. The latest on Hurricane Harvey. On Trump. The FBI got their hands on a letter he drafted but never sent to Comey. They'll need to prove intent to prove obstruction of justice. I stop and buy grapes and bananas and use the bathroom. I call Vana at 2:45, and she asks, "Are you driving? Did you leave a little early?" I say I'm already minutes from Bethany. She sighs, sharing in my relief.

Not long after three o'clock I'm on the beach in my blue chair with *The Cubs Way* in my hands. I read with the sound of the waves behind me. The book is about how the Cubs went from worst to best, seemingly overnight. Of course, there were many moving parts, aligning themselves for years, before they all converged. I read about the Zen of manager Joe Madden, and I feel inspired. I plan to put his quote on a poster in my room, "Never allow the pressure to exceed the pleasure," along with quotes by Thich Nhat Hanh, Joseph Campbell, Philip Roth...

When Ned Robbins finally returns my call about my not-exactly-imminent retirement, I don't tell him I'm sitting on the beach. I cup the phone in my hands to mute the wind. Ned confirms Dominica's unfortunate theory, that the new magic numbers for retirement-without-penalty are 35 years of teaching and 60 years of age. Not 30 and 55, as I'd been banking on. The future seems somehow stunted by this extension. Can I do this for *thirteen* more years? Eight seemed challenging enough.

I tell myself not to get too far ahead of things. To be *present.* I am *here,* on the beach, reading about a team of young talent, led by a veteran manager who understood, at age sixty, that success would be the result of decades of learning, and of a deep respect for all the influences that have made him the man he is. His principles come first. Character. Connection with his players. Faith in the mission.

VANA IN CHINA

Vana calls from Beijing, crying. I wonder where the rest of her cohort is. It's 6:30 a.m. Philadelphia-time. She's on speaker phone.

"I don't like it here."

"Okay," I say. "One day at a time."

"It's better when I'm with friends, I guess."

"That's good."

"I like Karen. And Hakeem. They're going for a walk now. I'll text you later. I need sleep."

She sounds delirious.

After I hang up, Michael cries "Mommy" for the next thirty minutes. He says his belly hurts. He tries to poop. He bawls, "I want to wear my Phillies shirt." He's howling now.

I say, "Yesterday's white one is filthy. It's in the washing machine. The gray one is clean."

"Not the gray! Gray shorts!"

"Huh?"

"Hugs." He holds his arms out. "I want the white one."

Talk about delirious.

I pick him up and hold him like a baby.

We've got thirty minutes to get dressed, eat breakfast, and fly off together in the Volvo—Christopher to Parker's house, where he'll catch the bus with his friend in an hour; Michael to day care, where he'll chatter with the teacher in the early-arrivals room; and I to Benfield, just in time for my first class.

Michael puts his head on my shoulder. We look out the window at gray skies.

"I want the white shirt," he says.

"I know, I know." Sure, we can pretend this craziness is about a baseball shirt. *I miss Mommy, too.* "You want baseball cards?"

He nods.

Out of nowhere, Christopher appears. "Can I have baseball cards, too?"

They open their packs. Michael sees that Christopher got a Phillie. It doesn't matter who it is.

"I didn't get any Phillies! He got all the Phillies. I don't have many Phillies!"

I look at Christopher. He knows the look: *Help? Please?*

Christopher hands him the Phillies card. "You want to pick a card to trade?"

Michael plucks the top card from his own pile and hands it over. He says, "Thank you."

I hug Christopher and tell him what a good guy he is. Great big bro. He dances off to his bedroom to get dressed for school.

In the kitchen Michael is wearing orange camper shorts and two T-shirts—his trademark layered look, even in the summer heat. He backs up into the mudroom, aiming himself at me like a fullback. This means big hug coming. He blasts forward and leaps. We've got this routine down. He's airborne. Beaming. Legs land spread around my hips. I lift him up for the big hug. Big kiss.

"Who's gonna have a great *day todayyy?"* I sing.

"Me."

"Good boy. Time for Cheerios."

I get three bowls. Michael, three spoons. Christopher zips up his backpack, gets the milk.

We got this.

Christopher's First Day of School

Christopher goes off to second grade today. Vana sends me a picture of Christopher and Michael on the sidewalk, beaming arm in arm. Another, of Christopher next to his buddy Parker in their seat on the bus. Vana must have climbed in and stood next to the bus driver to get the shot. She must have been carrying Michael in her left arm, which is carved like a bodybuilder's thanks to moments like this. I can picture the dip of her hip, Michael straddling a thigh, her right arm outstretched with phone aimed at the pair of second graders mirroring her big smile.

Last year, in first grade, Christopher reported that Parker, the boy who lives up the street, "doesn't like me." He said there were boys who didn't let him sit with them. I was skeptical. I theorized that this was the twisted excuse he offered when Mommy asked why it appeared he was sitting alone on the bus every day as she waved to him from the sidewalk and he waved solemnly back. Now, he and Parker are two peas in a pod. They're in the same class this year. They played on the same Little League baseball team. They took tennis lessons together in August. They're on the same soccer team this fall. Christopher reported to me recently that they've discussed plans to live together after high school. Christopher has already determined what cars they'll drive. Christopher will drive a Porsche, Parker a Ford.

I'm reminded of the Antonya Nelson short story I teach in AP Modern Lit, about a woman whose twelve-year-old son, Cole, devises a plan to buy a ranch with his next-door neighbor, the titular "Dick," before Cole's family moves from their house in California to higher ground in Colorado. After Dick runs away, having turned morose and isolated, Cole theorizes that Dick ran away because he didn't want to turn twelve. This nonsensical insight triggers the final epiphany in Anne, the protagonist, who realizes she can't think of how to convince her son, much less herself, that life is worth living, before or after one's innocence is lost.

Last night, Christopher asked me if I'd be picking him up from the after-school program, where last year he played basketball in the gym for an hour or two until I showed up on my way home from work. He asked if I remember where to pick him up. I said yes. He asked, "What if you forget?" and "Do you want me to draw you a map?" He drew me a map with a line stretching from a house to a school, and then, in a separate dimension, a figure descending steps into a basement, where the cafeteria and gym were clearly marked. I told him this would help, for sure. I set it on the passenger seat of my car. I would carry it with me inside so that he could see, when I arrived, how crucial his guidance was.

Today at school I miss Christopher and Michael more than usual. I feel so closely connected to them after a summer with so much time together. Yesterday, I trimmed four trees whose cut branches covered most of the walkway. Michael played trucks while I clipped and branches fell. Christopher tossed a ball into the air, leaping to catch it and rolling into the space where I was working. When it was time to fill the trashcan—four bags, as it turned out—Michael used his little rake. We sang as we worked. I sang randomly, "I'm going to kiss that belly all night long. I'm going to love that boy all my life long." Michael sang along. "I'm gonna kiss that belly..." When I went to the garage for another bag, he and Christopher followed.

Vana and her mother watched from the lawn chairs. "They're like puppies," they said to me, "how they follow you around."

The boys smiled, as did I, grateful that Mommy's announcement did not inspire in either of them some Oedipal impulse to peel off, to prove her wrong. Instead, they gathered closer to me.

Later, Christopher and I tossed his new oversized Eagles football back and forth in the front yard. He ran patterns. Repeatedly the enormous ball sailed into his arms and thumped off his chest and onto the grass. Unfazed, he sprinted back to the sidewalk, which was the line of scrimmage, and sprinted again toward the tree-lined end zone at the edge of the yard. Later he begged me to play one-on-one, swearing that we used to play some version where each of us passed the ball to ourselves, taking turns advancing up and down the field, which is the narrow strip of grass at the side of the house. I took out the trash and cleaned up—it was the last day of summer, and tasks kept presenting themselves to me—as Christopher followed and said, "When you're done with that, *then* can we play?"

I assured him we never played a version of football in which I passed the ball to myself. I didn't like myself sounding like an old dad making excuses. He said we could play rock, paper, scissors, and, if *he* won, we had to play *his* version and, if *I* won, *I* could pick the game. He won. Twice. Later, when I laughed and repeated that I was not going to play "pass-to-myself football," he screamed at me that I'd promised and now I was not being fair. I met him on the porch where, in protest, he threw the deck of UNO cards I'd brought from the kitchen. I started to pick them up. I said, "Is this fair that I pick these up? If you don't help me pick these up, then I won't play football." Without hesitation, he quietly got to his knees, picked up twenty or so cards, and handed them to me. I set the pile on the wicker table and walked to the yard. He threw himself a pass, over my head, zipped past me, and caught the ball for the game's first touchdown. Back and forth we went, raising our arms over our heads to make field-goal posts for the kicks we aimed at each other from the opposite side of the yard.

We managed to play without injury or interruption before Vana and her mother were finished cooking burgers and fries in the kitchen, where Michael, whipped from all the activity and no nap, watched Jack Jack play trucks in the YouTube videos he had become addicted to this summer. After dinner I gave Michael a bath. He was covered in dirt from playing in the mud earlier. I sudsed him up, behind and in the ears. Michael rinsed his own hair with the plastic pitcher, his little arms raising the pot above his large head. Next came Christopher. I lathered the washcloth, and he washed himself. I washed his hair. He asked if he could watch the Rangers-Blue Jays game on TV while I put Michael to bed. He found the Phillies, the afternoon game being rebroadcast. He asked why it was sunny in South Philadelphia when it was dark here in Bala Cynwyd. We went outside to look for the moon. I was procrastinating. I didn't want summer to end. Christopher recalled our moonwalks in the city, "back when I was two and three," he said. Tonight, the full moon, which later I would discover behind the tall trees, was hiding. "What do you mean, the moon must be low tonight?" he asked.

Michael and I read *Madeline at the White House* and *Goodnight, Goodnight, Construction Site.* When I went to leave his bedroom, he said, "I want you to keep me company." I paused at the door. He cried, "I had a fun day." I was puzzled by the seeming contradiction until I realized, as he repeated this, that he was nostalgic for the day and, though he didn't know it, nostalgic for the summer, which was over. "I want to have a fun day," he lamented, trying to capture the nuance of the emotion he believed he was failing to convey to me. "I want to stay here infinity days," he babbled, stunning me. Where had he learned the word infinity? Let alone the concept that at some point the numbers must run out, and time with it. My heart swelled with love for him. I said, "Me too," and lay down beside him. When he was asleep, I sneaked out, only to hear him cry out again when I closed the door. I re-entered. Lay down again. This time I waited for the deep sigh that marks deep sleep, and in no hurry, I slipped out.

We're Organizing a Bus

Emily, a red-haired girl with flushed face to match, says she woke up at 12:30 last night and stayed awake in bed until four, then just took a shower and got ready for school.

"Why?" I slug my coffee, oblivious.

The instant she shoots me a look, I know the answer.

She says, "Because of the shooting?"

I nod.

"I can't sleep," she says.

I wait to see if others will chime in or if she'll elaborate. A sudden blur of murmurs. No one takes the lead. I don't ask them to take turns speaking. I want to see where this goes without my steering. I pick up word of student walkouts being planned—two scheduled in the next two weeks. The first, they say, will be seventeen minutes long, one minute for each student killed at Marjory Stoneman Douglas High School in Parkland, Florida. Then a march in DC, along with simultaneous marches in other cities, including Philly, which many of them plan to attend.

Though I'm tuned into the news, I knew nothing of these behind-the-scenes developments. I'm impressed that my students are hip to such a movement springing up—and participating in it.

"I'm going to DC," says Emily. "We're organizing a bus."

I smile and refrain from announcing that I'm proud of them or that I'm sorry for these burdens they bear, because I don't want the last word. They've got the floor, and it's theirs to keep—for now and for the weeks and months and years ahead.

Others chime in that they'll be on that bus.

Despite being sleep-deprived, Emily is wide awake now, as I am.

Michael Wants a Snow Day

I wake up to the pleasant sounds of Michael singing, "Who lives in a pineapple under the sea? SpongeBob SquarePants, SpongeBob SquarePants."

We are all well rested, thanks to a two-hour delay due to light snow.

"No school?" Michael asks.

"Yes, school," I say.

We get dressed and take our time eating cereal together in the kitchen. Snow covers the leaves of the holly tree outside the window.

"I don't want to go to school today," Michael says. "I want to build a snowman. Can we?"

"We have to go to school," I say. "Plus, there's not enough snow to build a snowman."

"Please," he says. "A small one?"

At school, I'm walking through the main office, a shortcut to my classroom, when a call comes from a father saying his daughter has his permission to be excused early today. I can hear the forceful voice at the other end of the line. I lock eyes with the secretary who has taken the call. She seems to share my thought: we just got here. Freddy takes the phone from the secretary and says, "Knock it off, Darien." The caller ID displays the caller's phone number. The secretary and I laugh. Darien graduated last year. His girlfriend is a senior this year. Freddy hangs up, shakes his head, and mirrors our smiles.

LOCKDOWN

An email from Christopher's teacher:

Just wanted to let you know about one thing that came up today –

We had a lockdown/security drill this afternoon. Christopher and the student sitting next to him were being a little silly during the directions beforehand. During the actual drill, he said he got scared and was covering his head. Two students near him were apparently whispering a scary story to each other, and Christopher got upset. He hit them each in the chest or stomach. After we talked about alternatives to using hands, Christopher apologized to both students (and they did to him as well). Just wanted to keep you in the loop.

Thanks for your support,

Mrs. D.

Snowy Day

In bed, Michael and I are reading *Snowy Day.* The boy in the book is relieved when it turns out he only dreamed that the snow had melted, before “he headed back out into the big big snow.” Today, Michael improvises an extended ending in which the boy and his friend continue their trek through the snow, just as Michael, Christopher, and I did after their recent dentist appointments in the city, “and they went to the restaurant—” He pauses to ask, “What's the name of the restaurant we *go*ed to after the dentist? McCrossen's!” He revises, “And they went to McCrossen's and ate French fries and chicken wings...” He looks at me for something more.

“And hamburgers.”

“And hamburgers,” he happily adds, though it's something else he's reaching for. After a moment he's got it: *“all* afternoon.” This final phrase restores to our now-indoor ending a sense of the infinite.

Hours later I wake to Michael's whimpering. I'm alone in the king-size bed. Vana, nursing a cold, has at some point in the night left me alone with my snoring. I hear her sleeping peacefully behind the closed door of the guest room. I enter Michael's room.

“I'm scary,” he says.

“Why?”

“There's a monster under somebody's bed.”

“Oh.”

He stands up and latches onto me like a starfish. I carry him to my bed. Lying down, he keeps his body pressed against mine, as we sink back into a deep, deep sleep.

Ryan Returns

I blink, and it's May. I see Ryan Henry in the hallway, on his way back to class from the bathroom. I'm stunned. He's back. I was not expecting to see him again this year. Six months have passed since the last time he stayed after school to work in my classroom, the Wednesday before Thanksgiving. He has grown, filled out. He's muscular in a way that seems suited to his frame, in a way that makes me realize how the old body was insufficient in ways perhaps only his parents really understood. He lowers his head, as if to hide the boyish face that remains, under blond curls. There's the hint of a hardened scowl, which I expect to vanish when I say, "Ryan!" but when he looks up, his expression hardly changes. I say, "I was so excited about the story you shared with me back in the fall, and then suddenly you were gone for so long. I want to talk to you about it. I have notes for you and so many thoughts."

"Okay," he says. I'm waiting for more. The scowl is gone, but the impassive non-expression that lingers seems somehow more disconcerting. I can't help thinking of McMurphy in *Cuckoo's Nest,* post-lobotomy, hoping Ryan hasn't endured the pharmaceutical equivalent of such a procedure, despite his reentry into society and the beefed-up physique. I've stopped cold in the hallway, but he has shuffled on, maintaining what isn't exactly eye contact. "I have to go take a test," he says, aiming his thumb in the direction of the silent classrooms, from which I, too, just came, already having forgotten about the normal school-day business at hand.

"Oh, I'm sorry," I say.

"I'll stop by."

"Okay."

A moment later I'm alone, with no memory of what I was doing or where I was heading before seeing Ryan.

For a time, I make no move, consumed by the feeling that I've failed him. If only I'd tracked him down to talk about his story before things got so dire that his parents had to send him away to some institution in the Midwest. Maybe I could have prevented their need to resort to such dramatic measures. The short story he'd shared with me was more than a poetic revelation of his genius and his sadness and his madness. It was a volcanic manifesto, his signal, *to me,* I believed. And I waited casually for him to come back to see me, instead of snagging him urgently in the hallway and saying, "Ryan, I've read your story, and it's brilliant, and we need to talk about it *now,"* as if in this discourse there would have been healing and clarity and meaning and purpose and everything he needed to be made whole and healthy again.

I take a deep breath and, with no direction in mind, step into the space outside the one I've been occupying—a kind of progress, I tell myself—before returning to my classroom.

Town Hearing

At lunch we recap the CNN town hearing last night, where Senator Marco Rubio was faced down by Parkland survivors, who didn't believe his claims that his politics were not influenced by the NRA's campaign donations.

The NRA President has been warning all to be afraid of the socialists who want to take your guns away.

At a press conference, Trump accidentally exposed five talking points on a note card in full view. "I hear you" was number-five. Dean says it was written in a woman's handwriting—a woman whose job it is to remind the president to act sensitive. We wonder if he improvised the part about arming teachers. The local superintendents have already publicly expressed their disapproval of the idea, pointing out that teachers didn't sign up for this responsibility. We can't pretend we're not relieved to learn of our superintendent's reasonable view on the matter.

The students have gotten wind of Freddy's plan to oversee the walkout, starting with official signup sheets to see who's actually interested in participating.

Eighth period, the kids are both venting and cracking up, saying, "Doesn't this defeat the purpose? The purpose is to rebel. Protest. *Walk out.*"

I joke, "Don't forget your permission slips. Maybe ask your parents if they'd be willing to chaperone."

We dive back into *The Catcher in the Rye.* Our robust discussion seems halted for a moment when one student theorizes that Holden is gay. Others snicker, assuming this interpretation will be shot down by the teacher, who instead pushes them to explore the possibility. I want them to see just how far the kid will go to cure his loneliness. "All that stuff about 'flits' at the Wicker Bar..." The group tracks Holden's desperation since his arrival in New York, from stalling in the phone booth, to calling the stripper, to chatting up the cab drivers, to hiring a prostitute, to drunk-dialing Sally Hayes, to probing Carl Luce about his sex life, to talking in the bathroom with the wavy-haired guy who tells him to go home, bub, and how the hell old are you anyway?

"He thinks it's sex he wants," another student says, "but it's not. He begs Luce to stay for another drink."

"He says maybe even Luce is a flit."

Another says, "I think he just wants a connection, with *anyone.* It doesn't even matter anymore with who."

TWENTY QUESTIONS

After dinner I try to teach Christopher how to play Twenty Questions. On his first attempt he gets frustrated and wants to know the answer after asking only five questions. After ten questions I tell him to keep asking, and eventually he arrives at the answer, which is Odubel Herrera, the Phillies' centerfielder. We decide on a rule that you get twenty questions *plus* five guesses.

"Okay, ready?" he asks.

"Ready," I say. "Go."

He fires away. "Joel Embiid? No, wait—Nick Williams."

"Don't just guess names. Start with big, general questions. Like, is it a person? Is it an athlete? Or, is it an object?"

He nods. Got it. "Is it silver?"

I scratch my head. "How about a question like, Is it bigger than a bread box? Smaller than a tree?"

He winces. "A *bread* box? What's a *bread* box?"

"Or, a car," I say. "Whatever. Go ahead. Ask."

At bedtime, Christopher has a math-inspired breakdown. An hour earlier Vana had tried to calm him down after what sounded like a pretty rough homework session. Now she's struggling to get him to go to sleep.

Meanwhile, I get Michael to bed without a hitch after letting him play toys for five more minutes while I lie there fiddling with my phone.

When I slip out of Michael's room, I find Vana standing over Christopher's bed.

Christopher is crying again—unless he never stopped. "I like math, but I'm not good enough. I'm worried."

I say, "I'll take it from here."

Vana leaves and I sit down on the bed. Immediately Christopher and I are in hugging-crabs position, his legs around my waist. He lets it all out. "I'm not good. I'm afraid I'm not going to get into a good college."

Jesus. Another example of the downside of his precociousness. I tell him, "It's okay. That's crazy. Don't compare yourself to other kids."

"Mommy will be disappointed."

"Only if you give up," I say.

"She wants me to go to Princeton."

I say, "Just try your best. I'll email your teacher."

He likes this idea.

"Can I go to bed now?" he asks.

"Absolutely." I tuck him in and leave the room.

Minutes later he calls me back in. I brace myself for whatever form the manifestation of today's anxieties has taken.

He says, "I can't dream of anything."

I'm relieved. This complaint beats 'I can't get these scary images out of my head.'

He says, "It's just black."

I say, "Some people count sheep. The cow jumping over the moon."

He twists his face. "Count *sheep?* What *cow* jumping—?"

I say, "Think of baseball. Hitting, then running the bases."

"Okay," he says.

"Picture things you love. Seventy degrees, Saturday. You and me out there on the field..."

For how much longer, I wonder, will he welcome my dreams as his own?

WALKOUT

Second period, Logan seems upset. She's the leader of the class and chief organizer of the walkout scheduled for today. Freddy interrupts class with a follow-up to the morning announcement, clarifying where and when participating students will be directed to congregate outside and where the nonparticipants will be directed to congregate inside. Logan is clearly irked by Freddy's excessive involvement in the day's plans. She exits class early for a previously scheduled meeting, sullen, steaming.

The rest of us talk Robert Frost—"Miles to go before I sleep"—the mix of romantic and modern qualities in the work: the formal rhyme and meter but the natural speaking voice, the lovely natural settings but the loneliness lurking...

I admit I'm distracted—literally, I admit this, to the class—wondering if Logan is okay, if maybe I'm missing something. Is she just annoyed at Freddy? Sad about the events that have given purpose to today's demonstration? Anxious about such a terrifying event, from which, so far, we've been spared?

The kids explain that the student body has developed divisions and cliques over this event. A faction is protesting the protest, planning to shout down the protestors.

"Are they *pro*-violence?" I ask. "Pro-*murder?*"

"No," they say, it's just that they don't think that a walkout is a solution to the problem of loners and outcasts turning homicidal.

One says, "They think that students should just be nice to each other."

Another hisses, "Yeah, like we should just walk up to random people and try to be their friends."

I nod. "So, the protestors who protested the protest today just want everyone to be nice to each other?"

We all snicker at the blur of contradictions.

"Maybe there's some common ground here?" I offer.

Next period, the Walkout happens. Seventeen minutes. In memory of the seventeen killed at Marjory Stoneman Douglas High School in Parkland, Florida. I stay inside, in the cafeteria, and grade papers, while those who've chosen not to demonstrate congregate at the tables. Assistant Principal Serenity Davis barks at them to be silent. The kids grumble, feeling punished for not participating. Serenity walks by me and grins. "Sorry to be a bitch," she says, "but I just need to get them settled." After she passes, one nearby girl says, "I don't appreciate you talking to me that way," her volume perfectly calibrated so that Serenity Davis does not hear the complaint, or so that she can pretend not to hear, which is what she does. Serenity keeps walking. I turn to see the girl sitting down in a huff, satisfied to get the last word.

Later, in Creative Writing class, another girl announces, "I'm going to tell my dad that she yelled at us and we didn't even do anything."

I risk asking, "Is it possible she was just trying to get everyone quiet?"

My classroom goes silent. One boy appears dejected—by me?—as if I've just joined the ever-growing coalition of adult assholes. He lays his head down on his desk.

I clear my throat and then proceed with my presentation of the next writing assignment, which is to create sympathy, or, (new concept) *empathy,* for an otherwise unlikeable character, or, rather, a character whose behavior we don't condone but nonetheless *under-*

stand. First, they must find a real-life news story online featuring an unsympathetic character who, for example, robs a convenience store or shoots a cop. Then they must fictionalize the character in a compelling opening scene that takes place prior to that crime and builds to a hook, leaving the reader in suspense, making us wonder (with deep understanding of the character's personal plight) if, for example, she is actually going to steal that money, or if he is actually going to pull that trigger.

It occurs to me that the top story that will come up on their news searches for such unsympathetic characters will be that of Nikolas Cruz, heartbroken ex-boyfriend and now infamous wielder of the AR-15.

McDREAMY

A handsome kid I don't know comes into my classroom and asks if I'd be willing to take part in the sophomore skit at the pep rally Friday. Another two of his classmates follow him in. I have no idea why these sophomores I've never seen before would be asking me to participate. The answer is obviously no, I do not want to be in the sophomore skit. I do not want to be in any skit. The handsome kid asks, "You know the show *Grey's Anatomy?*"

I nod. "Sure." I'm thinking, *I watched that show before you were born. But not since.* Thanks to binge-watching on Netflix, these kids know shows like *Friends* and *The Office* better than their original TV audiences did more than a decade ago.

"Well, there's a character that sort of looks like you," the kid says.

"Who?" I ask. Twenty years ago, I was a shoo-in for McDreamy. But now? I brace myself for some grandpa character I've never heard of.

"Patrick Dempsey," the kid says.

I recognize the name. Wait a second. "McDreamy?"

"Yeah!" He's impressed I know.

I hesitate. By now several more of his classmates have arrived, and soon I'm surrounded by ten or twelve kids. They've all come from a Class Council meeting, they explain. One of them I taught last year as a freshman. I ask her, "Did you put them up to this?"

She's grinning, as are the rest of them, waiting for the answer they can see coming.

"Is it a speaking role?" I ask.

"Just a line, at most," says the handsome kid.

At this point we all know where this is heading, but I'm enjoying the feigned suspense.

"Fine, I'll do it," I say.

"Yay! Yeah!" they cheer. "Thank you!"

I don't tell them that I owe it to them. For the shot in the arm. To be seen as the cool young guy in the cast. The leading man. Flattery will get you far in life, I'm tempted to say, but they already know that.

They say they'll have my costume ready on Thursday for the rehearsal.

When they're gone, I google Patrick Dempsey and discover that he's as old as I am. The boost to my morale is only slightly diminished. The likeness isn't too far off, actually—the sunken eye sockets, crow's feet, peppery five-o'clock shadow, grooved forehead. This whole time I've been picturing him as the young heartthrob I remember from the last time I caught *Grey's Anatomy.* I had no idea the show was still running. The actors have aged, as I have. But McDreamy is still McDreamy.

COCO

Friday night and Christopher, Michael, and I can't wait to get going to Kids Movie Night at the Club across the street to watch *Coco,* this year's Oscar winner for best animated film. Dinner and popcorn will be served. Mommy is at Penn until tomorrow, so tonight it's just the boys.

We're killing time in the kitchen. Michael flips his Power Ranger mask upside down and pretends to be Darth Vader. He's huffing in tongues behind the solid plastic where the forehead should be. He dons a blue nylon cape, whips out the red "life saver," and asks, "Is Darth Vader a bad guy?" I nod. "How he dooz this? Like this?" He whips the light saber until, on the third try, the narrow red cones dart out to form a plastic laser. He whacks at a basketball on the kitchen floor. I've been talking to Christopher about Bucknell making the NCAA tournament—first-round game tonight—my alma mater on the brink of March Madness. Five minutes later Michael is dribbling the ball, wearing the Buccaneers cap I brought home recently from Tampa. "I'm rooting for the Buck-a-nells," he announces, confusing his loyalties.

It's my dad's birthday. He's eighty-two today. We call him on speaker phone, just as he never fails to call each of us, to sing, "Happy birthday to you..."

At the Club we fill our paper plates with hotdogs, French fries, and chicken fingers and find our spot on the floor in the banquet room. After toweling up a spilled pink lemonade, we settle in, eyes on the giant projector screen, as a musically gifted Mexican boy dares to defy his elders, only to find himself trapped in the Land of the Dead, where corpses and skeletons of his deceased relatives teach him lessons on loyalty and the value of family. Christopher seems for the most part untroubled by this morbid underworld, though I've got my eye on him while Michael takes great delight in the guitar-playing dead guys. But then, with about a half-hour left in the movie, Christopher buries his head in the pillow he brought from home.

"You want to leave?" I ask him.

He shakes his head no, then a few seconds later nods yes.

I wonder what tipped him over the edge. He won't talk, but he doesn't hesitate when I offer him my bed to sleep in tonight.

Michael says he wants to sleep with us too. I tuck them in on opposite sides of the king. Downstairs I watch Bucknell give the number-one seed a good run for their money. Then I slip into bed between the boys.

Christopher wakes up once or twice in the night, but when he sees me there next to him, he seems to get his bearings and goes back to sleep.

No night terrors, thank God, despite the last leg of the movie that sent us packing, where the kid discovers the truth about his great-great-grandfather, the boy's idol, a kind of Mexican Elvis, who poisoned his music partner to keep secret the fact that he was not the true author of the songs he sang to great fame and fortune. Pixar has worked miracles in the past, but I couldn't imagine how this morbid trip was going to end happily—and I would never find out.

The next day, Vana seems to detect that Christopher is not in the best of spirits. She invites him to accompany her on a "road trip" to pick up her coat at the cleaners, and then who knows what else—which seems like code for doing fun stuff.

Michael and I keep tossing the football on the front lawn.

"Can we go to Target?" he asks. He wants to go on a road trip, too.

In the street Vana hits the brakes.

I call out, "Everything all right?"

Apparently, Christopher is already crying in the back seat of the Volvo.

Vana says, "I really wish you wouldn't have taken him to that movie last night."

After they're gone, I reconsider my decision to take the boys to see a movie that had been specifically selected for an audience of children. The irony is that I actually hadn't trusted the praise of the Academy of Motion Pictures alone. I'd conducted additional research, alert to Christopher's sensitivities—and to the blame I might take for ignoring them. I asked my students about the movie. Not one flinched, despite the spooky subject matter. Good movie, was the simple consensus. Sure, there were ghosts. I asked the mother of Christopher's best friend. She had to think for a second why I might be concerned about *Coco* in the first place. Weeks ago, she'd taken Parker and his two little sisters to see it in the theater. In the Club's banquet room we sat next to our neighbors, whose kids are five and three. The room was filled with children ranging from babies in their mothers' arms to fourteen.

By complete coincidence, on our respective road trips, Michael and I run into Vana and Christopher at the nearby Starbucks. Michael is carrying the small box of Batman Legos I just bought him at Target.

I ask Christopher if he's still sad because of *Coco* last night. He looks at me with screwy eyes that say, "No, you moron, I'm just pretending to be sad because I'm about to flip a switch when I find out you bought Michael Legos and got me *nada*."

Once again I'm second-guessing myself, reconsidering my decision, just minutes ago, *not* to buy something for Christopher. It had been a *conscious choice,* not an oversight, on my part. Of course, by now I know that gifts, especially of the random sort like this, must be evenly, if not identically, distributed. Michael's was a seven-dollar minor expense. I reasoned that, out for a few hours on a road trip with Mommy pressing him to excavate the roots of his sorrow, Christopher would be the one returning with enviable gifts. I meant only to guard against that inevitable imbalance of riches.

Christopher lifts his sad little finger to Michael's Legos. "Did you...?" is all he says to me.

"You'll have to wait and see when we get home," I say.

His eyes brighten. Surprise.

In the car I'm slugging my coffee and gassing it back to Target. I tell Michael he gets to pick which set for Christopher. Michael is delighted with this plan.

When we get home, Christopher is shooting baskets at the Fisher-Price hoop he's outgrown.

Michael climbs the small hill to the porch. Clutched in his hands behind his back is the large box he selected for his brother. Michael beams. He could not be happier. "Look, Christopher!" Christopher smiles as Michael unveils the Ninjago set that puts his own seven-dollar job to shame.

"Aww, yeah," Christopher lets out. He takes the big box into his hands. "Yay. Awesome." He seems to be tempering his delight. He doubtless notices the incongruity as Michael retrieves from my hand the little Target bag containing his box.

Vana holds the door for us.

She grins as I enter. "Did you go *back?*"

I say, "Of course."

DEATH THREAT

On the first day back after Spring Break, two cop cars are parked at the curb outside the main entrance from the staff and student parking lots.

Last night at ten o'clock, on Easter Sunday, April 1, Dr. Haddock, the superintendent, sent out a recorded phone message to all district families and staff to announce that a student had posted on Snapchat threatening language addressed to all Benfield students. Dr. Haddock assured everyone that a thorough investigation was under way.

This cautionary message has proved effective. Not a single car sits in the senior parking lot.

In the mailroom Neil fills me in. He says that this is all an overreaction. That this could all be some kind of April Fool's prank. The accused, an eleventh-grade Vo-Tech student named Matthew, routinely posts lyrics from obscure death-metal bands. This one read "Kill u all" or some such thing. It's possible that a different kid created a fake Snapchat to frame Matthew, who, Neil says, used to be Public Enemy Number One back in middle school.

Third period, my students—the ten out of twenty-two in attendance today—report that the police were interviewing Matthew's friends, who say he posts evil stuff like that all the time, as if this should give the rest of us comfort. It turns out that Matthew got expelled from Benfield Middle School after being charged with having created a Kill List. He transferred to a nearby Catholic school before returning to the high school last year.

Later, at lunch, Neil explains that, by law, a kid cannot be expelled from a school for more than one year. He recalls the story of another current Benfield student who two years ago broke into a woman's house, beat her, wrapped her in plastic, and told her she was going to meet Jesus. He stole her car, went on a joyride, and got picked up in a Delaware beach town. He posted all of this on Snapchat. The woman survived. He went to juvey, where he bragged about his escapades.

I'm speechless, wondering how it's possible that someone with such a rap sheet could be walking these hallways—and that some of us, or at least I, don't know exactly who he is. But I suppose it's best, for the kid and everyone else, that he's not marked as a deadly threat.

"No conscience," Neil says.

Home again, the kid destroyed the family's refrigerator and electronics. Recently he fell off a bike and injured his arm. He didn't feel any pain, but his mom took him to the ER. He had a double break.

"What's concerning," Neil says, is that other students talk fondly of him. "He's charming. Classic psychopath."

When the bell rings, I hesitate before entering the hallway, kids streaming in both directions, opposing currents blending benignly.

McSTEAMY

After the pep rally on Friday, I'm hoofing it back to my classroom, still in my blue surgical scrubs, eager to beat the kids rushing to catch their buses. A short girl in black-framed glasses catches up to me and asks if I watch *Grey's Anatomy*.

"I used to," I say.

"I love that show." It's hard to read her expression behind the thick lenses. It's clear she's not peeling off to catch her bus just yet.

I nod politely. "I liked it, too."

"Don't take this the wrong way..." She waits for me to signal that it's okay for her to proceed.

My blank stare is apparently signal enough for her.

"McDreamy or McSteamy?"

I hesitate. I'd forgotten about McSteamy. I wonder how answering this question might be interpreted as condoning something I may not be grasping at the moment.

I throw caution to the wind. "They tell me McDreamy."

She shakes her head. "No. Definitely McSteamy." She gives me the once-over and smiles before departing for the bus.

My fifteen minutes are over.

BUTT-CHIN

Before I start the car, Christopher says, "Can I tell you what just happened?"

I say, "Of course."

He says, "Did you hear?"

I shake my head no.

"That one boy said, 'Bye, butt-chin.'" Before I can ask, he explains that earlier a fifth grader said his cleft chin looks like a butt.

I squeeze my chin and say, "Look, my hairy butt."

He laughs and then remembers he's upset.

He says, "Do you know why else I'm sad?"

It's time to go pick up Michael. I start the car. Christopher locks eyes with me in the rearview mirror. He says he's sad because it sounded like Mommy was mad at him last night—and Daddy too?—for coming into our bed again after a bad dream. I say no one is mad.

"Mommy said, 'This can't keep happening. We can't keep doing this.'"

I say, "I think I know the solution. You need to talk about it. Your dreams."

"It's not a dream," he says. "It's a movie I saw."

"*Coco?*"

"No, a different one. In school. *Mr. Peabody and Sherman.*"

I bite a smile. "And you keep thinking about it?"

He nods. "Mommy doesn't like to talk about..." He hesitates. "D-I-E and D-E-A-D. She skips the words in the books we read, like in *Madeline.*"

It's true. In Vana's versions, death is always averted. When Mommy's within earshot, Christopher dodges the d-word more readily than he dodges the f-word.

Spring has arrived, or so it seems. The windows are down. Christopher leans his face into the wind.

"It's okay," I tell him. We pull into the parking lot of Michael's school. "It's not a taboo subject. Not something you should feel uncomfortable talking about. Certainly not something that would get you into trouble."

"But I'm afraid I'm going to start crying if I talk about it."

"That's okay." I park, turn off the engine, and turn to him. "Let's have a good cry, right here in the car, right now, you and me—because otherwise you'll keep holding it in, like this"—I hold a fist at my chest— "and you'll try to go to sleep and all of those thoughts and feelings will bubble up in your mind just when you're beginning to relax. Can you please tell me what happened in the *Mr. Peabody and Sherman* movie? I've seen it," I lie, "so you can just remind me of the scene."

"Well, you remember the girl, and Sherman, they go in a time machine, back to ancient Greece, and they're in this giant horse..."

"The Trojan horse."

"Yeah, the Trojan horse, and they're about to fall off a cliff and Mr. Peabody saves them, but he's still inside the horse." He chokes up, buries his head in his hands. "And it falls off the cliff."

"And he dies?"

"No!" He hates the word. "But it makes me sad."

"Okay. That's it?"

He shakes his head. He gathers himself. "And then did Mommy tell you that I saw the movie Nana was watching?"

"No. Tell me."

"I don't want to. There are dead..."

"Bodies?"

"No! *Body.*"

"Does someone shoot someone?"

"Stop!"

"Okay. Sorry."

A few weeks ago, he awoke from a bad dream and refused to talk about it. But then he agreed to draw it. With his back to me, he drew a picture and handed it to me over his shoulder, as if in shame. There was a gun hovering in white notebook-paper space, with bullets storming down onto a stick figure bent back at the waist.

My theory is that Christopher's fears go beyond the obvious horrors. I think he recognizes in these frightening images his own worst impulses—which is to say, all of our worst impulses—and they frighten him. Not long ago, he lost it in the movie theater watching *Boss Baby* when the kid screams at his baby brother, "I wish you were never born!"

Just outside Christopher's open window, Artie, his Little League coach (whom I assist), is leaning over and smiling.

"Hey, Christopher," Artie says, "ready for baseball? How about this weather?"

Christopher quickly wipes his tears.

Artie says to me, "Wayne Cohn is out the first six games. Appendicitis. While he was on vacation with his family last week." He shakes his head.

"Oh no," I say. "Our first pick in the draft." As if we're talking big-money players here, disabled with a torn Achilles or strained ACL. We talk about the upcoming first practice, seeing live pitching. I suggest Wiffle balls. "Christopher has been chucking strikes in the front yard. That's how we've spent our time this week."

"Pitcher this year, huh, Christopher?" Artie says.

A smile emerges. Christopher is ready to play ball.

"Now they're calling for snow," Artie says. "Cold. In the forties Thursday and Saturday."

"Why can't it stay like this?"

Artie nods and ducks into his SUV.

In our short sleeves, Christopher and I head to Michael's classroom.

Inside, Michael hands me a tissue and says, "Blow my nose."

I hold the tissue for him, and he lets it rip. I fold it expertly with one hand and hold it firmly for the second blow. Then a third, with a squeeze, to finish off.

We're ready to head out. He waves goodbye to his friends and teacher.

"Nother tush-you," he says.

"What?"

Christopher says, "Michael, it's tish-you, not *tush*-you."

"It's okay," I say, as I hold the tissue again. I'm in no hurry for Michael to speak the King's English. The other day he asked me when he could grow *sideburners*.

"He's four years old," Christopher says. "He can say *tissue*. And why can't he blow his own nose? He says, 'Daddy, blow my nose.' It doesn't even make sense."

What luck to have a little brother to take some heat when you're feeling down about yourself.

Even if Michael understood how he was being used, he wouldn't remind his big brother why we missed the last thirty minutes of *Coco* the other night.

At home Christopher tells Vana, "The kids at school called me Butt Chin."

"What?" she asks.

I shake my head. "Explain to Mommy, please."

He tells her the full story.

Mommy says, "Forget them. Kids are mean. They're jealous because you're so handsome."

I want to pinch my chin again and say, "Tomorrow, tell them all to 'kiss my ass,'" but I resist.

Another Testing Day

My co-proctors, Charlie and Tom, are in full command when I arrive five minutes after the first bell. The test won't begin for another ten minutes, after the kids are in their seats and tests are distributed. Charlie, the shop teacher, sits on the radiator, reading the scripted instructions, as the students gear up for three hours of multiple choice. I'm in a chair holding a clipboard, poised to finish grading a stack of personal essays written by my creative writers, whose deeply intimate subjects draw me in.

The average teacher might dread these long stretches of standardized testing that interrupt classroom teaching, but for me they're a godsend—and precisely when I do my best work, when I can immerse myself in these sometimes heartbreaking, sometimes hilarious stories of loneliness and anxiety, of divorce and desperation, of suicide averted thanks to a friend who says come and play music with me after school, of discovering a yen to be a meteorologist while on a treacherous road trip with Dad, of being the adopted Chinese child of an otherwise stereotypical Italian-American family.

I remember an old Chemistry teacher friend enviously saying how different our jobs were, how precious were those moments when his students shared even a glimpse into their private worlds. Indeed, this work is my guilty pleasure, and in moments like this—reading silently in the company of colleagues (especially on a standardized test day)—I feel I'm harboring a secret I share only with my students: I'm the luckiest teacher in this place, and maybe on the planet.

The post-testing schedule is a condensed, gutted version of a normal day. After lunch I'm back in my classroom, hunkered down at my desk, when Ryan Henry pops in, I assume with permission from a study-hall teacher, though I don't ask to see a pass.

"I'm working on something new," he says. "I'm almost done."

"We still have to talk about your *other* story, 'Somebody Please Help Edwin.' It's great. I wrote notes, but we should look at it together so I can make sense of my comments for you—and of my handwriting."

He says, "Can I stay?"

Now, he means. I don't hesitate. "Sure."

He settles in at a nearby desk, opens his laptop, and gets to work. Apparently, producing new material right now is more important to him than revising.

At the end of the period, I ask, "How'd it go?"

He says, "Good. I want to keep working on this before I send it to you."

"Okay," I say. "You're welcome to write here anytime, and then we can meet and talk whenever."

"Can we meet next week?"

I nod. "Take your time. We're here all year."

Even as he gathers his things, there's a sense of urgency in him, suggesting that we've already wasted too much time, that the clock is ticking faster for him than it is for the rest of us.

I wish I could stop the clock so that I could give him all I have to give, as if it could ever be enough, before he has to leave this place and find his own way in the world.

WONDER

After school Christopher wants to pitch to me in the front yard. I say it's too cold. The temperature dropped last night. He says, "How about a movie?"

"Now? It's four o'clock in the afternoon."

"I want to watch *Wonder*. Remember we saw the commercial? The one with the boy...you know, with the face? You said he has a disease."

"You want to watch that? It's going to be sad. I'm not sure it's appropriate for your age."

"My classmates have seen it."

"You sure?" As I say this, I realize that maybe this request is calculated, if only unconsciously, to restore his manhood—or to take one giant step toward it. We find the movie on Netflix. I play the trailer. He nods. Ready.

He sits on the floor and eats Cheerios in chocolate milk. Twenty-five minutes in, when the kid asks his mom after a very distressing first day of school, "Why am I so ugly?", the dam bursts. I pause it.

I say, "You feel bad for him?"

"Yes." He catches his breath. Wipes his tears. "Also, I was thinking, if I looked like that, kids would make fun of me."

"That's called empathy. You put yourself in other people's shoes so you can understand them. There's no better quality to have. I'm proud of you." I aim the remote to continue.

He says, "Turn it off."

I hesitate.

Come on, Christopher. You can handle this. You wanted to watch...

Nooo! I said turn it off!

"Okay." I nod. "Let's go play baseball."

He's out the door, and I follow him.

Twenty-one years a teacher, seven a dad—maybe I'm learning something.

ACKNOWLEDGEMENTS

For your tremendous help in the editing process, thank you so much to Dan Loose, Kevin Maness, Julie Odell, Tony Knighton, Nathan Long, Kath Hubbard, Brad Mellinger, John Fried, and Robin Black; Rebecca Bernstein, Alisun Coldiron, Sam Kleiman, Tyler Kolmansberger, Leann Tang, and Olivia Truocchio.

For bringing this book brilliantly into the light of day, thank you to Jessica Bell and Amie McCracken at the singularly cool Vine Leaves Press. For your support from start to finish, my deepest thanks to Scott Gould, Kelly Simmons, Debra Spark, and Peter Turchi.

Two essays appearing in various sections of this book have been previously published. Thank you to *English Journal* for the publication of "Millennial Girl"; and to the Tom Howard/John H. Reid Fiction & Essay Contest for honoring and publishing "Changing Your Mind" at WinningWriters.com.

I've had more than my fair share of lucky breaks in life. One of them came in the form of a phone call while I was studying for a tax final in my third semester of law school in Philadelphia. The caller asked if I would be interested in a job next semester as a high-school English teacher in a nearby suburban school district. There's no uncomplicated way to tell this story, so I'll just say this: after finishing my exams, I took a leave of absence halfway through law school, and, after a sequence of more lucky breaks, I took the job I've enjoyed for nearly three decades. Thank you to all those people, including my first students, who helped create, and inspired me to take, that path. Had that call not come, I don't know what paths I might have taken in life, but I have spent exactly zero seconds wishing I had taken any other.

VINE LEAVES PRESS

Printed in the USA
CPSIA information can be obtained
at www.ICGtesting.com
CBHW010800111223
2492CB00007B/21